Builder's Essentials

Advanced Framing Methods

Scot Simpson

With original illustrations by
Mike Strecher

RSMeans

Builder's Essentials

Advanced Framing Methods

The Illustrated Guide to Complex Framing Techniques, Materials & Equipment

Scot Simpson

RSMeans

Copyright 2002
R.S. Means Company, Inc.
Construction Publishers & Consultants
63 Smiths Lane
Kingston, MA 02364-0800
(781) 422-5000
www.rsmeans.com

The editors for this book were Howard Chandler and Danielle Georges. The managing editor was Mary Greene. The production manager was Michael Kokernak. The production coordinator was Marion Schofield. The proofreader was Robin Richardson. The electronic publishing specialist was Sheryl Rose. Mike Strecher was a contributing illustrator. The book and cover were designed by Norman R. Forgit.

Library of Congress Catalog Number 2003266316

ISBN   978-0-87629-618-9

Reed Construction Data

Table of Contents

Acknowledgments

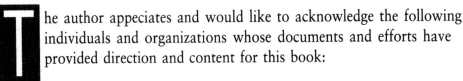

The author appeciates and would like to acknowledge the following individuals and organizations whose documents and efforts have provided direction and content for this book:

Glyn Boone; James Russell; Allan R. Simpson, Jr.; John E. Farrier; APA, the Engineered Wood Association; The Association of Mechanical Engineers (ASME); Digital Canal Corporation; The International Code Council (ICC); The International Conference of Building Officials (ICBO); The Mason Contractor's Association (MCAA); The Simpson Strong-Tie Company; Trus Joist, A Weyerhauser Business, Boise, Idaho; The Truss Plate Institute; and the U.S. Geological Survey National Seismic Hazard Mapping Project.

Introduction

I'm a framing contractor. I have been most of my life and probably will be for the rest of my life. I spent most of my career as a lead framer, directing framing crews and training workers to become framers. In my teaching, I found that much of the information I needed was not available in a good reference, so I wrote a book, *Framing and Rough Carpentry*.

Today I spend my time training and working with lead framers, and have again not found a reference with the information they need, presented in a framer-friendly format. This advanced book is a compilation of all the information I think is necessary for a lead framer to understand and have as a reference.

The three hardest framing tasks are getting started off the slab or foundation, framing stairs, and framing the roof. I have organized the process by giving the lead framer a procedure to follow. I also present lists and charts that make it easy to organize a job with less preparation time.

I remember the first set of circular stairs I struggled to frame. I was unable to find any written instructions. So I have written the instructions I was looking for in my chapter on stairs.

I think all framers struggle with roofs, especially if they don't cut rafters on a regular basis. The chapter on rafters can make this task much easier. After years of using different methods to find rafter lengths, I have settled on using what I call the *diagonal percent*. This is the relationship between the run and the diagonal. Using the diagonal percent makes it easy to determine the lengths before you touch a saw. This method also makes it easy to find stud heights of rake walls. The Rake Walls chapter includes forms with simple formulas that make the whole process easier.

I remember years ago, a builder said I was the only framer he ever knew who kept a code book on the dash of his truck. It's easy to understand why, since the code books, although very thorough, appear to be written more for lawyers than framers. That's why I extracted the information from the latest code books and made it framer-friendly in this book.

The code books are not the only regulations we have to be familiar with. New engineered wood products are coming on the market all the time, and they require special framing procedures. Just acquiring the right information on the job site for framing with this material can be a job in itself. The chapter on engineered wood products provides a lot of this information, as well as a feel for how to frame with these products.

I think there always will be some framers who will be able to enjoy the sunshine on their bare backs and legs. But most of us have learned the benefits of hardhats and saw guards and the need to be able to work in a safe environment. The Safety chapter discusses these issues and includes such things as illustrations of forklift hand signals.

Most lead framers don't look at themselves as managers. They would rather be wearing their tool bags and getting the work done. But whether they like it or not, they do manage their crews. The chapter on crew management gives direction on different approaches to, and aspects of management. It will help you to start thinking about your management style and how you can improve it. It also has tips for framing tasks that will help you organize your communications with your crew.

This book is written for lead framers, but the information is also valuable to superintendents and builders who work regularly with lead framers. The guidance in these chapters will also help framers who have a little knowledge, but a desire to learn more, and anyone who wants to learn more about framing wood buildings.

I hope you find this book beneficial and framer-friendly.

Chapter One

The Lead Framer

It is the job of the lead framer to get the building framed on time and within the budget. The lead framer must also make sure that the expected quality standards are met, and that the building is structurally sound, visually aligned, and ready for inspectors and for the other trades—all of this while maintaining a safe and congenial work place. To meet all of these goals is an impressive accomplishment. The purpose of this book is to help you get there. This book therefore covers all the major skills a lead framer needs to master.

Contents

Construction is a unique industry. It is always changing. Each new job or building has its own individual plan, timetable, and workers to do the job. The economy, local governments, codes, tools, and materials are also constantly changing, creating different work environments. The crew structure has to change, as necessary, to accommodate the particular requirements of a job. To be efficient, the lead framer must be aware of all factors that affect the job, and must be able to work successfully within them.

The management structure of a framing crew can differ from company to company. In some cases, the lead framer is the owner/builder. In larger construction companies, the lead framer may run only the framing crew. Either way, the lead framer leads the framing on the job.

This book is not intended to cover the functions of the framing contractor or builder that include office management, bids, payroll, or business organization. This book is written for someone who already has experience, knowledge, and skills in basic framing, and who wants to move up to the next level or become a better lead framer. This book gives you information you need to reach that goal, including:

1. Advanced framing techniques
2. Crew organization and management
3. Advanced framing procedures
4. Job organization
5. Lead framer job site relations
6. Material and equipment management
7. Quality control
8. Safety

The Lead Framer

As a lead framer, you need to have a different perspective from a crew member. When you are working on your own, the amount of work completed depends on you. When you are leading a crew, the amount of work finished depends on the whole crew. On your own, you have complete control over what can be done, whereas you have limited control over how much work your crew gets done. Nevertheless, you only need a little control and increased knowledge to make a big difference in how much work the crew finishes. This book is intended to give you that increase in knowledge—which can make your jobs run better.

Elements of the Lead Framer Job

1. Provide direction to framing crew.
2. Supervise crew.
3. Evaluate crew productivity.
4. Train crew.
5. Implement work goals for crew.
6. Maintain quality control on the framing.
7. Organize framing.
8. Organize framing material.
9. Read and interpret architectural plans and specifications.
10. Inform framing contractor or superintendent of discrepancies in plans and necessary change orders.
11. Make suggestions for the best and easiest solution for changes.
12. Create a job site atmosphere that promotes high productivity.
13. Maintain a safe working environment.
14. Conduct weekly safety meetings.
15. Coordinate framing with other trades.

Chapter Two

Preparing for the Job

T he best way to make a project start smoothly is to adequately prepare for the job. This means spending time looking over the plans, organizing information, and talking with the superintendent before you start working on the job site.

Often the lead framer does this preparation the night or morning before a job starts. You will find that your work will flow more smoothly if you begin preparation earlier and do it right.

If you are working for a framing or general contractor, many of the tasks listed in this chapter will be done for you. If, however, you are the lead framer, framing contractor, and builder all in one, then it's up to you to get these done. The word *superintendent* refers to the person on the job site who answers any questions related to the building. This person's actual title might be *superintendent, builder, owner,* or *framing contractor.*

In this book the word *building* applies to a house, a multi-unit, a commercial building, or any structure where wood framing is used.

Preparing to start at the foundation or slab involves these four steps:

1. Developing a job start checklist.
2. Reviewing the plans and making preparations.
3. Organizing the job site.
4. Conducting the pre-start job site review meeting.

Contents

Developing a Job Start Checklist

Using a job start checklist is a good way to prepare. Your framing will be organized and will move at a steady pace if all the items on this list are addressed. You can fill out the checklist in your pre-start job site review meeting with the superintendent. While the pre-start visit is not absolutely required, it is a very productive part of the preparation.

Following is a blank Job Start Checklist which can be photocopied for use at the job site review meeting. Following the checklist is an explanation of some points to consider as you check off each item. Although the items may vary from job to job, most items on this list are common to all jobs. You should also add your own items to this list.

Job Start Checklist

☐ 1. Power Source _____

☐ 2. Backfill _____

☐ 3. Lumber Drop Location _____

☐ 4. Material List _____

☐ 5. Anchor Nuts and Washers _____

☐ 6. Standard Framing Dimensions List _____

☐ 7. Plans—Two copies _____

☐ 8. Framing Hardware _____

☐ 9. Subfloor Glue _____

☐ 10. Mudsill Insulation _____

☐ 11. Hold-downs, Tie-downs, Anchoring Systems _____

☐ 12. Truss Plans and Delivery Schedule _____

☐ 13. Steel Plans and Delivery Schedule _____

☐ 14. Reference Point for Finish Floor _____

☐ 15. Reference Point for Wall Dimensions _____

☐ 16. Location of Truck on the Job Site _____

_____

_____

_____

_____

Job Start Checklist—Explanation

What to consider as you check off the job start items.

1. **Power Source**
   - Will you need more than one power source? Bigger jobs sometimes require more than one source.
   - What length of extension cords will you need for power tools? A cord that's too long can burn out your tools.
   - Will you need a heavy lead cord?
   - Is there enough voltage for your tools? A compressor, for example, may require 220 volts.

2. **Backfill**
   - Ask the superintendent to backfill all possible areas before you start. The more backfill completed, the easier it will be to perform your work.

3. **Lumber Drop Location**
   - Ask for lumber to be dropped as close as possible to the building, and in a central location. If a forklift will be available, you can have the lumber dropped in a more out-of-the-way location, as long as it's easily accessible.
   - Often the lumber you need first is on the bottom of the lumber load when it is dropped. Sometimes you can have the superintendent request that the lumber company load the lumber in the order you will use it.

4. **Material List**
   - Ask the superintendent for a copy of the material takeoff list. This list will help you figure out which size, length, and grade of lumber will be used for which part of the building. It is a good check, and helps prevent mistakes.

5. **Anchor Nuts and Washers**
   - The anchor nuts are generally delivered with the anchor bolts used by the foundation crew. Ask the superintendent to have the nuts located before you arrive on site, since trying to find them can be difficult.

6. **Standard Framing Dimensions List**
   - Go over the list (shown later in this chapter) with the superintendent. He may need to check with the architect, or door or window manufacturer, in order to verify rough openings.

7. **Plans: Two copies**
   - Ask the superintendent for a second copy of the plans. You will need one set for the job site. The second set can be used by the framing

contractor, by yourself off site, or by the layout framer on bigger jobs.

8. **Framing Hardware**

- If you purchase the framing hardware yourself, you can have good control of quantities and delivery. If you don't purchase it, request a hardware purchase list, which will help you identify quantities and type of hardware. It is common for the architect to specify a piece of hardware with a specific identifying number on it, then have the superintendent purchase an equivalent piece of hardware with a different identifying number. It helps to carry a hardware manufacturer's catalog with you for identification purposes. The Simpson Strong-Tie catalogs are most often referenced on plans.

9. **Subfloor Glue**

- Does the superintendent want to use subfloor glue? It may not be called out on the plans or specifications, but the superintendent may require it.

10. **Mudsill Insulation**

- Determine whether the superintendent wants to use mudsill insulation. Again, it may not be identified on the plans or specifications, but the superintendent may intend to use it.

11. **Hold-downs, Tie-downs, Anchoring System**

- It is best to install the hold-down studs when the wall is built, and it is easiest to drill the holes for the hold-down bolts before the hold-down studs are nailed into the wall.

- Have at least one hold-down of each size on the job site when you start. Because the hold-down sizes vary, it's good to have different sizes available so you can determine stud locations and bolt hole sizes and location. If you do not have the hold-downs, you can use a hardware catalog to determine hole sizes, locations, and stud locations.

12. **Truss Plans and Delivery Schedule**

- Many buildings have truss plans in addition to the plans provided by the architect. Because you want to line up the studs, floor joists, and roof trusses where possible, it is important to know where the truss manufacturer started the layout. You should use the truss layout and align the studs and floor joists. Truss plans typically call out where the layout starts.

- Often the truss plans are not drawn until shortly before they are needed. It is best to request the plans early so that they will be available when you need them.

- Check on the delivery date. Depending on the economy and the local truss manufacturers, the lead time for trusses can vary from days to weeks. You don't want to get to the roof and have to stop because the trusses aren't yet built.

13. **Steel Plans and Delivery Schedule**
- Typically if you have steel on the job, it should be in place before the wood framing is started. Check with the superintendent to see when it will be ready.

14. **Reference Point for Finish Floor**
- When you check the floor for level, it helps to have the benchmark used for the concrete work. If you don't have the benchmark, then you have to take a number of different readings to come up with an average before you can determine whether the concrete work is within tolerance. Sometimes the superintendent will be able to give you the benchmark.

15. **Reference Points for Wall Dimensions**
- Having the reference points will save you time in determining where the lines are actually supposed to be. Since the concrete work is seldom exactly where it is supposed to be, you will have to decide by how much the concrete is off and the best way to compensate for it without doing extra work or compromising the building.
- If you don't have reference points to work with, you will have to spend extra time taking measurements to determine where the mistakes are located in the concrete.

16. **Location of Job Site Truck**
- Be sure to locate your truck, trailer, or storage container close to the job site. Planning ahead with the superintendent can often open up a location that later could be occupied by other trades, material, or supplies.

Reviewing the Plans and Making Preparations

Plan review will save you time and energy, and make your work more productive. If you are framing a house with a plan you have used before, then you have already done the review. But if you are framing a new house or, particularly a multi-unit or commercial building, then it becomes very important to review the plans. Here are some of the most common ways of reviewing plans:

1. **Study the plans.** Sit down with the plans and figure out how the building is put together. Read the specifications. Most often they are standard and you can skim through them, but make sure to note anything that is new or different. Know enough about the new material so that you can

understand the architect's explanations. If you can't figure it out, ask the framing contractor, superintendent, or architect about that particular element. If you are on a large job where the specifications come bound by themselves, you should know that they are probably organized under the Construction Specification Institute's (CSI) MasterFormat. Under this system, rough carpentry is listed in Division 6 as 06100. This section contains the basic specification information about framing this job.

2. **Make a list of questions.** While you are studying the plans, have a pad of paper and pencil handy so you can write down any questions. Go over these questions with the superintendent at the pre-start job site review meeting. Often, getting a question answered or a problem solved before the job begins saves an interruption in the framing. Even a little thing like the architect's missing a dimension on the plans can cause a delay. If the superintendent okays scaling the missing dimensions, there won't be a problem; but if you need verification on missing dimensions, it's best to get them before you begin.

3. **Highlight the plans.** It's a big help to highlight easy-to-miss items on your plans. Use the same color highlights on all jobs so that it becomes easy to identify items for you and your crew. An example would be:

   Orange—Hold-downs
   Pink—Shear walls
   Green—Glu-lam beams
   Blue—Steel
   Yellow—Special items

4. **Establish framing dimensions.** Most rough openings are standardized, but because of exceptions and differences in floor covering, it's important to go over the rough openings with the superintendent before the job begins. The information sheets that follow can be used for reviewing these dimensions with the superintendent.

   There is a sheet for 88⅝" studs and one for 92⅝" studs. These can be adjusted for different size studs. Go over each item with the superintendent. Ask him/her to review the sheet and indicate that you will be using the rough-opening dimensions listed unless you are instructed differently. Note that 88⅝" studs are standard because with a 4 × 8 header, they leave a standard 82½" door opening. Note, too, that 92⅝" studs work with a 4 × 12 header.

   These sheets apply to residential framing. Commercial framing is not so standardized. Note that the use of hollow metal (H.M.) door and window frames is common in commercial framing. The frames are usually 2" in width. Rough openings (R.O.) for H.M. frames would typically be 2" for the frame plus ¼" installation space. As an example, a 3'-0" door would have a R.O. width of 3'-4½" which is made up of

3'-0" for the door opening, 4" for the frames on each side, and ½" for the ¼" installation space on each side. The R.O. height would be 7'-2¼" which would be made up of the 7'-0" for the door opening, 2" for the frame, and ¼" for installation space.

5. **Tape the plans.** Plan deterioration can be a problem, particularly at the end of a job. Use the same set of plans when possible so they include your highlighting and any changes that you have marked. When possible, request water-resistant print paper for the plans. If you're in a rainy area or season, this will keep the lines from running. Plastic covers are made to cover plans, but they can make it difficult to turn the pages. Clear plastic adhesive covering can be used, but then you can't write on the plans to note changes. A good system is to use clear plastic wrapping tape to tape the edges of the plans. This treatment usually provides the stability to make it through the job while still allowing for notes written on the plans.

Taping the Plans

		Header Size	Trimmer Size **
Stud height .... 88⅝"			
Wall height .... 93⅛"			
R.O. windows .... Width—nominal			
	Height—nominal	4 x 8	81⅛"
		4 x 10	79⅛"
R.O. exterior doors .... Width—nominal + 2½"			
	Height—82⅝"	4 x 8	81⅛"
	Height—82⅛"	4 x 10	80⅝" cut T.P.***
R.O. sliding glass doors ... Width—nominal			
	Height—6'-10" door 82⅛"	4 x 8	81⅛"/ ½" furr*
	82⅛"	4 x 10	80⅝" cut T.P.
	Height—6'-8" door 80⅛"	4 x 8	81⅛"/ 2½" furr
	80⅛"	4 x 10	79⅛/ ½" furr
R.O. interior doors .... Width—nominal + 2" (nonbearing)			
	Height—82⅝"		81⅛"
R.O. bifold doors .... Width—nominal + 1¼" for ½" drywall / —nominal + 1½" for ⅝" drywall			
	Height — 82⅝"		81⅛"
R.O. bypass doors .... Width—nominal			
	Height—82⅝"		81⅛"
R.O. pocket doors .... Width — 2 x nominal + 1"			
	Height—84½"		83"
Bathtubs .... Width—nominal + ¼"			
Tub fire blocks .... 14½" from finish floor to bottom of block			
Medicine-cabinet blocks .... R.O. 14½" × 24"			
	Height—48" from finish floor to bottom of R.O. 3" minimum away from wall corner		

These dimensions should be checked with the job site superintendent before beginning each job.

* Furr = furring under header after header is in place.

** Trimmer heights will increase by 1½" if lightweight concrete is used or ¾" if gypcrete is used.

*** Cut T.P. —Cut the top plate out and leave the double plate.

R.O. (rough opening) – Any opening framed by the framing members.

Standard Framing Dimensions 92⅝" Studs

		Header Size	Trimmer Size **
Stud height .... 92⅝"			
Wall height .... 97⅛"			
R.O. windows .... Width—nominal			
	Height—nominal	4 x 8	85⅛"
		4 x 10	83⅛"
R.O. exterior doors .... Width—nominal + 2½"			
	Height—82⅝"	4 x 8	85⅛"/4" furr*
	Height—82⅝"	4 x 10	83⅛"/2" furr cut T.P.
R.O. sliding glass doors ... Width—nominal			
	Height—6'-10" door 82⅛"	4 x 8	85⅛"/4½" furr
	82⅛"	4 x 10	83⅛"/2½" furr
	Height—6'-8" door 80⅛"	4 x 8	85⅛"/6½" furr
	80⅛"	4 x 10	83⅛"/4½" furr
R.O. interior doors .... Width—nominal + 2"			
(nonbearing)	Height—82⅝"		81⅛"
R.O. bifold doors	Width — nominal + 1¼" for ½" drywall — nominal + 1½" for ⅝" drywall		
	Height — 82⅝"		81⅛"
R.O. bypass doors .... Width—nominal			
	Height—82⅝"		81⅛"
R.O. pocket doors .... Width — 2 x nominal + 1"			
	Height—84½"		83"
Bathtubs .... Width—nominal + ¼"			
Tub fire blocks .... 14½" from finish floor to bottom of block			
Medicine-cabinet .... R.O. 14½" x 24" blocks			
	Height—48" from finish floor to bottom of R.O. 3" minimum away from wall corner			

These dimensions should be checked with the job site superintendent before beginning each job.

* Furr = furring under header after header is in place.

** Trimmer heights will increase by 1½" if lightweight concrete is used or ¾" if gypcrete is used.

R.O. (rough opening) —Any opening framed by the framing members.

Organizing the Job Site

After the plan review, you need to organize the job site. Figure out what your initial manpower needs and schedule are, and what tools you'll need for the job. The first day on the job site is usually a challenge.

1. **Manpower needs.** Typically, on the first day, your crew is ready to go to work and will be looking to you for instruction. At the same time you may not be sure if the concrete is level or the right size. Meanwhile, the superintendent is on his way over with his list of things you need to take care of. If you have too many framers, everyone might be standing around until you get the job organized. If your schedule allows, start with just a two-man crew to check the foundation or slab for level and size and to get some lines chalked and some detailing done.

2. **Manpower tasks.** Knowing which jobs you want each framer to do before you get there always helps. Also, keep a couple of back-up tasks (such as cleaning out the truck or fixing tools) in mind in case something prevents you from starting right away. First-day jobs might include:

   - cleaning the slab or foundation
   - checking concrete dimensions
   - checking level of concrete
   - cutting makeup and headers
   - nailing makeup and headers
   - chalking lines
   - setting up chop saw (radial arm or similar)
   - building plan shack
   - detailing plates

3. **Tools.** Not having the right tools can be like trying to cut the Thanksgiving turkey with a table knife. The tool list that follows will help you determine what you need. For example, you can look at the plans to find out what size bolts are being used so you can be sure to have the appropriate drill bits and impact sockets ready.

   It's easy to show up the first day without some of the necessary tools. Also, you might use different tools at the beginning of a job and at the end of a job. Highlighting the tools you need on the Tool List before the job starts will help you prepare and save time.

   Note that the "Location" column on the Tool List at the end of this section refers to the location where the tools are kept (see legend on tool list). The locations listed can be adjusted to your own situation.

4. **Plans.** Any time you can devote to the plans before you start the job is probably well spent. Two things are particularly important for getting started. First, decide where you are going to pull your layout from (see

Tool List

Tool	Location	Quantity
Framing saw	SB	1 per framer
Saw blades	H	Many
Cut saw	TB	2 per crew
Cut saw blades	FB	5 per crew
Impact wrench	TB	1 per crew
Impact sockets		
⅜" for SDS ¼"	MB	1 per crew
¾" for ½" bolt	MB	1 per crew
¹⁵/₁₆" for ⅝" bolt	MB	1 per crew
1⅛" for ¾" bolt	MB	1 per crew
1⁵/₁₆" for ⅞" bolt	MB	1 per crew
1½" for 1" bolt	MB	1 per crew
1¹³/₁₆" or 1⅞" for 1¼" bolt	MB	1 per crew
Drill	TB	2 per crew
Drill bits		
⅝"	FB	2 per crew
¾"	FB	2 per crew
⅞"	FB	2 per crew
Router	TB	1 per crew
Router bits		
Panel pilot	FB	2 per crew
½" round	FB	1 per crew
Router wrench set	MB	1 per crew

Legend:

SB = Saw Box	H = Box	FT = Front of Truck
TB = Tool Box	SR = Screwdriver Rack	JH = Jay Hooks
MB = Metal Box	T = Truck	LB = Lock Box
FB = Flat Box	TT = Top of Truck	

Tool	Location	Quantity
Chop saw	TB	1 per crew
Beam saw	TB	1 per crew
4-way electric cord	H	1 per crew
100' electric cord	H	1-½ per framer
Nail gun	LB	1 per framer
GWB nail gun	LB	1 per crew
Air compressor	TB	1 per three framers
100' air hose	H	1-½ per framer
2' level	TT	1 per crew
4' level	TT	1 per crew
8' level	TT	1 per crew
Sledge hammer	FT	2 per crew
Crowbar	FT	2 per crew
Framing square	TT	1 per crew
Stair nuts set	FB	1 per crew
Glue gun	TB	2 per crew
Wall pullers	TB	2 per crew
Hand saw	H	1 per crew
Transit stand	FT	1 per crew
Transit	LB	1 per crew
100' tape	FB	1 per crew
String line	TB	2 per crew
Water jug	T	1 per crew
Step ladder	T	1 per crew
Extension ladder	T	1 per crew
First aid kit	FT	1 per crew
Microwave	FT	1 per crew
Stereo	T	1 per crew

Tool	Location	Quantity
Broom	T	1 per crew
Chalk bottle	T	1 per crew
Knife blades case	H	1 per crew
Vice grip	MB	1 per crew
5" crescent wrench	MB	1 per crew
8" crescent wrench	MB	1 per crew
Allen wrench set	MB	1 per crew
Screwdriver		
Standard	SR	2 per crew
Phillips	SR	2 per crew
PLUS		
Retractable safety line	JH	2 per crew
Lanyards	JH	4 per crew
Regulators	FB	½ per gun
Compressor oil	TB	1 per crew
Gun oil	TB	1 per crew
Plumb bob	FB	1 per crew
Electric three-way	FB	2 per crew
Air three-way	FB	2 per crew
Saw guides	FB	1 per crew
Screwdrivers	FB	Misc.
Chain saw	SB	1 per crew
Chain saw blades	FB	1 per crew
Palm nailer	LB	1 per crew
Ear plugs	FB	Misc.
Back support	JH	Misc.

Chapter 5), and second, decide which lines you are going to set for reference (see "Getting Started" in Chapter 3).

Looking at plans on the job site can be like trying to read a map on a motorcycle: there is always the sunshine, wind, or rain. On the job site you'll be juggling a number of things. Your crew will be asking you what to do next and you'll have to think about the material you need, and if you have enough nails, for example. It will take you about an hour to absorb as much information from the plans on the job site as you can in fifteen minutes off the job site. A good habit is to review the plans for ten minutes every morning away from the job site. You'd be surprised at how many mistakes are avoided by doing this.

5. **Schedule.** Developing a schedule is a difficult task, and one that should be a responsibility of the framing contractor. If, however, the framing contractor does not provide a schedule, the lead framer should create his own. It is a valuable tool that will help you organize the job and then analyze how the work is going.

6. **Plan shack.** On bigger jobs a plan shack is a good tool to have. It doesn't have to be fancy, but if it keeps your plans dry and helps keep the job organized, it is worth the time and material.

Plan Shack

Conducting the Pre-Start Job Site Review Meeting

Meeting with the superintendent before you start work at the job site is the next step. Scheduling this visit a week before you start gives the superintendent adequate time to acquire the information and material you will need. At this meeting you can go over the questions developed while you were reviewing the plans. You'll also be able to go over such items as the location of the temporary power supply and material delivery dates—items common to all new jobs. The job start checklist shown earlier in this chapter should be used to review these points with the superintendent.

Conclusion

Following the four basic steps for job preparation (developing a job start checklist, plan review and preparation, job site organization, and pre-start job site review meeting) will make the job run a lot more smoothly.

In addition, the lead framer must juggle a number of tasks—from managing and instructing a crew, to making sure the needed material is on the site at the right time. Being prepared and aware of the various elements is vital to the lead framer.

Chapter Three

Getting Started

Certain activities must take place before you begin framing. The dimensions and level of the foundation and slab need to be checked. If they are not perfectly level (which is not unusual), you must determine how far from correct they are, whether they are within tolerances, and what types of adjustments you must make. It is important that the dimensions are accurate, and the building is square before you start. Note, too, that the cabinets, floor covering, drywall, roof trusses or rafters, and much more depend on the measurements being accurate and square.

The four steps to getting started are:

1. Checking the exterior wall dimensions.
2. Checking the reference lines for square.
3. Adjusting the reference lines to correct dimensions and square.
4. Checking the building for level.

Contents

Checking the Exterior Wall Dimensions

If the superintendent gives you the concrete-work reference points, getting started will be easier for you. If you are not given these, establish reference lines of your own. Be sure to mark these lines well, since you will be using them throughout the job. Using clear marking paint in inverted cans makes it easy to protect your lines on the concrete.

You will want to use the reference lines to find any deviations from plan measurements or any out-of-square parts of the foundation. Start by stringing dry lines that will allow you to measure. The more of the building you can measure from these lines, the more likely you are to find any mistakes. Look at the plans and string two dry lines perpendicular to each other and covering as long a distance of the building as possible. If you can add two more dry lines, one on each side and opposite to the first two, that will help. (See "Start-Up" example below.) Once you have established your lines, take measurements between the lines and to the major exterior walls in the building. Make a quick footprint of your building, and as you measure the distances, write them down on the footprint (see "Footprint Sketch Dimensions" example later in this chapter).

Start-Up Example

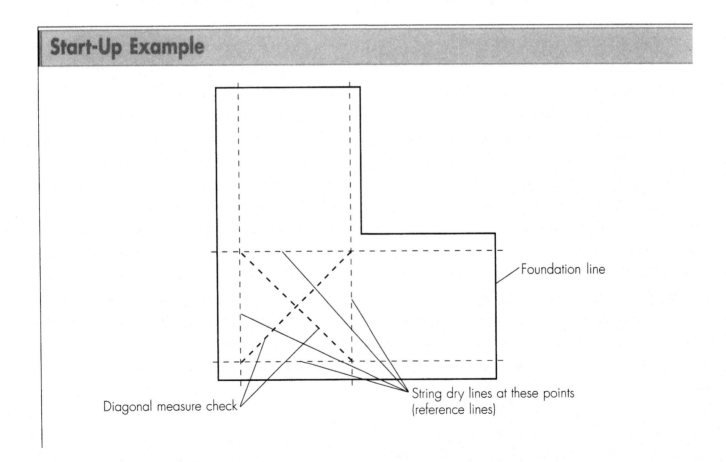

Foundation line

Diagonal measure check

String dry lines at these points
(reference lines)

Summary:

To check the exterior wall dimensions:

First, string dry lines to create reference lines.

- Select lines that are as long as possible.
- Locate line ends at extreme ends of the building.
- Locate lines so that they reference the entire building.

Next, use reference lines to measure the building dimensions.

- Check the exterior wall locations and note any discrepancies.

Checking the Reference Lines for Square

To check using four reference lines, measure the two diagonals, then write down the measurements on the footprint you used for measuring the dimensions. If the corner points are set correctly, then the diagonals will be the same length. If the reference dry lines are square, then the diagonals will be the same length. (See "Start-up" example on preceding page.)

If you have only two reference lines to work with, you'll need to use a triangle to help you check for square. The two reference lines will be "square" with each other if they create a right angle (90°). You can use a 3-4-5 triangle or the Pythagorean theorem to determine whether the two

3-4-5 Triangle

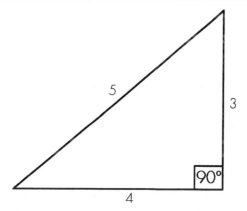

A 3-4-5 triangle will help you establish when two lines are square or at right angles to each other. To establish square, just follow these steps:

1. Start from the 90° angle and measure out 3 units on one line and 4 units on the other line.
2. Measure the diagonal length from the end of the 4-unit line to the end of the 3-unit line.
3. If the 5-unit line is not exactly 5 units, then adjust the 4-unit line or the 3-unit line as described in the "Adjusting the Reference Lines to Correct the Dimension and Square."

reference lines create a 90° angle. In each case the three (the rise, run and the diagonal) of a triangle must have a certain length relationship for the reference lines to be "square." Since we can let the two sides of the triangle be the reference lines and make them any length, it is the third line (the diagonal) which will determine if the reference lines are at a 90° angle. A 3-4-5 triangle works well because as long as one angle is a right angle (90°), and the lines on either side of the right angle (the rise and run) have a relationship of 3 to 4, then the third side (the diagonal) is a 5 in the same relationship.

To use the triangle, use your reference dry lines to replicate a right angle, then create a triangle using the 3-4-5 relationship for the sides. To do this, measure a distance out on each reference string line from the point where the two lines intersect. The measurements of each leg should be a multiple of 3, 4, or 5. Note that the longer the length, the better assurance you have of accuracy. So if you are using a 25' tape, for example, measure out 20' on the one side and 15' on the other side. The distance between these two points—across the diagonal—should be 25'.

The Pythagorean theorem system sounds a lot worse than it is. If you use a calculator like a Construction Master®, all you need to know is that the three sides of the triangle are represented on the calculator by a run button, a rise button, and a diagonal button. You'll need to find the length of the third side of the triangle (diagonal) that is required to make the two reference lines square (90°). If you enter the lengths of the two sides of the triangle that are next to the angle that needs to be 90° into the calculator (by pressing the run button for the one side and the rise button for the other side), pressing the diagonal button will give you the length of the third side of the triangle. This length is the distance needed to have the reference lines square and the angle to be exactly 90°.

If the diagonal length is not what it is supposed to be, then write on the footprint how much over or under it is.

Summary:
- If you use four reference dry lines, check the diagonals. (See "Square Correction" example.)
- If you use two reference dry lines, use a triangle to check for square. (See example.)
- Check for and note any discrepancies.

Adjusting the Reference Lines to Correct the Dimensions and Square

Common sense and experience are the best decision-making tools for approaching and correcting errors. Once you have your footprint sketch with the dimensions and square checks on it, you'll be able to determine if there are any errors.

If a diagonal line is too long, then some of the lines at the end of the diagonal must come in to make the diagonal the right length (see "Square Correction" illustration below). Check the wall dimensions lines to see which lines can be shortened. Once you've determined the best way to make adjustments, it's best to speak to the superintendent about your suggestions. Typically a fix will involve moving the wall in or out on the concrete foundation. Depending on the finish, there is a certain tolerance that will allow for moving the walls without affecting the appearance. It is common to have finish material that overhangs the foundation, so moving the wall out slightly may not be noticeable. It is also common to have the sheathing on the outside of the foundation, so that if the wall needs to come in, it can be adjusted in the thickness of the sheathing without affecting the look of the finish.

If corrections would cause visible errors in the finished building, then consider alternative measures. An example of a visible error would be if the concrete finish wall sticks out past the siding on the finished exterior wall. There are three methods that can be used for correcting errors in the foundation. These are as follows:

- Correct the foundation wall. This is the best solution, but often cost-prohibitive.

- Change the dimensions of the building. This is easy, but very often causes problems later on. Make sure to check that the change does not affect truss span if using roof trusses. Also check to see that the change does not affect dimensions of such items as bathtubs or cabinets. If a change is made, make sure it is made on all copies of the plans.

- Do not correct the errors. Correcting the errors might cause more problems or imperfections in the building than the errors will.

Square Correction

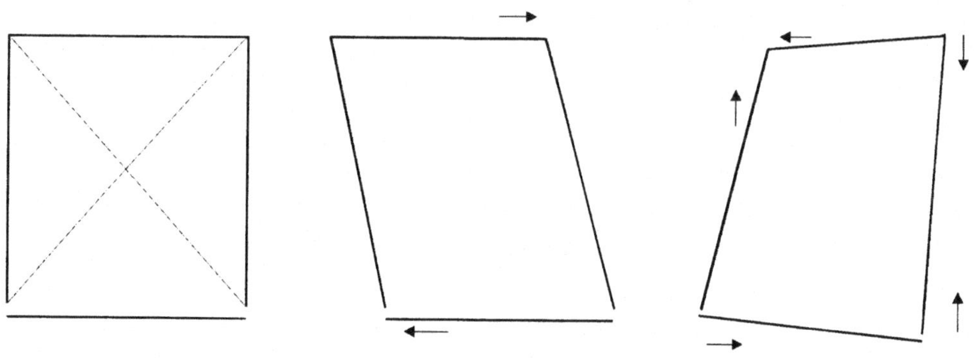

Arrows indicate direction to move reference lines to help make reference lines square.

The "Footprint Sketch Dimensions" illustration (on the next page) is made on the job site. It will help determine how to best adjust your reference lines to make the building square. In this example, four dry lines are established to form a square. The diagonal distances that should be the same are then checked. Because they are different, the reference lines will need to be moved to make the diagonals square. By comparing the actual and the planned dimensions of the walls that the reference lines are measured from, you can determine which reference lines should be moved. When you move a reference line, the other lines are affected.

If you have all the information down on your footprint sketch, you can come pretty close to knowing exactly how much to move each line, and keep making adjustments until you are comfortable with your accuracy. Once your reference lines are established, you can set all the other lines in the building from them. The measurements in circles on the sketch show the distance that the reference lines would be first moved. It is difficult to determine exact amounts because of the proportions, but if you study the footprint for a little while, you can come pretty close.

Checking the Building for Level

Using a transit is the best way to check for level. A water level can also be used. Once a level foundation has been established, you are ready to cut, drill, and set the mudsill in place.

The foundation and/or slab should be ready for you to start framing when you first arrive. Sometimes, however, this is not the case, and time will be needed to "shoot" (measure using a transit) a foundation and slab. Time must also be allotted to fix any problems in the concrete. Although the framing contractor will address the costs of these adjustments, it will be your responsibility to check and make a suggestion if you think corrective work is necessary. Start by checking and recording your findings. Record your findings in a way that lets you use the information if you decide the concrete needs corrective work. To record your findings, make a footprint sketch similar to the one you used for dimensions and squaring, and write the transit readings on the footprint. (See "Footprint Sketch Elevations" later in this chapter.)

To take the measurements, one framer should hold a tape measure at the spots to be measured, while another framer uses the transit to record the height to the transit line from the concrete. If the concrete work is done well, typically a variance of ¼", then just shooting at strategic locations on the concrete should be sufficient to check the concrete. If you quickly find out that the concrete is not level, you will need to shoot the concrete every four to eight feet along the walls. Either way, be sure to record the measurements on the footprint sketch. Mark the locations where the measurements were taken. When you start building walls, you will use the measurements in the footprint and the marks on the concrete to determine stud heights. The marks are only made every four to eight feet because when you are laying out walls a level can be used to find the heights between the marks. Another way to find the stud heights between marks is to use a chalk line at the top of the wall to rub studs against and mark the heights. (See photo "Chalk Line at Top of Wall" on the next page.)

Once you have finished a footprint with the elevations marked, you can determine if any corrections need to be made. With the elevations written down, you can show the footprint to the superintendent or owner to let them decide what tolerance they will accept on their building.

If you look at the "Footprint Sketch Elevations" illustration, you will notice that most of the building elevations center around 49¼" and are within ¼". The top wall on the sketch, however, appears to be low, with the lowest point at 49⅝". Although 49⅝" is more than 49¼", it actually represents a low point because the measurement represents the distance from the transit line down to the concrete.

Footprint Sketch Dimensions

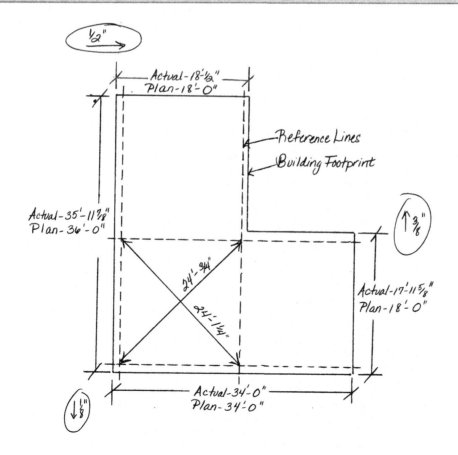

Chalk Line at Top of Wall

Transit Line from Concrete

On this footprint sketch example, you would probably want to use a height of 49¼" and recommend adjusting the section of the building that is low.

The X's on the footprint represent the position of your tape measure when you shoot the height with the transit. Mark the X on the concrete so that when you start building walls you will have a reference point if your heights need adjustment. Also keep your footprint sketch for this purpose.

Conclusion

Before you begin framing, it's crucial to check your foundation and slab to make sure they are square. Once you have done this, you can move to the next level, the actual framing.

Footprint Sketch Elevations

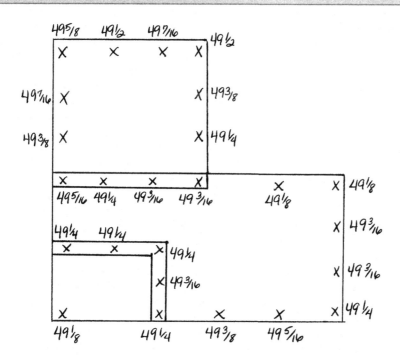

Chapter Four

Managing the Crew

Managing a framing crew is a task like no other. The job changes every day and is always full of new surprises. The lead framer should be good at "multitasking." A typical day might include trying to make sense of plans that don't provide enough information, dealing with an owner who is focused more on cost and schedule than framing, and organizing a group of framers who have different levels of knowledge and experience into an effective team for framing your building.

The most valuable tools you can have in managing a crew are common sense, framing knowledge, the ability to evaluate a situation objectively, and an understanding of your crew's abilities and personalities. You probably already have a preferred management style, based on what you have learned in your experience in the field. This chapter will help you better understand that management style and improve upon it.

Contents

Different Types of Management

There are many ways to manage framers. It is important to know the different management styles and the effects that they have on employees so that you can create the most productive framing crew. There are three main styles of management: *autocratic, bureaucratic,* and *democratic.*

Autocratic: The lead framer has the decision-making power and does not delegate authority. Discussion and suggestions are generally not permitted. This system sometimes motivates framers to please the lead framer instead of to improve productivity. It also discourages framers from finding creative solutions.

Bureaucratic: The lead framer enforces established rules, regulations, policies, and procedures to run the crew. This style does not allow for creative solutions.

Democratic: Framers help determine the goals of the company. The lead framer organizes and directs the framers as part of his job as a crew member. If a problem comes up between the lead framer and a framer, they work together to find a solution they can both accept. This style usually creates a congenial work atmosphere.

Most lead framers use a combination of the three styles. This lets them have authority when they need it, while getting the help from their framers in developing the most productive methods for accomplishing their work.

Managing a framing crew can be compared to playing quarterback on a football team. Your team has to have confidence in your ability to direct them. The team expects you to tell them when they make mistakes, but they also expect you to tell them what they need to know to do a good job and to be considerate of them. In effect, you have to develop a working relationship with each framer.

Autocratic Lead Framer

Different Types of Framing Crews

There are different types of framing crews, which require some adjustment in style. They are:

1. Hourly employees
2. Piece workers
3. A combination of the two

Hourly workers are paid by the hour. Their goal is to keep their employer happy with their work. They typically are more concerned with quality of work than with speed. Piece workers are paid by the amount of work they finish. Their main goal is to get as much work as possible done within a certain time frame. A combination of the two allows for the employee to be paid for each hour he

A Democratic Lead Framer Acts Like a Quarterback

or she works, then to receive a bonus for completing extra work within a defined time frame. A combination system can provide the motivation to maintain speed, while still allowing you a great degree of control over the job.

Motivation

Motivation is the intangible factor that can make or break a crew, and probably the single most important factor that affects framers, yet it is not something you can demand of your crew. As a lead framer, you want to support individual framers and maintain a high level of motivation in the crew.

Ideas for Building Relationships and Motivation

1. Honesty is a basic. It doesn't take long for a framer to determine whether or not you are honest. A framer will observe not only what you say and how you treat him or her, but what you say to others and how you treat them. Keep your framers well informed. If there is a slow-down coming up and some framers might be laid off, let them know. You risk the chance of their quitting before the job is finished, but if you want them to be on your side, you have to be on theirs.

2. The first day on a job is the most important time for setting a new framer's attitude toward his or her job. Take time to introduce him to the whole crew and show him where he can find tools, the first aid kit, and portable toilets. Allow time for him to acclimate to the job.

3. Developing relationships takes time and a conscious effort. While your time is valuable, and you have to balance it, try to listen to what your framers have to say, and show patience. If you want them to support your interests, you have to be concerned about theirs. Make yourself available and easy to talk to. Encourage open and free resolution of problems, and make every effort to use your framers' suggestions, or explain why if you decide not to. This gives the framers positive feedback and gets them thinking about better and faster ways to accomplish tasks. If you constantly reject their suggestions, you reduce their motivation.

4. Use power discreetly. The more you have to display authority, the less valuable it becomes. Persuasion and guidance can be more effective than a show of authority.

5. Assign more responsibility and train framers to take on new tasks whenever the job allows. This will motivate framers to take on more duties.

6. Teach framers how to solve problems.

7. Praise framers for good work. This helps create a positive attitude, especially when it is done publicly. Compliments are a good

relationship-builder, especially when framers first start working with you. Go out of your way to find something they have done well. Hopefully you can get a couple of positive compliments in before you have to start pointing out any mistakes.

8. Making mistakes and learning on the job are everyday occurrences and should not create fear in a framer. Your framers need to know that you are there to teach and direct them, and that you will be fair and reasonable.

9. Criticism should be made into a learning experience and given in private. When a framer makes mistakes or is sloppy, don't assume it's intentional. Calmly explain what he did wrong. Direct the criticism at the action, not the person. Be specific, for example, "Your nails are not sunk deep enough," instead of, "You are a horrible nailer." If the framer does not improve or change, then you may have to tell him that he is not suited for the work and should look for work elsewhere.

10. You should not feel that any task is beneath you. Pitch in and be a good example, especially if the job is one that nobody wants to do.

11. Be courteous. Everybody likes to hear "please" and "thank you." Saying "thank you" is a good way to finish up without giving the workers the sense that they are dismissed.

Respecting your framers will help keep them motivated, and help get the job done right.

Competition as a Motivator

It is sometimes possible to create competition that will provide enjoyment for your framers and increase productivity. Here is an example:

A while ago, I had a couple of hammers left over from tools I had purchased for a training class. On the job, we were framing a two-story hotel with two long walls on either side. I woke up one morning asking myself, "How can I make these walls go quicker?" I decided to create a competition by splitting the four framers into two teams, with one team on each side of the hotel. The winning team—the one that got their wall up first—would get the hammers. With the competition, the framers enjoyed the day and got a lot more wall framed than normal. Healthy competitions can help provide motivation.

Goals

One of the best management tools is goal-setting. It develops motivation by creating a reason to work productively; gives you a good tool for judging the productivity of a framer; and provides a good benchmark for discussing each framer's daily tasks. Goals should be set for different time periods, ranging from the entire length of the job, to daily or task goals. Goals can be written down, or you can go over them in a conversation with your framers.

Goals for the job are usually defined in the beginning by your schedule and manpower.

It helps to break down your overall project goals into goals for each part of the job, like the first-floor walls, the joists, and the rafters. Once you know the goals for the major parts of the job, you can begin to set your daily goals.

Set daily goals the first thing in the morning. You might want to think about them and who you will assign to each task, on your way to work. After assigning the tasks, ask each individual to set their own goals for the day, which you can review with them.

Framers sometimes think they can get more work done in a day than they actually can. In this case, all you have to do is agree with their goals, and encourage your framers to achieve them. If, on the other hand, they set their goals at a lower rate of productivity than you expect, review their goals with them, and see if you can teach them faster ways to achieve them. You might do a little of their work for them so they can see how fast it is supposed to be done.

If you can't agree on a goal with a framer, give him another task, and assign his original task to someone else. At the end of the day you can compare how much work the other person accomplished with what you and the first framer expected, then determine which one of you was more on-target. This takes time and effort on your part, but sometimes that's what's needed to create motivation—which will save time in the long run.

It's important to review goals when your framers are done with their tasks—either at the end of the day or the next morning before you set new goals. This will show framers that goals are important. It also lets you determine when and if improvement is necessary.

Set goals that are realistic, obtainable, but still challenging. When you review the goals with a framer, you want to be objective, constructive, and make it a learning experience.

When setting goals, consider the learning curve. Studies have found that when you double the amount of similar work that someone does, their productivity increases by 20%. Even experienced framers have a learning curve.

The more experience you have, the clearer your goals will be. The more you set goals, the better you will become at setting goals.

Communication

Communication is to a lead framer what a hammer is to a framer—one of your most important tools. Before you were a lead framer, you had to communicate with only one person—the lead framer. As a lead framer, you have to communicate with all the framers on your crew, the framing contractor, the superintendent, and possibly the architect, engineer, and owner.

Each one of these people comes from a different environment, has different knowledge and experience, and different goals related to the job you are framing. Good communication is based on honesty, trustworthiness, openness, and effective listening skills. Keep in mind that bad communication creates problems, while good communication solves problems.

Communicating with Framers

Each framer who works for you will have his or her own unique characteristics, personality, background, and place of origin. It's probably impossible to know all the sides of a single framer, but the more you know about each framer, the easier it will be to communicate with and teach him or her.

Communicating with the Framing Contractor, Superintendent, Architect, Engineer, or Owner

We all know how to talk—some better than others. What we don't always know is what to say and who to say it to. That will vary depending on the size of the job and the organizational structure of the companies doing the building. If you say the right thing to the wrong person, or the wrong thing to the right person, you might end up causing yourself delays and/or additional work.

Solving Problems on the Plans

The nature of the construction industry lends itself to communication errors. With each new building, you might be working with a completely new group. In many cases an owner will select the team that will design and build the building. The architect may have a great sense of how the finished building will look and feel, but probably won't be familiar with framing slang and concepts. The architect may hire an engineer to design the structural members of the building. Once the plans are complete, the owner will hire a builder who subcontracts the framing to your employer. You'll then have to frame the building based on plans that may have been passed around, worked on, and changed by a group of people who may not have worked together before, and who may have varying degrees of experience or knowledge of what you have to do to frame the building.

Chances are, there will be some mistakes, omissions, and/or details on the plans that just don't work. The parties involved in the design of the plans are capable of making mistakes in the same way you and your crew can make mistakes. Be ready to deal with these problems as they arise.

Good communication is probably your biggest strength when it comes to resolving mistakes or processing changes. The smaller the building, the easier it will be to navigate mistakes, and thereby reduce extra cost and time delays. Sometimes all it takes is a quick conversation with the superintendent. On bigger jobs, however, it may be necessary to get input from all members of the building management team, all the way back to the owner. In these cases, be sure to present the information in an organized way to prevent delays. The following five steps organize the process of solving problems with the plans.

1. **Identify the problem:** The information may be missing from the plans, or it may just not work. It could also be that the information you need may be in another part of the plans, not where it is usually located.

2. **Have another framer review the situation:** When you find a mistake, make sure it really is a mistake. One way to do this is to have one of your crew look at it. Even if he doesn't have the knowledge to fully analyze the situation, just explaining it to him helps you review it in your own mind.

3. **Develop a solution:** It is usually worth your time and energy to develop an easy solution and write it down. Very often your suggestion will be accepted. This saves the person who made the mistake from having to work out a solution—which could take days or even weeks and could be more difficult to frame than need be. Along with your proposed solution, you should note extra costs that result from the correction.

4. **Identify and seek out the person responsible:** Typically if the mistake is in the architectural plans, it will be an architectural mistake. If it's in the structural plans, it's probably an engineering mistake. Quite often, however, it's a coordination mistake between the architect and the engineer. If you're lucky enough to have direct availability to the parties involved, a quick phone call might provide an easy solution. Remember that framing contractors, general contractors, architects, engineers, and owners all have relationships. Go to the source whenever possible, but be careful to go through proper channels for communication. Get permission if necessary, to directly contact the appropriate party.

5. **Propose the solution:** Each job has its own chain of authority. Sometimes the general contractor takes responsibility for solutions; sometimes it's the owner or architect. Direct the suggested solutions to whoever accepts the authority. If the solution doesn't come in writing, you should be the one who writes it down, along with the name of the person who proposed the solution, as well as the date. Write it on the plans for easy reference. Do this while the person is still there to make sure you understand their interpretation of the solution. This way, you'll be protecting yourself in case of any future confusion.

Delayed Communication

Organizing your communication is another important task of a lead framer. For example, you might realize that you need more material or hardware, but the person who orders it is not on the site. By the time you see that person, however, you are onto another task and forget to let them know what you need.

The easiest way to avoid this problem is to carry a small notebook in your pocket, and write down what you need, whether it's information or materials. Get used to checking your notebook whenever you talk to the people who supply your material or process your change orders, or when you are making phone calls. The notebook acts as a memory aid; this to prevent forgetting items due to delayed communications.

Pick-Up Lists

Pick-up lists are important to keep things organized at the end of the job. The superintendent typically creates this list of tasks that have to be done before you are finished with the job. When the list is first given to you, review it to make sure everything is clear to you. It is sometimes easiest to ask the superintendent to accompany you around the site to make sure you understand exactly what he is trying to communicate.

You may have to consult the plans to get all the information you need in order to understand the work that needs to be done. If the superintendent does not have a written list, make your own list as you walk around the site discussing each task.

Difficult Personalities

Chances are you will have to work with a difficult framer at some time. Common sense and creative thinking are good tools in these situations. Here are some difficult personality types:

1. **The Complainer:** Looks for problems and whines instead of looking for solutions. **Suggestion:** Determine the problem, then discuss the solution. Tell the framer that complaining is not helpful, and that you would rather he look for a solution himself first. Also tell him that if he gets stumped on a solution, you are there to help.

2. **The Back-Stabber:** Would like to be lead framer or just likes degrading another framer. Commits disrespectful acts in an attempt to replace the lead framer or insult another framer. **Suggestion:** Confront any disrespectful acts or well-founded suspicions and talk openly about them. Tell this person how his actions can affect the whole team. If you can't resolve the issues, speak with the framing contractor about the situation.

3. **The Talker:** Is probably one of your nicer framers. As long as he can keep you talking, he doesn't have to work. **Suggestion:** Be considerate, but after you've listened for a while, excuse yourself because you have to get some work done. He will understand.

Clear Descriptions are Important on Pick-Up Lists

4. **The Perfectionist:** Typically motivated to get every task right. If things go wrong, this framer lets everybody know and brings everybody down with him. **Suggestion:** The perfectionist can be a great resource, as he tends to look for any potential problems. You can use him as a sounding board for new tasks, and for work you have already begun.

To deal with difficult people, it helps to understand them as much as possible. Some framers who seem difficult may just have different kinds of personalities that require different ways of relating to them. Understand that there are differences in personalities, and that you can use the strength of each framer for the betterment of the whole team.

Assigning Framers Tasks

As a lead framer, your most important job is to assign framers to tasks. If they are unfamiliar with the tasks, it's part of your job to teach them how to do the work. On the one hand, you can only put your tool belt on and work if the rest of the crew is working productively on its own. It may be tempting to grab the right tool and take care of the problem yourself. On the other hand, doing the task yourself means your crew is not learning, and you are not available if you are needed elsewhere.

Organizing your crew and assigning tasks can be the easiest part of your job, or it can be the most difficult. A lot of it has to do with the framers you have working for you, and the way you manage them. For example, one individual with a bad attitude can disrupt a whole crew, or a crew without proper direction can work all day and get little done.

When you first start leading, you'll quickly realize that it takes a lot of preparation to keep the whole crew busy all the time. As each framer finishes a task, you must have another task ready. If a task isn't ready, the framer(s) will have to wait around while you get it ready for them.

If you are working on a task and one of your crew needs something to do (and you don't have anything else for him to do), show him what you are doing so that he can help you or take over. Or have him get started on the next phase of the job. The point here is that if anyone is going to be standing around scratching his head, it should be you, because you can always use the time to plan for the next step.

Analysis of Crew Performance

For your framers to become better framers, they should have an understanding of how well (or not) they are performing their jobs. Crew analysis is the process of answering this question. It is important to know the capabilities of each framer, so you can assign him to the kind of task where he'll be most productive.

When you assign the task, you need to know how much supervision or instruction your framers need. You need to know their capabilities, and how they interact with the rest of the crew. Discuss these things with your framers. Their feedback will help you understand and evaluate them.

The "Framer Analysis" form in this chapter can be used to evaluate your crew and to show your framers what aspects of their work are important to you. This is also a good format for deciding wage increases based on performance. The framer who consistently gets high ratings may get more money if he reaches a certain skill level.

To use the form, give the framer a rating from 1 to 10 for all the items listed. The "Value Factor" column in this form is an estimate of the comparative value of the productivity items. You can change these values to your own preferences. Enter your rating in the column titled "Framing Rating 1 to 10." Multiply the rating by the various value factors and put the results in the column labeled "Total." Add the total ratings. This will give you a value you can use to compare your framers' performance. You can use the Framer Analysis form for your own planning purposes or to show framers where they need to make improvements.

Quality Control

In framing, the question of speed versus quality always comes up. You want to get the job done as fast as possible—but you must have a quality building, and quality takes time. The most important thing to consider is the structural integrity of the building. Once that requirement is satisfied, the faster the job can be done, the better.

It is a lot easier to talk about the importance of quality than it is to define it for a framer. Quality to one framer can be the product of a "wood butcher" to another framer. Framers learn under different lead framers who have different goals and objectives, and different standards of what quality workmanship is. You need to establish your own definition of quality of workmanship for the framers working for you.

The best way to do this is by observing or auditing their completed work, then giving them feedback on what you saw and what you would like to see. To audit the work, check a portion of what has been done. If that sample is done well, most likely the rest is done right. If you find a mistake, find out why it was made, correct any similar errors, and make sure the framer knows why this happened.

A checklist is helpful when you audit individual tasks. It will help you remember all the parts that need checking. For example, the following list could be used for shear walls.

Shear Walls Checklist

1. Nailing pattern for sheathing.
2. Blocking, if required.
3. Distance between sheathing nails and the edge ($^3/_8$" minimum).

Framer Analysis

	Value Factor	×	Framer Rating 1 to 10	=	Total
Productivity					
1) Speed	7	×	_____	=	_____
2) Framing Knowledge	6	×	_____	=	_____
3) Framing Accuracy	5	×	_____	=	_____
4) Ability to use Framing Flow	4	×	_____	=	_____
5) Endurance	3	×	_____	=	_____
6) Consistency	2	×	_____	=	_____
7) Rate of Learning	1	×	_____	=	_____
Effect on Productivity of Other Framers					
1) Respect for Lead Framer	3	×	_____	=	_____
2) Cooperative	2	×	_____	=	_____
3) Positive Attitude	1	×	_____	=	_____
Effect on Efficiency of Company					
1) Attendance	4	×	_____	=	_____
2) Positive Attitude	3	×	_____	=	_____
3) Follows Safety Rules	2	×	_____	=	_____
4) Truck and Job Site Neatness	1	×	_____	=	_____
TOTAL					_____

4. Nails are not driven too deep.

5. Lumber grade, if specified.

6. Hold-down sizes and location.

7. Hold-down bolt sizes.

8. Tightness of bolts.

The following guidelines can be used to control the quality of experienced and new framers' work, and the work at the end of the job.

For an experienced framer you have worked with before:

1. Casual observance as part of routine.

2. Audit work after completion, or at regular intervals.

For new-to-the-task framers:

1. Review framing tips (at the end of this chapter).

2. When possible, demonstrate work.

3. Watch as the new framer gets started.

4. Ask the new framer to get you for review after the first piece is finished.

5. After a half hour to an hour, review the work.

6. End of day: review the work.

7. End of task: audit the work.

End of job:

1. Audit 10% of each individual task.

2. If mistakes are found, review all task work.

3. Correct all mistakes.

4. Check for omissions.

In the hustle of framing, things can get missed. An end-of-job pick-up list will help you remember to check everything. You can start with the following and add your own items for each job.

Pick-Up Checklist

1. Studs under beams.

2. Drywall backing.

3. Fireblocking.

4. Nailing sheathing.

5. Headers furred out.

6. Thresholds cut.

7. Crawl space access.

8. Attic access.

9. Dimensions of rough openings on doors and windows.

10. Drop ceilings and soffits framed.

11. Stair handrail backing.

12. All temporary braces removed.

13. Joist hangers and timber connectors.

Remember that quality control is not just for the owner's benefit in the finished product. Quality control also makes your work go more smoothly. When your framers' cuts are square and true to length, the framing fits together a lot more easily. If the building is square, when you cut joists and rafters, you can cut them all at once, the same length, instead of having to measure each one. When you get to the roof, the trusses will fit.

Organizing the Crew's Use of Tools and Materials

In addition to organizing and teaching the crew, you will have to organize your tools and materials. Each crew and job will require a different type of organization. To give you an idea of how to go about this, we will discuss three aspects: *tool organization, material storage,* and *material protection.*

Tool Organization

Following is an example of how the crew's tools might be organized using a job site tool truck.

General

Put tools away, in their designated place, after using them.

- Hang safety harnesses and lines on hooks.
- Stand sledge hammers and metal bars in corner.
- Place saws on saw table.
- Place nail guns in safety box.
- Place electric tools in wood box.
- Hang up screwdrivers.
- Place metal wrenches and sockets in metal box.
- Place nails out of weather.
- Place trash in designated container.

Roll-up

Roll up largest, bulkiest items first.

- Four-way electric extension cords.
- Air hoses.
- Electric cords.

Take equipment to truck in following order:

- Miscellaneous hand electric tools.
- Air hoses and electric cords.
- Circular saws and old saw blades.

- Air compressors. (Drain every Friday.)
- Ladders.

The person responsible for the truck should:

- As soon as roll-up begins, start picking up and taking tools to the truck.
- Take tools from framers and put them in their place in the tool truck.
- Clean truck when not busy putting tools away.
  —Put similar nails together.
  —Hang up rain gear.
  —Put tools in proper place.
  —Check and account for number of tools.
  —Put all loose garbage in bucket.

Nails

- Use up partial boxes of nails first.
- Follow established storage procedures.

For example, starting at the right-hand side of back of truck

  —1st—16d sinkers   4th—joist hanger nails
  —2nd—8d sinkers   5th—concrete nails
  —3rd—roofing nails   6th—fascia nails
  —On right-hand side under seat, 10d gun nails
  —On left-hand side under seat, 8d gun nails

Roll-out

- Check oil in air compressors every morning.
- Oil nail guns every morning.
- Check oil in circular saws the first of every month.
- Check staging and ladders.
- Check safety devices in all tools.

This list should be discussed at the first crew meeting on the job, then the list should be posted on the tool truck.

Material Storage

The following five items are important to consider for material storage.

1. If your lumber is being dropped by a truck, check to make sure the lumber is loaded so that the items being used first are on top. You might need to contact (or have the superintendent contact) the lumber company to make sure they think about the loading order. Sometimes it helps to make up a quick list to help them out. For example:

   - Treated mudsill plate
   - Floor joists
   - Floor sheathing

- Wall plates
- Studs
- Headers
- Wall sheathing
- Rafters
- Roof sheathing

The lumber company may not be able to load the material exactly the way you want, but a little concern for the loading order can make a big difference in the amount of lumber you have to move.

2. When using a forklift, store like items together so that you do not have to move other material to get at what you need.

3. When storing items, always think about where you are going to use them. If you don't have a forklift, store them as close to where you are going to use them as possible.

4. If you have to store items in front of each other, make sure the items needed first are available first.

5. Consider using carts or other mobile devices for moving lumber in the building.

Pallet Jack and Drywall Cart for Moving Lumber

Material Protection

Material protection also requires you to consider accessibility and time. You can spend a lot of needless time moving and protecting material. You can also end up reducing the quality of your building by not taking care of your material. Consider the following:

1. If the specifications indicate a certain procedure for protecting your material (usually the case on larger jobs), then you need to follow them.

2. Use scrap lumber to keep your material out of the dirt.

3. If lumber is left in direct sun, the exposed sides will dry out more than the unexposed sides, and cause it to warp. The warp will make framing difficult, and walls curved.

4. Moisture loss or absorption from lumber causes shrinkage or swelling. If the shrinkage or swelling is uneven or happens too quickly, the wood fibers can break and cause the lumber to warp.

5. Fungal growth occurs when moisture content reaches 20%, and the air temperature is between 40 and 100 degrees. Fungal growth causes decay and stain.

6. The moisture content of green lumber is little affected by rainfall. But if it is not used right away, green lumber is more susceptible to fungal decay and stain.

7. Posts, beams, and timbers are always green. Seasoning checks will occur, but will not affect the structural performance. The more this lumber is protected, the less it will check, and the easier the installation will be.

8. Always cover lumber if you are expecting snow or other bad weather. It is easy to lift the cover to remove the snow when you need to use the lumber. On the other hand, if the lumber is being used up quickly and is not adversely affected by the environment, covering it may be a waste of time.

9. If lumber is delivered with covers already on, leave them in place as long as possible. If you are using only small quantities at a time, consider pulling the lumber out at the ends to leave the cover on. With engineered wood products such as glu-lam beams, you may be able to just uncover the ends for bearing.

10. If moisture absorption is expected on full bundles of sheathing, cut the banding to prevent edge damage due to expansion of the sheathing.

11. When lumber is covered, allow ventilation so that the sun does not create a greenhouse effect that will promote mold growth.

Teaching Framers

You have to take training seriously if you want your framers to take learning seriously. You are a teacher whether you want to be or not. The only question is whether you are a good teacher.

Being a good teacher means that you have to have a degree of self-confidence and security that comes from understanding yourself and those working for you. You need to have confidence in your own knowledge. As a teacher, it is also good to remember the following five learning concepts.

- A picture is worth **10,000** words.

- A demonstration is worth **100** pictures.

- **Tell** your framers what you are going to tell them, **tell** them, then **tell** them what you told them. Repetition makes learning easier.

- It is important that framers understand the structural significance of their work.

Some of your teaching will apply to all of your crew. For example, special nailing may be specified for double wall plate joints for the whole building. A crew meeting is a good time to inform the whole crew all at once.

Hold a crew meeting before you start a job, then once a week after that. Monday morning meetings can help ease everyone back from the weekend. You can have these meetings right before or after your safety meetings, while you already have everyone together. It's nice if the crew meeting can be a relaxed time, while still covering important points such as:

- Task assignments

- Crew procedures (crew organization)

- Tool organization (tool truck)

- Job-specific items

Teaching While Assigning Tasks

Most of your teaching will occur when you are assigning tasks to framers. You won't have to say anything to your experienced framers, but new or apprentice framers benefit from seeing you follow a certain procedure (outlined below) to make sure you don't forget anything.

When assigning a task:

- Always assume that they are seeing the task for the first time.

- Explain everything you know about the operation.

- As you're explaining the operation, tell your framers why it's done this way.

- Ask them if they understand. (Have them explain it to you.)

- If they ask you a question and you don't have the answer, tell them you'll find out and get back to them.

Check on them:

- After five to ten minutes.

- Repeatedly until you're confident that they know what they're doing.

When you're teaching a framer trainee, remember that they're learning as a student, so expect that it may take a little while for them to catch on. Don't expect all trainees to learn instantly, but always assume they want to learn.

The best way to communicate how to do a job is to actually do the job, and let the trainee watch. At the same time, explain as much of what you're doing as possible. If you were showing an apprentice how to nail off plywood, you would use the following sequence:

1. Tell them the nailing pattern.
2. Ask them if they know what "nailing pattern" means.
3. Tell them about keeping the nail $3/8$" away from the edge of the plywood.
4. Tell them to angle the nail slightly toward the edge of the plywood.
5. Tell them when they need to use a regulator or depth gage, and show them how.
6. Tell them how to avoid breaking the plywood surface.
7. Demonstrate use of a nail gun.
8. Watch them while they shoot a couple of nails in.
9. Ask them to come and get you to check their work after they have finished two sheets.
10. Check their work closely to make sure it's done properly.

Using this type of checklist will help you remember all the items that should be covered. This list also helps with assigning framing tasks.

You might want to review certain parts of each framing task with a framer if he is not familiar with them, or hasn't performed them in a while. Go over these points with a framer when you assign a task. Each lead framer has his own tips and should develop a list for each task. Writing them down makes it a lot easier to remember. Following are some common framing tips for common framing tasks. Start with these and add your own.

Building Wall Tips

Material Movement for Walls

1. Locate wall framing so that once the wall is built, it can be raised into position as close to where it finally goes as possible.

2. Spread the headers, trimmers, cripples, and sills as close to their final position as possible.

3. Eight is an average number of 2 × 4 studs to carry.

4. You can use your leg to stabilize the studs you are spreading. Stabilize them with one arm and one leg to free up your other arm so that you can spread them one at a time. This way you won't have to set them down, then pick them back up to spread them.

5. Select a straight plate for the top and double plates, and position any crown in the double plate in the opposite direction of the top plate crown. This will help straighten out the wall.

Using Your Legs to Support Studs While Spreading

Teaching Wall-Building

Nailing Walls

1. Nail the headers to the studs first. Make sure that they are flush on top and on the ends of the headers.

2. Nail the trimmers to the studs. Make sure that they are up tight against the bottom of the header and flush with the sides of the stud.

3. Nail the studs and cripples to the plates. Nail sills to the cripples and the trimmers. Make sure that all the connections are tight and flush.

Squaring Walls

1. Align the bottom plate so that when it is raised, it will be as close to the final position as possible.

2. Attach the bottom plate to the floor along the inside chalk line for the wall. Toenail through the bottom plate into the floor so that the sheathing won't cover the nails. If the wall is in position, it can be nailed on the inside, and the nails can be pulled out after the wall is raised.

3. Use your tape measure to check the diagonal lengths of the wall.

4. Move the top part of the wall until the diagonal lengths are equal. Example: If the diagonal measurements are different by one inch, then move the long measure toward the short measure by one half inch diagonal measure. Make sure the measurements are exact.

5. Once the diagonals are the same, check by measuring the other diagonal.

6. Temporarily nail the top of the wall so that it will not move while you are sheathing it. Make sure you nail so that your nails won't be covered by the sheathing.

Teaching Joisting

Joisting Tips

Material Movement for Joists

1. Material movement is a major part of installing joists.

2. Always carry the joists crown-up. This way, you can spread the joists in place, in the right direction, without having to look for the crown a second time. It's easier to look for the crown on the lumber pile than when it is on the wall.

3. Check on the size of joists and positions needed. Try to spread the joists on the top of the pile first so you won't have to restack the joists.

4. Check your carrying path for the joists. Sometimes you can reduce your overall time by making a simple ramp or laying a joist perpendicular to those already in place.

Cutting Joists to Length

1. Cut joists after spreading.
   - Spread joists on layout, and tight to rim joists.
   - Chalk cut line.
   - Lift and cut each joist in sequence.

2. Cut joist on lumber stack.
   - Measure joist lengths.
   - Cut multiple joists on lumber pile.

Nailing Joists

1. Position joist on layout and plumb.
2. Nail through rim joist into joists, making sure joist is plumb.
3. Toenail through joist into double plate. Nail away from end of joist to prevent splitting.

Rafter Tips

Cutting Rafters

1. Figure cut lines for rafters, and check measurements before cutting.
2. Install common rafters first.
3. Cut three rafters.
4. Check two to see if they fit. If they fit, leave them in place and use the third as a pattern for remaining cuts. If they don't fit, cut to fit or save for hip or valley jacks
5. Cut balance of common rafters and install.

Teaching Rafters

Installing Ridge Board

1. Figure height for ridge board.
2. Install temporary supports for the ridge board.
3. Install ridge board.

Nailing Rafters

1. Toenail common rafters on layout into double plate.
2. Nail on layout through ridge board into rafter.
3. Cut hip and valley rafters.
4. Cut jack rafters.
5. Set and nail hip or valley rafter.
6. String line centerline of hip or valley.
7. Layout hip or valley rafter.
8. Toenail jack rafter on layout through rafter into double plate.
9. Nail jack rafter to hip or valley rafter.

Sheathing Tips

Floor Sheathing

1. Make sure the first piece goes on square.
2. Chalk a line using a reference line and the longest part of the building possible.
3. Align the short edge of the plywood with interior joists, the long edge with the rim.
4. Pull the layout from secured interior joists.
5. Nail the plywood to align with the chalk line and layout marks.

Wall Sheathing After Walls are Standing

1. Make sure the first piece goes up plumb. If you are installing more than three pieces in a row, use a level to set the first piece plumb.
2. It is easier to install the plywood if you are able to fit a 16d nail between the concrete foundation and the mudsill.
   a. Place two nails under each piece near each end.
   b. Remove the nails when you are finished.
3. The easiest and fastest way to handle an opening in the wall is to just sheath over it, then come back and use a panel pilot router bit to cut out the sheathing.

Roof Sheathing

1. Make sure the first piece goes on square.
2. Chalk a line from one end of the roof to the other.
   - When measuring for the chalk line, make sure you consider how the plywood intersects with the fascia. The plywood may cover the fascia, or the fascia may hide it.
3. If the sheathing overhang is exposed, the sheathing could take a special finish.
   - If the exposed sheathing is more expensive than the unexposed sheathing, then often the exposed sheathing is cut to fit only the exposed area. In this situation, cut the sheathing so that it breaks in the middle of the truss or rafter blocking.

Nailing Sheathing

1. Read the information on the stamp on each piece of plywood. Make sure you are using the right grade. Sometimes the stamp will tell which side should be up.
2. There should be at least a $1/8$" gap between sheets for expansion.
3. The heads of the nails must be at least $3/8$" from the edge of the sheathing.
4. Make sure that the nail head does not go so deep that it breaks the top veneer of the sheathing. Control nail gun pressure with a pressure gage or depth gage.
5. Angle the nail slightly so that it won't miss the joist, stud, or rafter.
6. Use the building code pattern for walls, floors, and roofs. Always check the plans for special nailing patterns. (Most shear walls have special patterns.)

Teaching Sheathing

Installing Hold-Downs (After Walls Are Built)

1. Select a work area (large, close to material).
2. Check the plans for the location, quantity, and other details of hold-downs.
3. Collect all material and tools needed.
4. Spread hold-down posts for common drilling (cut if necessary).
5. Mark hold-down posts for drilling.
6. Drill for posts with holes $1/16"$ larger than the bolts.
7. Loosely attach hold-downs, bolts, washers, and nuts to posts.
8. Spread hold-downs to installation location.
9. Drill holes for through-bolts if necessary.
10. Place hold-down in wall.
11. Place through-bolts into hold-downs where required.
12. Tighten all nuts.
13. Nail posts to plates.
14. Nail sheathing to posts.

**Installing Hold-Downs
(After Walls Are Built)**

Installing Hold-Downs (While Walls Are Being Built)

1. Locate wall hold-downs on plans and check details.
2. Locate holes to be drilled for hold-downs, anchor bolts, and through-bolts.
   - Measure location for through-bolts.
   - Center hold-downs on plates.
   - Center hold-downs in post or align with anchor bolts.
3. Drill holes.
4. Nail post into wall.
5. Nail sheathing to wall.
6. After wall is standing, install hold-downs, bolts, washers, nuts, and through-bolts.
7. Tighten all bolts and nuts.

**Installing Hold-Downs
(While Walls Are Being Built)**

Removing Temporary Braces

1. Remove temporary braces only after the walls have been secured so that they will not move.

2. A sledgehammer provides a fast and easy way to remove the braces.

3. Knock a number of the braces off at one time. Be careful that no one steps on the nails before you remove them.

4. Put the removed braces together.

5. Hit the point end of the nail to expose the nail head.

6. Use a crowbar to remove the nails.

7. If you do not have many braces, a hammer is an easy way to remove them.

Removing Braces

Material Organization and Cutting

Material Organization, Mitre Saw

1. Set up your table in convenient locations for moving lumber in and out.

2. Place the incoming material as close as possible to the side of the saw where you will be positioning it to cut.

3. As it is cut, stack the lumber in a pile that is neat and easy to pick up and carry or lift with a forklift.

4. Put scrap wood that you will be cutting into blocks nearby, maybe under the saw table.

Cutting With a Mitre Saw

1. Set your length gage for multiple cuts.

2. Cut your first piece, then check the cut for square (both vertical and horizontal) and correct length.

3. Check the second and tenth piece for square and length.

4. Check every tenth piece after that for length.

5. Keep lumber tight against lumber guides, but don't bang them so that they move.

6. Remove any sawdust near the guides.

7. Respect the saw! If you don't, there is a good chance you will hurt yourself or your fellow framers.

Mitre Saw

Fractions

Many apprentice framers are not familiar with fractions, and some might be embarrassed to admit this. It doesn't take long to teach him or her fractions. Ask him to show you where ¹¹/₁₆" is on the tape. If he can't do it easily, draw a duplicate of a tape showing the different length lines. Mark the fractions on each line, and tell him to take it home and memorize it. Review as frequently as required to develop proficiency.

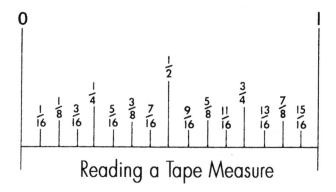

Reading a Tape Measure

Looking Ahead

While lead framers are not responsible for developing project costs or schedules, they are asked for input into the decisions of others who must estimate and schedule construction. The superintendent, for example, might need to know if he can meet a deadline with the crew that is in place; you as lead carpenter might need to know if there is enough material available to complete the job; or the framing contractor might need to know if any labor can be spared to send to another job.

To answer these questions, the lead carpenter must understand and appreciate the importance of the construction schedule and budget. This means thinking ahead and looking at the project as a whole, while also focusing on the details. It means evaluating the crew's ability to perform its job at a particular time under a given set of conditions.

Using the Crew Effectively

A crew includes both labor and equipment required to install materials. On any given day, the makeup of the crew can change. One person may not show up or may be sent to another job. At other times you may have to absorb extra manpower on short notice. Equipment you expected to have available may not be there or, with little notice, you may have the benefit of equipment. When faced with these situations, a seasoned lead framer draws on his or her experience and makes the necessary adjustments to either *push* the job or, at the very least, maintain the momentum.

The lead framer should understand the labor hours required for each task, and be able to know in his or her mind if the schedule is realistic and can be maintained. Perhaps more important is recognizing potential problems before they become real problems. In a matter of hours, what seems to be a minor glitch can become devastating to the schedule. For example, if fuel has not been requested for a piece of equipment, production may be forced to stop while waiting for a fuel delivery.

Never underestimate the importance of measuring realistically the crew's ability to perform the work. Keep in mind that most jobs, unless very short in duration, are scheduled well before the work begins, and job durations are usually based on optimistic job site conditions. During the course of construction, a monthly schedule is broken down to weekly schedules, and weekly schedules are broken down to daily schedules.

Before committing the lead framer to a schedule, the framing contractor normally has agreed to the means and methods that will be followed for the job. If the estimator has based the estimate on a crew that performs differently than an average crew, the schedule may or may not have allowed enough time for the work.

Avoiding Slow-Downs

Once a productive and effective crew has been assembled, nothing can slow that crew down faster than a shortage of material. Construction project estimators and schedulers often look at past project costs for material, labor, and equipment needs and costs. They may make adjustments to these figures based on input from the field allowing for factors such as a more experienced work force, or new equipment that will make the work go faster. Nevertheless, material shortages can still occur. The lead framer needs to keep an eye on the rate at which materials are being used, and communicate material needs to the superintendent.

Waste

Project estimators perform quantity takeoffs that are really a best guess of how much material will be needed for the job. Waste is a concern in the quantity takeoff for any area of construction. There is some inevitable waste in framing lumber, depending on spans, wall heights, and the grade of lumber. A rule of thumb for lumber waste is 5–10%, depending on material quality and the complexity of the framing.

Making Sure You Have the Correct Stock

The lead framer should be made aware of any material lists, structural framing drawings, shop drawings, engineered drawings, or cut lists that have been prepared for a framing project. This information is critical to ensure that the correct stock (lengths and widths) is used in the assembly of the frame. Read all notes on the drawings and find out whether the plans being used are the most recently amended or approved.

Using the plans and shop drawings, the lead framer can determine which material to use for cripples, jacks, headers, blocking, and other miscellaneous members.

"Short" or "Will Call" Deliveries

Keep in mind that many initial stock deliveries are "short," meaning that as the project nears completion, someone is responsible for ordering just enough materials to complete the frame. This is sometimes referred to as "will call." The lead framer needs to know in advance if this strategy is being used.

On some projects where material storage and handling are restricted, a "just-in-time" delivery schedule may be necessary. This means that the lead framer must in some cases anticipate material and equipment needs on a daily basis.

In "will call" or "just-in-time" situations, the lead framer must be made aware of any problems in deliveries and must estimate and plan material use in order to maximize the productivity.

How Change Orders Affect the Schedule

A lead framer may be given instructions to perform change orders with little regard for how the change will affect crew productivity. (A better scenario would be that the lead framer is asked for his or her input on what, how, when, and why the change has been requested and what the effects will be.)

The cost of change order work varies according to how much of the installation has already been completed. Once workers have the project in their mind, even if they have not started, it can be difficult to re-focus. The lead framer may spend more time than usual understanding and explaining the change. Modifications to work in-place, such as trimming and refitting, usually take more time than was initially estimated. Post-installation changes generally involve some demolition. The change may come after finishes and trim are installed and may require protection of in-place work.

When faced with a change or a rework situation, the lead framer must break down the typical day into segments and estimate the impact on each segment. Say a change involves reframing an opening or creating a new opening in a wall that has been completed. The estimated time for the change should account for demolition, possible salvage of original materials to be reused, procurement of new materials required, and possibly a reluctance of the crew to perform the change. The time spent on the change will generally add time to work in progress. If the lead framer anticipated four openings per day and now has to reframe two, productivity for framing openings may drop to three per day until the change is complete. This will delay setting windows or installing exterior sheathing and other tasks.

Recordkeeping

Recordkeeping is quite possibly one of those tasks that you thought you were getting away from when you started framing. The reality is that recordkeeping is an important, but not necessarily major task for the lead framer. There are three things you will want to keep records for: timekeeping, changes to the plans, and extra work.

Timekeeping

Timekeeping is easy, but you have to record it every day. If you don't, it's easy to forget and make a mistake that is not caught until the payroll checks come out. Most companies provide forms that can be filled out at the end of every day. You will need some type of an organizer to store your time cards and other records. For a small job, an aluminum forms folder, similar to what the UPS drivers use, works well. These folders are durable and keep the rain out. If you are working on a big job, you will probably need something like a builder's attaché to keep all your papers organized.

Keeping Your Papers Organized

Your time cards can be kept in your organizer so you always know where they are.

Changes to the Plans

Changes to the plans should always be recorded when they occur. Changes may be conveyed in conversation or in writing. Because the time when you receive the changes is not always the time you will be doing the work, it is important to record the information so that you will not forget it. The best place to record changes is on your plans. Write it on the sheet where you will see it, then write the date and the name of the individual who gave you the change. If it was given to you on paper, keep that document in your organizer after you have written the change on the plans. You can also tape the change to the plans. If there is not enough room to record the changes on the appropriate sheet, tape the information on the back of the prior sheet so you will see it when you are reading the sheet involving the changes.

Extra Work

The third recordkeeping task is recording change orders. This is important because if work is done that wasn't originally figured in the framing bid or contract, it must be documented in order to obtain payment. This can be a sensitive issue. Many times there is controversy over payment for tasks that are not clearly defined in the bid or contract. If at any time you are asked to

Plans with Taped Changes

perform work that you consider a change order, you should inform the person asking you to do the work right away that this extra work constitutes a change order, and that you expect to be paid for it. The person requesting the extra work can then decide whether they still want to make the change, knowing the extra cost it involves.

When you actually perform the change order work, make sure you record the work done and the cost to be billed. If you are to be paid on a time and material basis, you need to keep accurate time records showing the hour of the day and the day the work was performed.

Conclusion

When you started reading this chapter, you were probably hoping for some nice clean answers on how to manage a crew—answers that you could put to use tomorrow. Now you are probably thinking that you have more questions than you did when you started reading—and that's the way it should be. Managing a crew is a never-ending job that will challenge you every day. The information presented in this chapter should give you a base for the common-sense decisions you will have to continually make in response to the questions that come up as you manage your crew.

Chapter Five

Advanced Framing: Layout

The construction industry is unique. On every job a group of participants must be assembled to get the structure built. The participants include people with varying backgrounds, knowledge, training, and experience—from the owner, architect, and engineer to the builder, superintendent, material suppliers, and skilled craftsmen of every trade. In some cases, some or all of the participants may have worked together on a previous job. In most cases, however, the organizational process starts from scratch with each new building.

Layout for framing requires the lead framer to bring together the desires of the owner, the written instructions of the architect and engineer, instructions from the builder and superintendent, and materials from the supplier—then write them on job site lumber in a legible manner so that the framers can build the walls, floors, and roofs without continuous interpretation. This chapter describes this process, and explains the written words and symbols the lead framer uses—known as *layout language*.

There are many different styles and variations of layout language. The approach you use will depend on the size of the job, the area of the country you are working in and, most of all, the style of the person who taught you framing layout. This chapter presents a common style of layout and variations of this style. Any style you use is good, as long as the framers can read and understand it, and you have provided all the information they need to frame the building completely.

Contents

Wall Layout

On many jobs the basic skeleton of the walls is built, and then the blocking, hold-downs, and miscellaneous framing are filled in as a later operation. There are some disadvantages to installing miscellaneous framing after the basic framing. For example, you may have to notch around wires and pipes. You may even have to come back and set up a separate operation after you have already left the job site. This chapter describes a system that includes everything possible in the layout, so the walls can be framed, complete, all at one time. To do this takes organization and pre-planning, which includes gathering all the information you need before you do the layout.

The positioning of the top plate and bottom plate for layout detailing is a variable that depends on personal preference and the type of operations. The plate can be positioned vertically so that the 1½" width is on top, which makes it easy for marking on the plate. The plate can also be laid flat (horizontally) on top of the chalk lines so that the plates are in the same position as when the walls are standing. This system makes it easy to keep the walls in the proper position, particularly when you have angled walls. A third option (for some exterior walls only) is to position the bottom plate where it will be once the wall is standing, then tack the top plate to it, hanging over the side. This system works well if you want to attach the bottom plate to the floor and then stick-frame the wall.

The layout language varies, but all layout styles are similar. The language chart later in the chapter shows the basic layout language. Although the parts of the walls are typically the same in different areas of the country, quite often they are referred to by different names. For example, a *backer* is also known as a *channel* or *partition*. Even the term "layout" can have different meanings. Sometimes layout is understood to be the total process of chalking the lines for the wall locations (snapping), cutting the plates, and writing the layout language on the plates (detailing). It is not important what terms are used, as long as there is clear communication.

Wall Plates Positioned Vertically for Layout

Miscellaneous Wall Framing Layout

Each building has unique characteristics that require special attention. Hold-downs, shear walls, blocking, backing, special stud heights, and posts are some of the more common miscellaneous framing items. The framing language for miscellaneous framing items is not well-defined because the operations frequently change and are not always used. The Miscellaneous Layout Language Chart later in the chapter gives you an idea of how these framing tasks can be communicated.

Hold-Downs

Hold-downs are probably the most difficult to mark correctly. They vary from location to location and require different studs or posts for connecting.

Wall Plates Positioned Horizontally for Layout

Top Plate Tacked to Bottom Plate Hanging Over Edge of Concrete for Layout

Wall Layout Language

	Layout	**Studs** (Cutaway, looking down on wall from above)
Corner	`COR`	
Backer	⊠	
Stud trimmer	`X` `T`	
Double corner	`D COR`	
Double backer	`DB`	
Stud	`X`	
Double stud	`X` `X`	
Staggered studs	`U` `D` `U` `D` U = Up D = Down	
Beam	81⅛T `X` `T` `T` Write trimmer height (T) next to layout	
Nonbearing flat header	36" F	
Nonbearing L-header	39" L	
Nonbearing cripple header, more than 4'	60" C	
Bearing walls, solid header, sizes vary	39" (4 × 8)	
Header layout	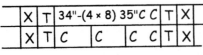 C = Cripple	

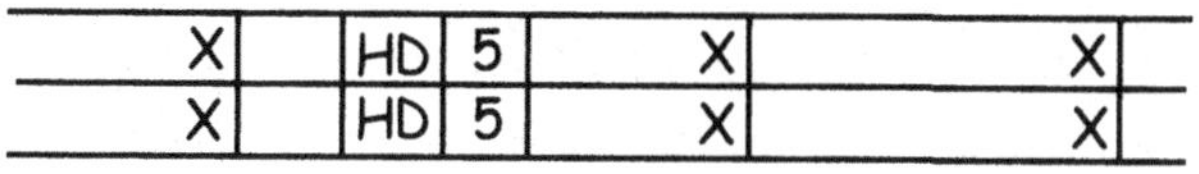

Miscellaneous Layout Language Chart

X		HD	5		X			X	
X		HD	5		X			X	

Holdown 5

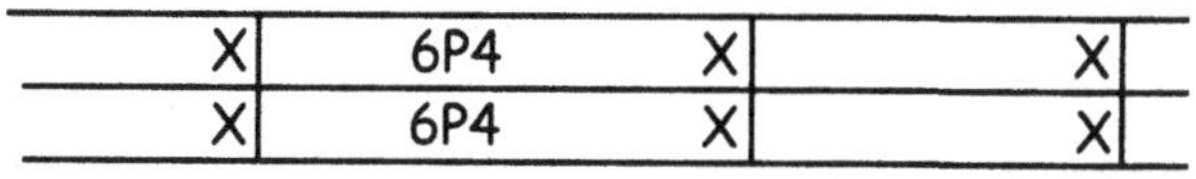

X		6P4		X			X
X		6P4		X			X

6" O.C. plate nailing
P = Plywood sheathing
4" edge nailing

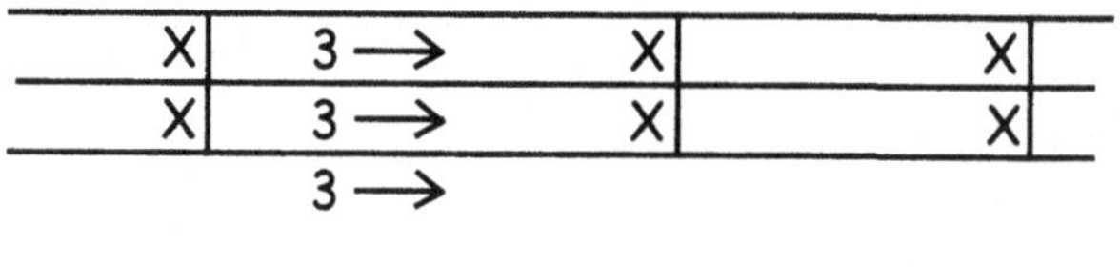

X		3 $\longrightarrow$		X			X
X		3 $\longrightarrow$		X			X
		3 $\longrightarrow$					

Location mark

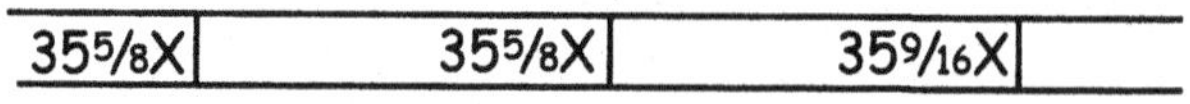

$35^5\!/\!_8$X	$35^5\!/\!_8$X	$35^9\!/\!_{16}$X	

Special length studs

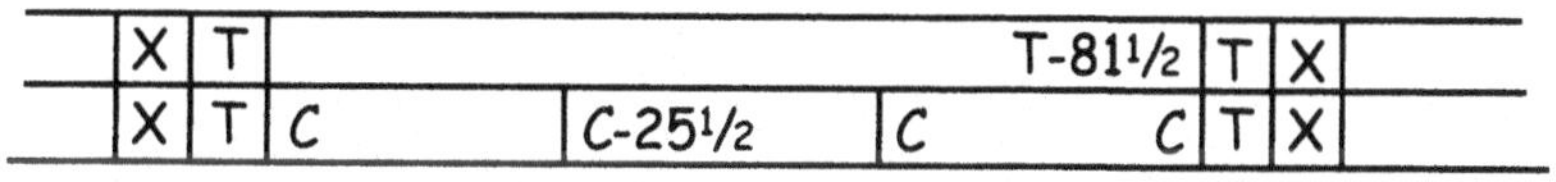

X	T				T-81½	T	X
X	T	C	C-25½	C	C	T	X

Cripple heights

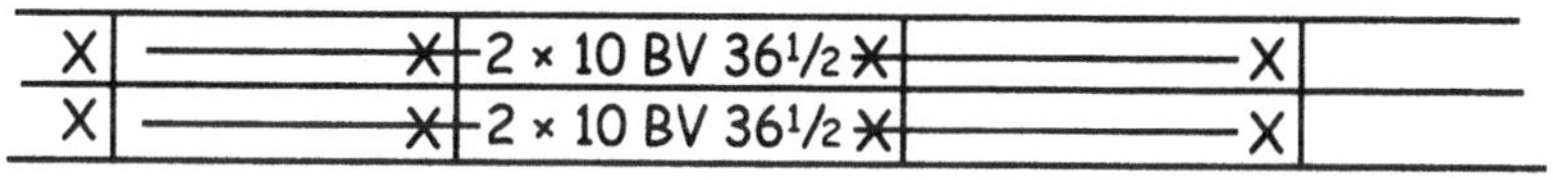

Blocks
2 × 10
B = Block
V = Vertical
36½" = Center height from floor
——— = extent of blocking

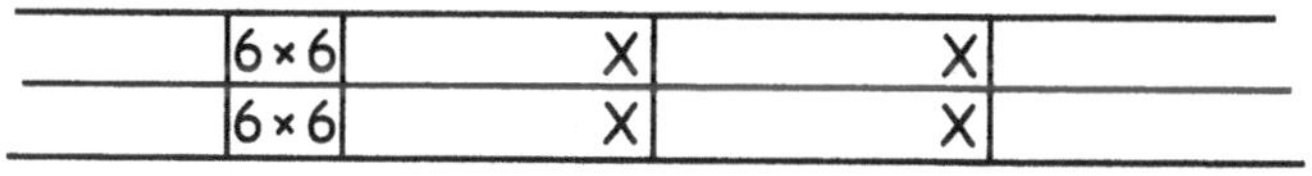

X	———	X	2 × 10 BV 36½	X	———	X	
X	———	X	2 × 10 BV 36½	X	———	X	

6 × 6		X		X		
6 × 6		X		X		

Posts

X			X	
X			X	

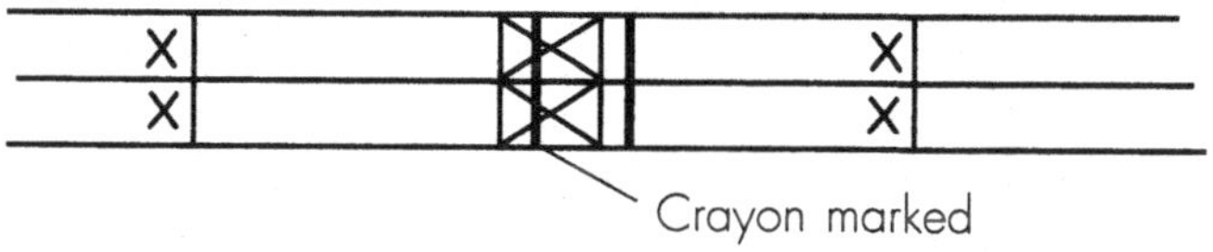

Offset backer

Crayon marked

There are also different types of hold-downs, and each manufacturer has its own identification system. There are, however, four basic styles of hold-downs that you need to show in your wall layout.

1. This is the basic hold-down, which bolts, nails, or screws to the hold-down post or studs. This type is typically attached to an anchor bolt in the foundation, or bolted to an all-thread rod that is connected to a hold-down in the wall below. (See "Hold-Downs with Floor Between" illustration below.)

2. This hold-down is already embedded in the concrete and needs only to be attached to the wall. (See "Hold-Down in Concrete" illustration on the next page.)

3. This is a strap used to connect the top of one wall to the bottom of the wall above. (See "Strap Wall to Wall" illustration on the next page.)

4. This hold-down is continuous between all floors from the foundation to the top floor that is being secured with hold-downs. (See "Hold-Down, Continuous" illustration later in chapter.)

The difficulty for a lead framer in laying out for hold-downs is knowing what to write on the plates so that the requirement will be easily understood. The best thing to do is to explain to the framers at the beginning of each job what symbols you are using to indicate hold-downs.

Hold-Downs with Floor Between

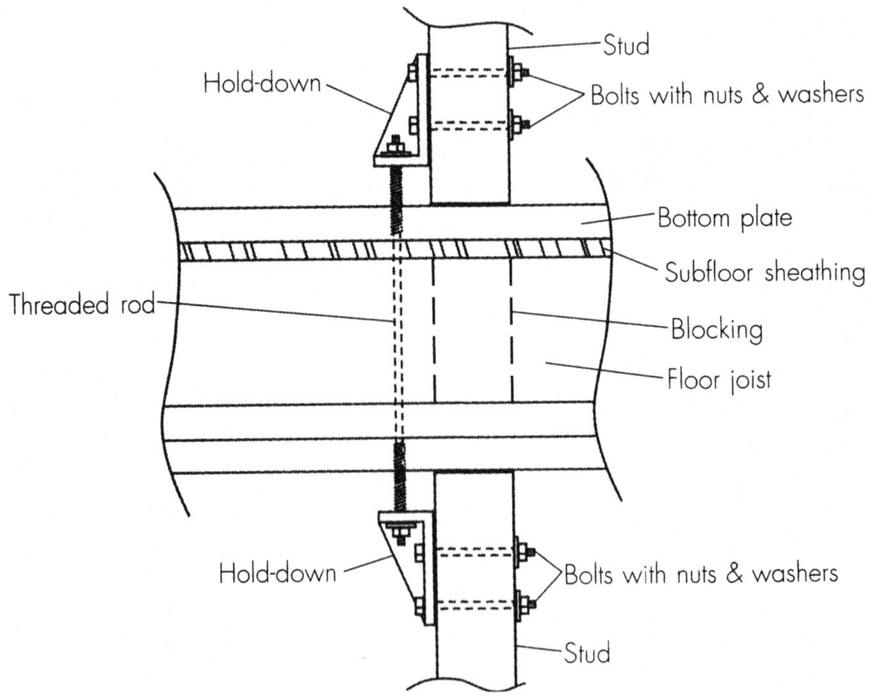

Hold-Down in Concrete

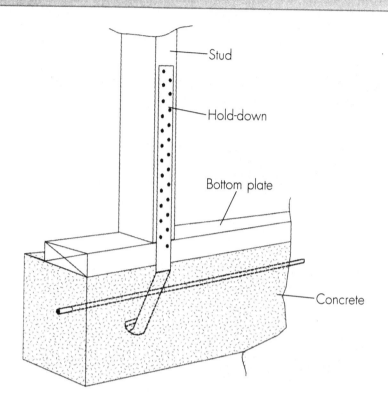

Stud

Hold-down

Bottom plate

Concrete

Strap Wall to Wall

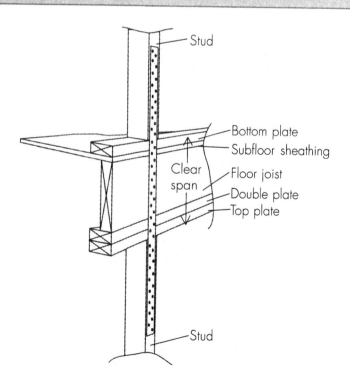

Stud

Bottom plate
Subfloor sheathing
Floor joist
Double plate
Top plate

Clear span

Stud

Use the same language when possible at different jobs. The most common symbol for hold-downs is HD, followed by the number representing the size of the hold-down—for example, HD2 or HD5.

When you are laying out for hold-downs, it's important to get the layout in the right location. Since the purpose of a hold-down is to connect the building to the foundation, the hold-downs must line up with the anchor bolt in the foundation below them. Hold-downs are typically found at the end of shear walls. Engineers sometimes position hold-downs attached to posts at the ends of walls or within a specific distance from the ends of walls. If that information is not specified, keep the hold-down as close to the end of the wall as possible. If the hold-down anchor bolt is already in the concrete, then you can only position it in two locations—one on either side of the hold-down anchor bolt. (See "Hold-Down Either Direction" illustration below.)

If you are using the epoxy system and installing the anchor bolts later, you have more options. A good rule of thumb is to keep the hold-down within one foot of the end of the wall. However, the shorter the wall, the closer the hold-down should be to the ends of the wall.

When laying out for a hold-down, you want the studs or post to be in the correct position in relation to the anchor bolt or hold-down in the wall.

Hold-Down Either Direction

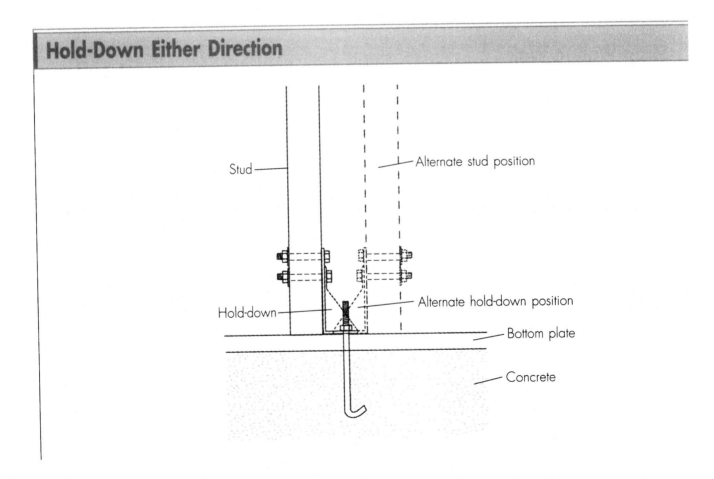

A good way to make sure the distance from the studs to the anchor bolt is correct is to use one of your hold-downs to mark the pattern and location of the studs or post. (See "Hold-Down as Pattern" illustration.) If you do not have a hold-down available for this purpose, you can use the manufacturer's hardware catalog to find the distance from the anchor bolt to the studs.

When you are laying out for the hold-downs on an upper floor, it is helpful to mark the location of the hole to be drilled in the plate and the floor. You have to locate the hole anyway to lay out the studs. By marking its location, you are saving someone else from having to locate it again. It is easiest to go ahead and drill the holes through the floor then, before the walls are built. These holes can be oversized to make alignment easier.

Shear Walls

Shear walls have unique characteristics, but the most common information a framer needs to know about them is the type of sheathing, the edge nail spacing, and the nail spacing for nailing of the bottom plate. The sheathing used is typically either plywood or OSB, identified as "P," or gypsum, identified as "G." The edge nailing is designated as a number after the P or G, and the floor nailing as a number before the P or G. An example could be "6P4," meaning that the bottom plate is nailed at 6" on center, the sheathing is plywood, and the edge nailing is 4" on center. The language for shear walls can be written on the plates with the other language, but it is

Hold-Down as Pattern

best to also write it on the top of the bottom plate. That way, when you get around to nailing the wall down, the nailing pattern will still be visible.

Different Length Studs

Some walls will have studs of different lengths. Examples are rake walls or walls where the concrete is not level, and the studs are cut to compensate. In such cases, you will want to write the stud lengths on the plate next to the studs.

Cripples

The cripples to be framed over and under the windows and doors will be laid out on the same layout as the studs. You will mark them with a line and a "C," and indicate their lengths on the plates—for example, "C-25½"." Mark the cripple height for the cripples that go below the window on the bottom plate, and the cripple height for the cripples that go above the window or door on the top plate.

Blocking

Many kinds of blocks are installed in walls. Some common blocks are fire blocks, medicine cabinet blocks, cabinet blocks, stair rail blocking, curtain rod blocking, and wainscot blocking. The hardest part of laying out for

Hold-Down, Continuous

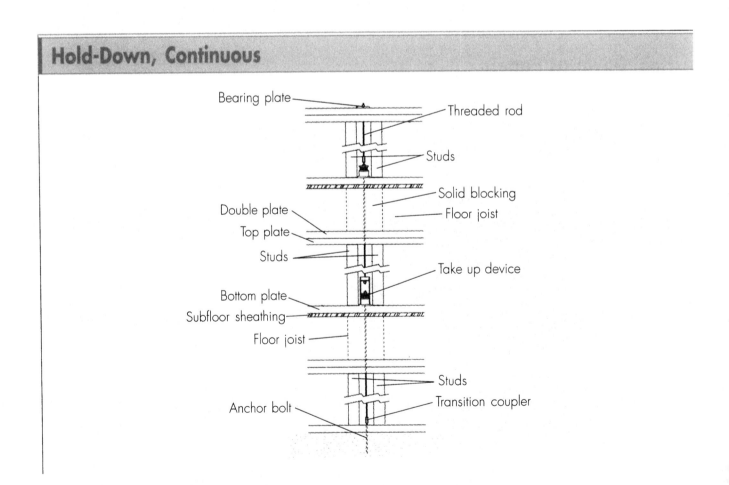

these blocks is getting the right information so you can figure out their location. You might as well find this information before you build the wall, since it is easier and more efficient to install the blocks as you build the walls than afterwards.

Two basic types of blocks are installed in walls. One is a horizontal block that fills the whole stud space as a fire block does. The other is a vertical block that is flush with one side of the wall.

The vertical block is more often used for backing to provide a greater area for attaching other fixtures. To position a block in the wall, a framer needs to know if the block is vertical or horizontal, the height of the block, and the size. This information is written with a "B" first, indicating blocking, and then either a "V" or an "H," indicating a vertical or horizontal position. The height is then written following the V or H, indicating the center height of the block from the subfloor sheathing or the concrete. If the block is the same width as the studs in the wall, then that is all the information that is necessary. However, if the block is a different width than the wall, then the size of the block should be written before the "B." If there are a number of blocks in a row, as is the case with fire blocking, you can just mark one stud space and (with a carpenter crayon) draw a line in both directions to indicate the extent of the blocking.

Vertical and Horizontal Blocks

Backer Layout

Normal backer layout has the layout marks for a backer aligned with the position of the wall that will be nailed into the backer. This isn't always the case, however. Sometimes it is better to move the backer so it does not line up. For example, you might have a door next to the backer, with only 2½" between the backer and the rough opening of the door. Instead of having a 1½" trimmer and a 1" king stud, you just attach a 1½" trimmer to the backer and move it over ½". The best way to mark this on the wall layout is to mark both positions of the backer. The first position is where the backer would align with the wall, and the second is where the backer was moved and where it will be nailed. A good way to distinguish the two positions is to mark over the one line with a carpenter's crayon (keel or lumber crayon). This layout information will help when the walls are nailed together. It will also help when you are cutting the double plate of the joining wall to overlap. (See "Backer Move" illustration on next page.)

Special Stud Layouts

It is important to be aware of special stud layouts, such as might be required for shower or bathtub center valves. Showers and tubs are typically 30" wide. Space must be allowed in the middle for the valves. It's usually easy to find the center and then set a stud 8" on center each way (see "Plumbing Studs" illustration). Recessed medicine cabinets are another special layout. They typically require a 14½" rough opening and could fit between standard 16" O.C. spaces. More often than not, however, the design requires installation in a particular location that requires special layout.

Backing for Siding

Different types of siding require different types of backing. For example, bevel siding with a wide window will require an extra stud or extra backing along the window to attach the siding.

Structural Support

Often a beam or girder truss, or some other structural member, requires structural support all the way to the foundation, but that support is not shown on the plans. Check and lay out for upper floor structure support when laying out walls.

Location Marks

Another mark you might need to make on your walls is for location. If you have to move the plates to make room to build walls, then you need to mark the location for all the walls to make sure you know where they go when you are ready to build them. It is best to use a crayon and mark a number and an arrow on each plate. The top and bottom plates will be marked with the same number. The arrows will point in the same direction as all the

Backer Move

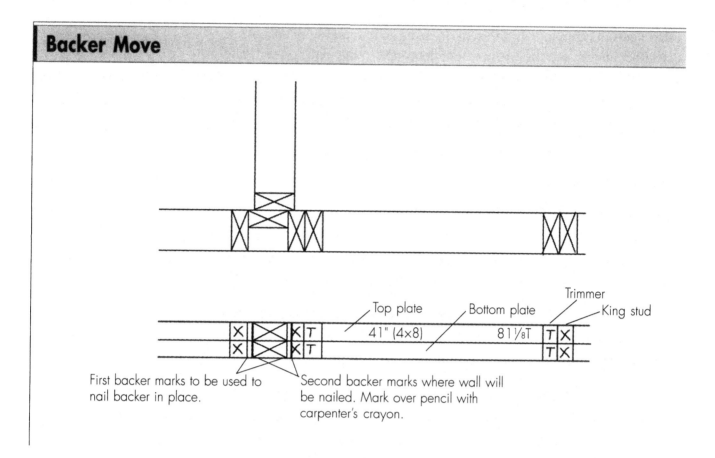

Trimmer

King stud

Top plate

Bottom plate

41" (4×8)

81⅛T

First backer marks to be used to nail backer in place.

Second backer marks where wall will be nailed. Mark over pencil with carpenter's crayon.

Plumbing Studs

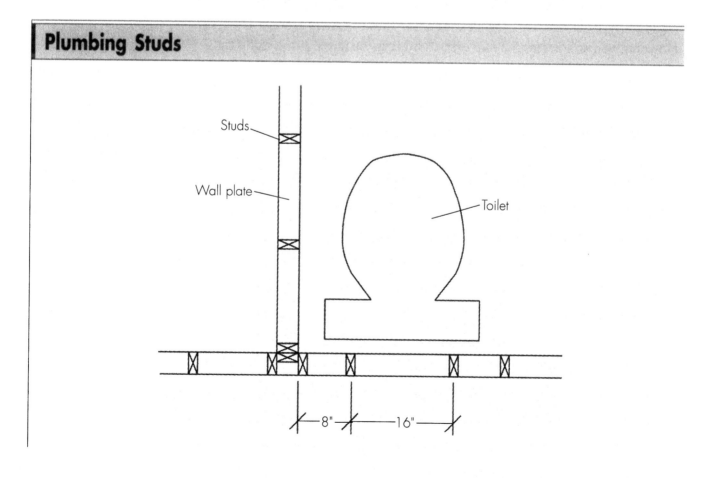

Studs

Wall plate

Toilet

8"

16"

other walls that run in that direction. In addition to marking the plates, mark the number and the arrow on the floor next to the plates. (See "Plate Location Marks" photo below.)

If you are laying out walls on a concrete slab, then you will have to contend with plumbing and electrical pipes. Before you start your layout, notch the bottom plate to fit.

Layout Methods

Use the Correct Order

When you perform the layout, follow a prioritized order. For example, trimmer and king studs for doors and windows take priority over studs. That is because if a stud falls on the location of a trimmer or king stud, then the stud is eliminated. Using a certain order for layout also helps you keep track of where you were if you are pulled off layout and have to come back later to pick up where you left off. The order should be doors and windows first, then bearing posts, backers and corners, then hold-downs—followed by special studs like medicine cabinet studs, then regular studs, and finally miscellaneous framing, such as blocks.

Align Framing Members

It is good practice when laying out studs to align the roof trusses, floor joists, and studs. This is not entirely possible in most cases because the studs are typically 16" O.C., while the roof trusses or rafters are 24" O.C. However, you will at least line up every third truss or rafter. If the studs are

Plate Location Marks

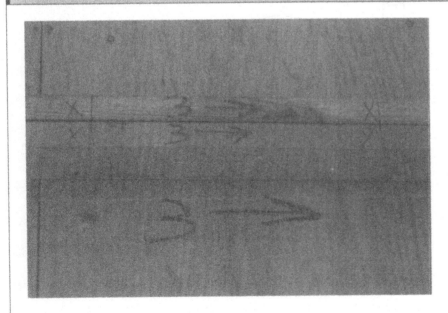

24" O.C., then they need to align with the trusses or rafters. Aligning the studs, joists, and trusses or rafters not only makes good sense structurally, but makes it easier for the plumbers and electricians to run their pipes and wire between floors.

Consult the Roof and Floor Drawings

To start laying out your studs, you need to know the layout of your roof and floor systems. If you are using dimensional lumber, then you can most likely start the layout for your roof and floor wherever it is convenient. If, however, you are using I-joists or roof trusses, the layout will probably be defined on a set of shop drawings provided by the supplier. You should receive a set of these shop drawings before you start laying out your studs, so that you can align wherever possible. Once you have decided on a starting point for your layout in each direction, use the same layout throughout the building. Although it is not structurally necessary to align nonbearing interior walls with multiple floors, it is helpful to have the studs aligned for the plumbers and electricians.

A Word of Caution

Some production framing techniques speed up the layout process, but be careful, if you use them, not to sacrifice quality. For example, instead of using the X with a line next to it to indicate a stud, a single line can be used to represent the center of the stud. Be careful with this designation, because the studs need to line up with the middle of the wall sheathing. If you figure that you allow ⅛" for expansion between the sheets of sheathing, that only allows ¹¹/₁₆" for nailing each side. You cannot afford to be off by even a small amount and still get enough stud to nail to. If you use this system, you also have to be sure that your framers are competent and can align the studs properly.

Other Tasks That Can Be Done Along with Layout

Some items can be attended to while you are performing the layout. One is to cut a kerf in the bottom of the bottom plate at door thresholds when they are sitting on concrete. This kerf (about half the thickness of the plate) allows you to cut out your bottom plate after the walls are standing without ruining your saw blades on the concrete. [See "Kerf Cut (Threshold Cut)" photo next page.]

You can take care of another item while drilling the bottom plate to install over anchor bolts. When the bottom plate is taken off the bolts to do the layout, it can be turned over and accidentally built into the wall upside-down. This problem can be prevented by using a carpenter crayon to mark "UP" on the top of the plate before it is removed from the bolts. Angle walls have the same potential for getting built with the plates backward. You can also mark them as they are being laid out.

Layout Tools

There are some tools that can help with layout, particularly with multi-unit or mass production-type framing. One of these is the channel marker, a template made to assist in laying out corners and backers. Another is a layout stick. The layout stick is 49½" long and is placed on the plates to act as a jig for marking studs. (See "Channel Marker and Layout Stick" photo below.)

Kerf Cut (Threshold Cut)

Channel Marker and Layout Stick

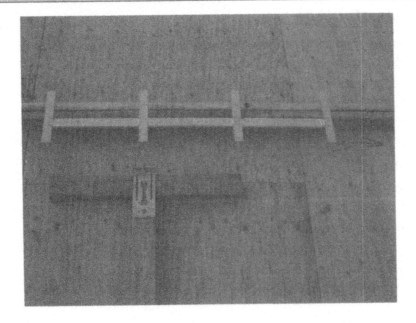

Floor Joist Layout

Joist layout is relatively easy compared with wall layout. It uses the same basic language as walls.

Special layout for joists includes the area under the toilet and shower drain. It is easier to move a joist a couple of inches or even to add a joist than to come back and header out a joist because the plumber had to cut it up to install pipes. On larger buildings, there may be shop drawings for the floor joists which can be used for your layout. The shop drawings should show the locations of openings and how they should be framed. (See "Joist Layout Language" illustration next page.)

Rafter or Truss Layout

Rafter or truss layout, like floor joist layout, is relatively easy compared with wall layout. Sometimes it is helpful to lay out for rafters or trusses on the top of the double plate so that once the wall is standing, the layout will already be done, and you won't have to do it from a ladder. (See "Rafter Layout on Walls Before the Wall is Stood Up" illustration next page.)

Special layout is often required for ceiling can-lights. Check on necessary clearance to make sure you provide enough room.

Conclusion

Writing layout is just like writing anything else. If the person reading it understands what you want to say, then you've done a good job. When you are done with the layout, take a look at it to make sure you can read it. If your writing is not showing up clearly, you might try a different brand of carpenter pencil. There are different leads, and some write better than others, depending on the condition of the wood. You can also use indelible marking pens, which are especially good on wet lumber.

Review the layout with the framer who will be reading it before they start. If a framer doesn't understand your layout, it takes more time for him to try to figure it out than for you to explain it to him. A little extra time spent on layout is usually a good investment. It's not easy taking information from all the different sources that combine in the construction of a building and making it legible for framing, but if the layout is communicated clearly it will help the framers do their work in an organized and productive manner.

Joist Layout Language

Joist	X
Tail joist	T
Double joist	X X
Beam	6 × 12

Roof Layout Language

Rafter or truss	X
Tail rafter or truss	T
Double rafter or truss	X X

Rafter Layout on Walls Before the Wall is Stood Up

Chapter Six

Advanced Framing: Rafters

The angles and pitches of a roof are as varied as the colors in a child's crayon box. Just as some colors have certain characteristics in common, so do rafters. This chapter covers the common characteristics related to the cutting of rafters.

Contents

Important Considerations for Cutting Rafters

When cutting rafters, you need to consider the following four factors:

1) The length
2) The adjustment to the length at the top and bottom
3) The angle of cuts at the top, bottom and the bird's mouth
4) The height at the bird's mouth

You should note the following about each factor:

1. Length is determined by two factors—distance spanned and slope.

2. The top and bottom adjustments can depend on a number of factors and are almost always a little different. The two main factors are the distance from the true ridge or framing point, and the connection with other framing members.

3. The angle cuts relate to the pitch of the roof and the position of the framing member the rafters are attaching to.

4. The height of the bird's mouth can be set by details on the plans, for bearing, or to keep the roof level at the plate height.

There are many different ways to cut and set rafters. It doesn't matter which method is used as long as the completed roof is structurally sound and looks the way it was intended. Different approaches work best on different types of roofs. Sometimes a combination of methods works best.

This chapter will not discuss the specifics of all the different rafter cutting methods, but will instead describe what is possibly the easiest way for figuring the information needed to cut rafters. Using this method, you will be able to "cut and stack" a roof. That is to say, you will be able to cut all the rafters on the ground and stack them ready for installation before the first one is installed.

First we need to define some basic terms.

Span—the distance between two supporting members, typically measured from the outside of two bearing walls.

Run—horizontal distance.

Rise—vertical distance.

Diagonal—the distance between the far point on the run and the high point on the rise. (Similar to hypotenuse in mathematical terms.)

Hip or valley run—the horizontal distance below the hip or valley of a roof, from the outside corner of the wall to the center framing point.

Overhang hip run—the horizontal distance below the overhang hip of the roof, from the outside corner of the wall to the outside corner of the fascia.

Hip or valley diagonal—the distance between the far point on the hip or valley run and the high point on the hip or valley rise.

Overhang diagonal—the distance between the far point on the overhang run and the high point on the overhang rise.

Diagonal percent—equals the diagonal divided by the run.

Hip-Val diagonal percent—equals the hip or valley diagonal divided by the hip or valley run.

Rise percent—equals the rise divided by the run.

Pitch—The slope of the roof, or the relationship of the run to the rise. Typically defined as a certain height of rise for 12 units of run for a common rafter, and 17 (16.97) units of run on a 90° hip or valley rafter.

Framing point—The point where the center lines of connecting rafters, ridges, hips, or valleys would meet.

Cheek cut—An angle cut that is made to bear against another rafter, hip, or valley.

Common rafter—A rafter running from a wall straight to a ridge board.

Jack rafter—A rafter running to a hip rafter or a valley rafter.

Hip rafter—A rafter at an outside corner of a roof that runs in between and joins jack rafters that bear on corner walls.

Valley rafter—A rafter at an inside corner of a roof that runs between and joins with jack rafters from each side.

Ridge end rafter—A rafter that runs from the end of a ridge.

Pitch angle—The vertical angle on the end of a rafter that represents the pitch of the roof.

Connection angle—The horizontal angle at the end of a rafter needed to connect to other rafters, hips, valleys, or ridge boards.

There are calculators that are made specifically for assisting with construction math. These are very helpful in finding rafter lengths. Construction Master IV® is one available calculator, which we will refer to and use in this chapter to demonstrate the process of finding rafter lengths. These calculators make it easy to do the complicated math, working in feet and inches. The sequence of buttons takes a little time to master, but once you are familiar with them, you will never go back to pencil and paper.

1) Figuring Rafter Length

The length of a rafter can be found by determining the horizontal length (run) that it covers, and the pitch of the roof. The constant relationship between these factors is defined as the **diagonal percent**. This percent is constant for any common or jack rafter on any roof that has the same pitch. To find the length of a rafter, multiply the length of the run by the diagonal percent. For example, if you have a roof with a 6/12 pitch and a run of 6'-11¼", you multiply 6'-11¼" by 1.118 (diagonal percent for a 6/12 pitch) and find that your rafter length is 7'-9¹/₁₆". With a construction calculator, enter 7' × 1.118, and it will read 7'-9¹/₁₆". The following illustration provides the diagonal percent for common pitch roofs. To figure the length of hip and valley rafters, use the hip-val diagonal percent shown on the Diagonal Percent Chart.

Diagonal Percent Chart

PITCH	RP-Rise Percent	DP Diagonal Percent	SAW ANGLE	HDP-Hip Diagonal Percent		
1/12	0.083	1.003	4.5	1.002		
2/12	0.167	1.014	9.5	1.007		
3/12	0.25	1.031	14	1.016		
4/12	0.333	1.054	18.5	1.027		
5/12	0.417	1.083	22.5	1.043		
6/12	0.5	1.118	26.5	1.061		
7/12	0.583	1.158	30.25	1.082		
8/12	0.667	1.202	33.75	1.106		
9/12	0.75	1.25	37	1.132		
10/12	0.833	1.302	40	1.161		
11/12	0.917	1.357	42.5	1.192		
12/12	1	1.414	45	1.225		

Rise Percent

RP = Rise Percent = Rise divided by run = Rise/Run

Diagonal Percent

DP = Diagonal Percent = Diagonal divided by Run = Diagonal/Run

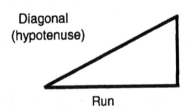

Hip Diagonal Percent

HDP = Hip Diagonal Percent = Hip or Valley Diagonal divided by run = Hip Diagonal/Run

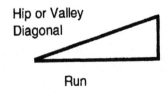

When you use the diagonal percent, the most difficult part of figuring rafter length is finding the length of the run. The adjustments that need to be made at the top and bottom of the rafter should be added and subtracted from the run before the rafter length is calculated. In finding the run, it is best to start with the full run distance from the outside of the bearing wall to the framing point of any connecting framing member. Use the framing point for consistency, and then make adjustments from there.

2) Figuring the Adjustments to Rafter Length at Top and Bottom

Because there are so many different types of connections for rafters, it helps to establish certain standard ways to connect them, and measure them in order to find the proper adjustments to length for the top and bottom. Following are some standard connections and their adjustments. They will not apply to every situation, but they will work for the most common roofs.

Adjustments for Common Rafters

1. Subtract half the thickness of the ridge board at the top.
2. At the bottom measure to the outside of the wall framing (not the sheathing).

Adjust Length for Top of Common Rafter Before Finding Rafter Length

Rafter length
Overhang diagonal
Run diagonal

1½" Ridge board

12
6

2 x 12

10⅛"

6'-11¼"
7'-0"

22½"
24"

Span 14'-0"
Adjustment
Subtract ½ the thickness of the ridge board.
This example = ¾"

Diagonal percent found on chart

This example
Plumb cut height at bird's mouth = 10⅛"
Run diagonal = 6'-11¼" × 1.118 = 7'-9⁹⁄₁₆"
Overhang diagonal = 22½" × 1.118 = 2'-1¹⁄₁₆"
Rafter length = Run diagonal + Overhang diagonal
= 9'-10⅗⁄₁₆"

Adjustments for Hip and Valley Rafters

1. Subtract half the 45° thickness of the ridge board. (See "Connection # 1 (Close-Up) illustration below.)

2. At the bottom, measure to the outside corner of the two connecting walls.

Adjustments for Jack Rafters

1. Measure to the framing point where it meets the hip or valley it is connected to. (See "Adjusting the Top Length for Jack Rafters" illustration later in this chapter.)

2. Subtract half the 45° thickness of the valley rafter.

3. When the rafter rests on an exterior wall, measure to the outside of the wall framing.

Adjustments for Rafters Running Between Hips and Valleys

1. Measure to the framing points where it meets the hip or valley it is connecting to. (See "Adjusting the Top Length for Jack Rafters" illustration later in this chapter.)

2. Subtract half the 45° thickness of the hip or valley rafter at each end.

Connection # 1 (Close-Up)

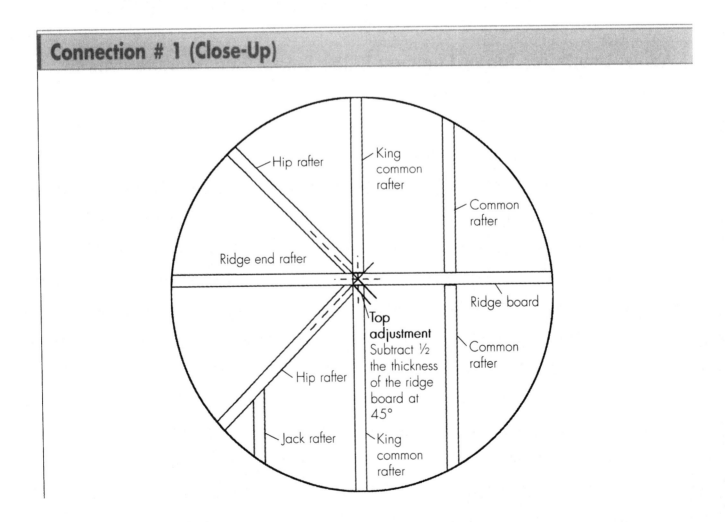

Adjustments for Miscellaneous Connections Between Hips, Valleys, Ridges, and Rafters

1. Find the combination of cuts that provides the greatest number of standard cuts and still provides a sound structural connection.

2. Measure to the framing point for making adjustments.

3. Connection #2 is an example of a miscellaneous connection where a ridge board, a common rafter, a hip rafter and a valley rafter connect. (See "Connection #2" illustration later in chapter.)

Connection # 1

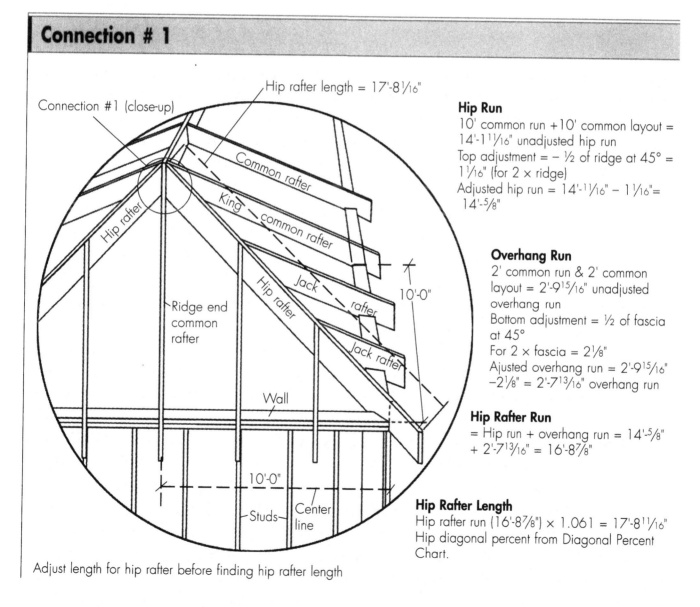

Hip rafter length = 17'-8$\frac{1}{16}$"

Connection #1 (close-up)

Common rafter

King common rafter

Hip rafter

Jack rafter

Jack rafter

Hip rafter

Ridge end common rafter

Wall

10'-0"

10'-0"

Studs

Center line

Hip Run
10' common run + 10' common layout = 14'-1$\frac{1}{16}$" unadjusted hip run
Top adjustment = – $\frac{1}{2}$ of ridge at 45° = 1$\frac{1}{16}$" (for 2 × ridge)
Adjusted hip run = 14'-1$\frac{1}{16}$" – 1$\frac{1}{16}$" = 14'-$\frac{5}{8}$"

Overhang Run
2' common run & 2' common layout = 2'-9$\frac{15}{16}$" unadjusted overhang run
Bottom adjustment = $\frac{1}{2}$ of fascia at 45°
For 2 × fascia = 2$\frac{1}{8}$"
Ajusted overhang run = 2'-9$\frac{15}{16}$" –2$\frac{1}{8}$" = 2'-7$\frac{13}{16}$" overhang run

Hip Rafter Run
= Hip run + overhang run = 14'-$\frac{5}{8}$" + 2'-7$\frac{13}{16}$" = 16'-8$\frac{7}{8}$"

Hip Rafter Length
Hip rafter run (16'-8$\frac{7}{8}$") × 1.061 = 17'-8$\frac{11}{16}$"
Hip diagonal percent from Diagonal Percent Chart.

Adjust length for hip rafter before finding hip rafter length

3) Finding the Angle Cuts at the Top, Bottom, and at the Bird's Mouth

It is easy to figure the angle cuts if you break them down into two separate angles. The first is the **pitch angle**, and the second is the **connection angle**. The pitch angle is either a common or a hip/valley. If you use a speed square, you don't even have to calculate it. If you are cutting a rafter that is not a hip or a valley, then use the common scale on a speed square for the pitch of your roof and draw your pitch angle line on the rafter. If you're cutting a hip or valley rafter, then use the hip-val scale on the speed square. The pitch angle line will be your cut line for your saw cut.

The connection angle depends on a lot of factors, but 45° and 90° are the most commonly used angles. Basically, you will be setting the angle of your saw at the connection angle and cutting the cut line created by the pitch angle. For 90° corners on hips and valleys, the connection angle for jack rafters will be 45°. For standard, common rafters, the top connection angle is 90°.

Adjusting the Top Length for Jack Rafters

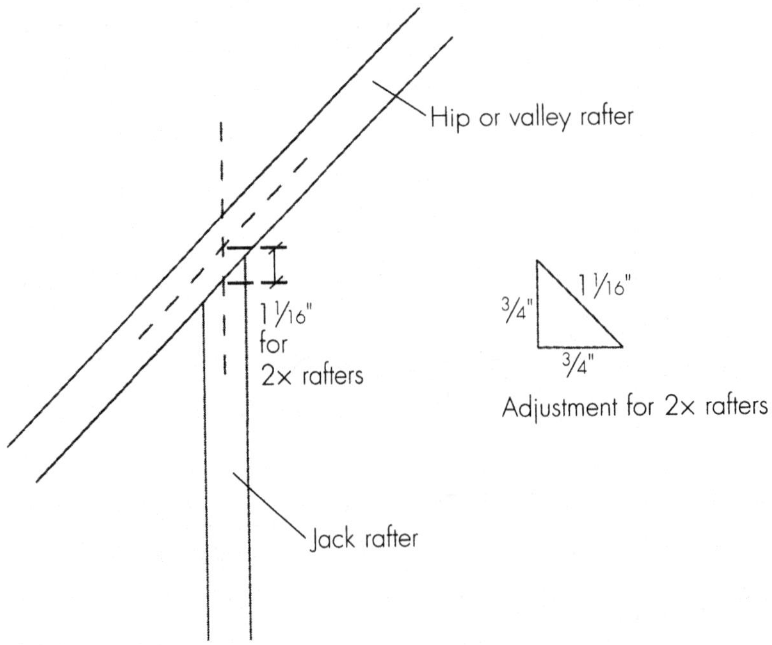

Hip or valley rafter

1 1/16"
for
2x rafters

Jack rafter

1 1/16"

3/4"

3/4"

Adjustment for 2x rafters

Connection #2

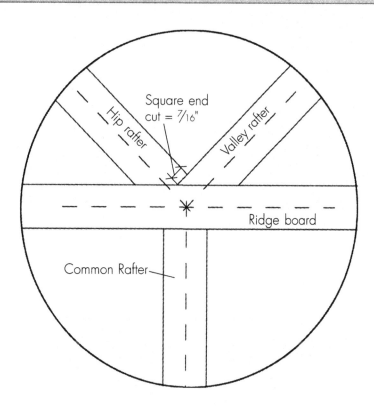

Square end
cut = 7/16"

Hip rafter

Valley rafter

Ridge board

Common Rafter

Pitch and Connection Angle

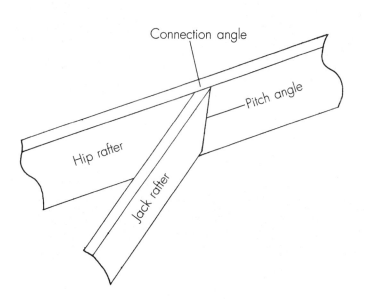

Connection angle

Pitch angle

Hip rafter

Jack rafter

4) Finding the Bird's Mouth Height

The height of the bird's mouth will affect the height of the roof and possibly the interior design of the ceiling. The most common detail for a bird's mouth has the bird's mouth cut starting at the inside corner of the wall.

On a hip and valley, the inside corner won't align with the wall. Since the height of the hip and valley bird's mouth must be the same as the common rafter bird's mouth, you can simply measure the common rafter height and transfer it to the hip and valley bird's mouth. The following chart shows some common bird's mouth heights.

Bird's Mouth Chart

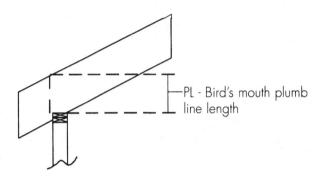

PL - Bird's mouth plumb line length

Bird's Mouth Plumb Line Lengths

2 × 6 Walls

Rafter Size	11¼	9¼	7¼	5½
Pitch				
3/12	10¼	8 3/16	6⅛	4 5/16
4/12	10 1/16	7 15/16	5 13/16	4
5/12	9⅞	7 11/16	5 9/16	3 5/8
6/12	9 13/16	7 9/16	5 3/8	3 3/8
7/12	9 13/16	7½	5 3/16	3 3/16
8/12	9 13/16	7 9/16	5	2 15/16
9/12	9 15/16	7 9/16	4 15/16	2 3/4
10/12	10 1/16	7½	4 7/8	2 5/8
11/12	10 3/16	7½	4 3/4	2 3/8
12/12	10 9/16	7 9/16	4 3/4	2 1/4

2 × 4 Walls

Rafter Size	11¼	9¼	7¼	5½
Pitch				
3/12	10 ¾	8 11/16	6 5/8	4 13/16
4/12	10 11/16	8 9/16	6 7/16	4 5/8
5/12	10 ¾	8 9/16	6 7/16	4 ½
6/12	10 13/16	8 9/16	6 3/8	4 3/8
7/12	10 15/16	8 5/8	6 5/16	4 5/16
8/12	11 3/16	8 13/16	6 3/8	4 5/16
9/12	11 7/16	8 15/16	6 7/16	4 ¼
10/12	11 11/16	9 1/8	6 ½	4 ¼
11/12	12 1/16	9 5/16	6 5/8	4 ¼

On hip rafters, you measure the height to the outside edge of the hip. Whereas on valley rafters it's a little tricky. You need to measure to the center of the valley, which is slightly higher than the outside edge.

Finding Rafter Length: Examples

Breaking the process of cutting rafters into the four basic characteristics described in this chapter helps to organize the task, but it is still a complicated process. Probably the best way to learn is to work through the steps in figuring individual rafters. The following illustration is an example of a roof that has a number of different rafters and a ridge board identified. Nine additional examples explain how to find the lengths for these rafters and ridge board based on the illustration.

Roof Example

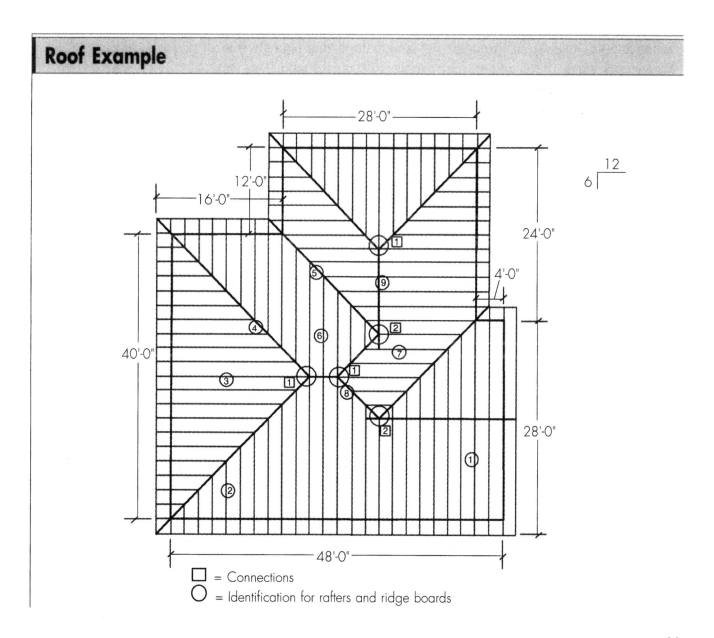

□ = Connections
○ = Identification for rafters and ridge boards

Finding Common Rafter Length—Item ① on Roof Example Illustration

The roof span at this area is 28'-0", making the run equal to ½ the span of 14'-0" minus half the thickness of the ridge board (¾"). That makes the adjusted run 13'-11¼". Multiplying that times the diagonal percent for a 6/12 pitch roof (which is 1.118) gives a run diagonal length of 15'-7". If you add that length to the overhang diagonal of 2'-1⅛", the rafter length is 17'-8⅛". The overhang diagonal is found by subtracting the fascia (1½") from the 2'-0" overhang, which gives (22½"), and multiplying by the diagonal percent 1.118.

Finding a Jack Rafter Length—Item ② on Roof Example Illustration

Most hip rafters are on 90° corners, with the hip runs in the middle of the corner. Because the two sides of a triangle made by a 90° angle and two 45° angles are the same, the run of the jack rafter can be easily found.

The distance of your layout to the center of your rafter is the same distance as your run to the center of your hip. Just subtract one half the thickness of the hip at a 45° angle (1¹⁄₁₆") from the run, and multiply that figure by your diagonal percentage. Then add on your overhang diagonal length. This will give you your rafter length. In this example, the rafter is on layout at 8'-0", so we subtract 1¹⁄₁₆" (half the thickness of the 1½" hip at 45°), giving 7'-10¹⁵⁄₁₆", which is multiplied by the diagonal percent of 1.118. The result is 8'-10⅛". Add this to the overhang diagonal of 2'-1⅛" (same as common

Find Jack Run

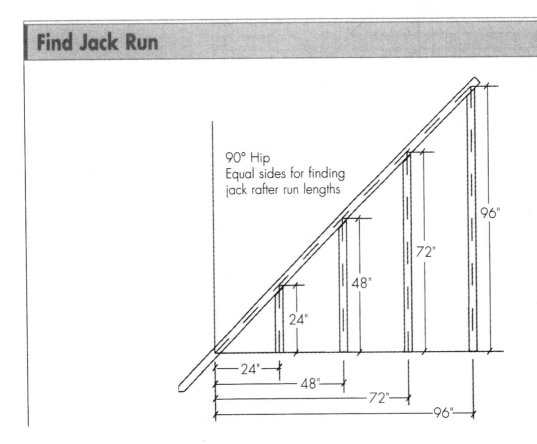

90° Hip
Equal sides for finding jack rafter run lengths

96"

72"

48"

24"

24"

48"

72"

96"

rafter overhang), and we get a jack rafter length of 10'-11¼". Note that because the connection angle is 45°, the measurement should be taken to the center of your cheek cut.

Finding a Ridge End Common Rafter Length—Item ③ on Roof Example Illustration

As long as you use the top cut illustration in "Connection # 1" then this rafter will be cut the same length as the king common rafter adjacent to it.

Finding a Hip Length—Item ④ on Roof Example Illustration

Finding the hip length requires an additional step and uses the hip-val diagonal percent. First find the hip run. It is the diagonal created by a triangle in which the other two sides are the run of the ridge end common and the line from the hip corner to the ridge end common. In this case, the span is 40', so the run is 20', and the distance from the corner is also 20'. Using the calculator, enter 20' for the run, 20' for the rise, and press the diagonal button. The result is 28'- 2³/₈". This distance is the run of your hip. Subtract half the distance of the ridge at a 45° angle, which for a 1½" ridge is 1¹/₁₆", leaving an adjusted hip run of 28'- 3⁵/₁₆". Then find the hip overhang length using a similar procedure. The sides are 2', which leads to a 2'-9¹⁵/₁₆" diagonal. Then subtract 1½" at a 45° angle for the fascia (which is 2¹/₈"), so the hip overhang run is 2'-7¹³/₁₆". Add this figure to the 28'- 2³/₈" hip run, and you get a hip rafter run of 30'-10³/₁₆". Multiplying that number by the hip-val diagonal percent of 1.061 results in a hip rafter length of 32'-8³/₄". Remember, these lengths are to the middle of the rafter, and each end has two 45° connection angle cuts at a 6/12 hip-val pitch angle.

Finding a Valley Rafter Length—Item ⑤ on Roof Example Illustration

This valley will be the same length as the hip rafter for the 28'-0" span section, except for the end cuts. On the bottom, the 45° cuts will be concave (<) instead of convex (>) like the hip. At the top, there will be a full-width 45° cut. The top-end adjustment will require you to subtract one half the thickness of the ridge at 45°, which is 1¹/₁₆".

Finding the valley rafter length is similar to finding the hip length, and requires the following steps:

- Span = 28'-0"
- Run = 14'-0"
- Top adjustment = subtract ½ ridge board at 45° = 1¹/₁₆"
- Hip run = 19'-9⁹/₁₆" = On the calculator enter 14'-0"
  –Then press the *run* button, enter 14'-0"
  –Then press the *rise* button and then the *diagonal* button
- Overhang hip run = 2'-7¹³/₁₆"
  –On calculator enter 1'-10½" *run* then 1'-10½" *rise,* then press *diagonal*

- Add the hip run and the overhang hip run =
  19'-9^{9}/16" + 2'-7^{13}/16" = 22'-5^{3}/8"
- Subtract for the top adjustment ¾" on a 45° = 1^{1}/16" (See "Connection #2" illustration.)
- Adjust the hip rafter run = 22'-5^{3}/8" – 1^{1}/16" = 22'-4^{5}/16"
- Hip rafter length =
  22'-4^{5}/16" × 1.061 (hip-val diagonal percent) = 23'-8^{11}/16"

The top will be a 45° saw cut for the connection angle at a 6/12 hip-val cut for the pitch angle.

The bottom will be concave (<), two 45° saw cuts at a 6/12 hip-val cut.

Finding a Valley-to-Ridge Jack Rafter—Item ⑥ on Roof Example Illustration

There are a couple of ways to find the length of this rafter. The ridge location is easy to establish as half the span of 40', making it 20'. The valley point can be determined by figuring the distance the valley runs before the rafter starts. In this case, since the rafters all conveniently line up and run at 24" O.C., the easiest method is to count the rafter spaces from the other side of the roof. In this example, there are seven rafter spaces; therefore the run will be 14'. Subtract half the distance of the 45° bottom cut for the valley rafter (1^{1}/16"), and half the thickness of the ridge board (^{3}/4"), and the run will be 13'-10^{3}/16". The rafter length will be 13'-10^{3}/16" × 1.118 (diagonal percent) resulting in a 15'-5^{13}/16" rafter length. The connection angle at the top will be a 90° saw cut, and the pitch will be at a 6/12 common cut on the speed square. The bottom will be a 45° saw cut at a 6/12 common cut. The measurement will be to the center of the 45° cheek cut.

Finding Valley-to-Hip Jack Rafter Length—Item ⑦ on Roof Example Illustration

Although there are different ways to find the run length, the following example shows a way that has not yet been illustrated. In this example, run length will be figured from the 28' span length. The run for the 28' span is 14'. The top of the rafter is 2' past the end of the ridge board, which will add 2' to the run going up the hip that it connects to. The run at the bottom will be shortened by 4' because it extends up the valley the equivalent of 4' of run. This leaves 12' of run. Adjust for top and bottom by subtracting one half of a 45°, angle for top and bottom cuts or two times 1^{1}/16" (2^{1}/8") = 11'-9^{7}/8" times 1.118. This makes for a rafter length of 13'-2^{5}/8". Both the top and bottom would have a 45° cheek cut for the connection angle and would be marked at a common 6/12 for the pitch angle.

Ridge-to-Ridge Hip Rafter—Item ⑧ on Roof Example Illustration

In this example the rafters are so conveniently arranged that we can see the hip rafter goes from the center of one rafter to the center of another rafter with two in between, resulting in a distance of 6'. Another way to find this length is to calculate the difference in the runs for the ridges that establish the height difference. One has a span of 28'-0" for a run of 14'-0", while the other has a span of 40'-0" for a run of 20'-0". The difference is 6'-0", the same as figured above.

Once you have the 6'-0" of run, then you follow the same procedure as with a hip and make the necessary top and bottom adjustments. First establish the hip run. Enter 6'-0" run and 6'-0" rise on the calculator and press *diagonal*, which gives you the hip run of 8'-5¹³/₁₆". The top will be a standard hip connection. Therefore one half the ridge at a 45° angle (1¹/₁₆") will be subtracted. At the bottom it will be a #2 connection. Therefore subtract one half the thickness of the ridge at a 45° angle, or 1¹/₁₆". The bottom will also require a square cut ⁷/₁₆" deep on the end. You can establish the thickness of this square cut by finding the diagonal for the triangle in which the other two sides are the same and created by the balance of the difference between half the distance of the ridge board at 45° and half the distance of the ridge board at 90°.

Miscellaneous Connection #2

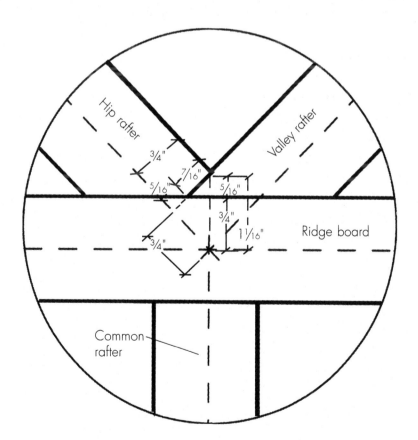

The $^7/_{16}$" square cut will not affect your hip run. This means that you can subtract the $1^1/_{16}$" and $1^1/_{16}$" to get an adjusted hip run of 8'-3$^{11}/_{16}$". Multiplying 8'-3$^{11}/_{16}$" × 1.061 (hip-val diagonal percent) gives you the ridge to ridge hip rafter length of 8'-9$^3/_4$". The top cut will be a regular hip cut with convex (>) 45° cuts at a 6/12 hip-val pitch. The bottom will be a 45° cut at a 6/12 hip-val pitch with a $^7/_{16}$" square cut end.

Finding the Ridge Board Length—Item ⑨ on Roof Example Illustration

The ridge board runs parallel with the wall at the other end of valley #5 and the hip of the 28'-0" span. That length is 12'-0", so the length of the ridge is 12'-0" with adjustments at the ends. The hip connection is a number 1, so one half of the thickness of the common rafter ($^3/_4$") is added. At the other end, it is a connection #2, and the ridge will extend to the next rafter, adding 23$^1/_4$" to the length.

The ridge board length therefore is: 12'-0" + $^3/_4$" + 23$^1/_4$" = 14'-0". Both ends will be cut at 90° with square ends.

Let the Computer Do the Work

Using the methods described above to find the lengths and angles for cutting rafters is not easy, but it is at least organized—and with a calculator that works in feet and inches and that figures the diagonals automatically, the process is straightforward. However, the easiest method is to use the computer. There are software programs currently available that will do all the work for you and produce a sketch of each rafter. Solid Builder is one of these programs. The following illustrations are done in Solid Builder. "Roof Production" identifies the type of roof parts, the quantity, lumber, and strength. "Rafter Profiles" illustrates the individual rafters with the balance of information you will need for cutting the rafters.

The hardest part of producing these computer-generated diagrams is learning the software and then entering the information needed for each structure in order to generate the diagrams. However, for the architect who has already drawn up the plans, or the builder who is working with computer-generated plans, it is an easy task to produce these rafter profiles. If computer-generated rafter profiles were prepared and attached to plans, it could really make framing roofs a breeze.

Conclusion

Until you have framed many roofs, cutting rafters is always going to be a challenge. Three ways to make it easier are:

- First, use the diagonal percent to find the rafter length.
- Second, figure lengths to the framing points and then make the adjustments.
- Third, become familiar with and use a construction calculator for the math.

If ever you get stumped, you can always organize your thinking by using the four basic characteristics of cutting rafters:

1. Find the length.
2. Adjust for the top and bottom.
3. Figure the angle cuts for the top, bottom, and bird's mouth.
4. Figure the height of the bird's mouth.

Roof Production

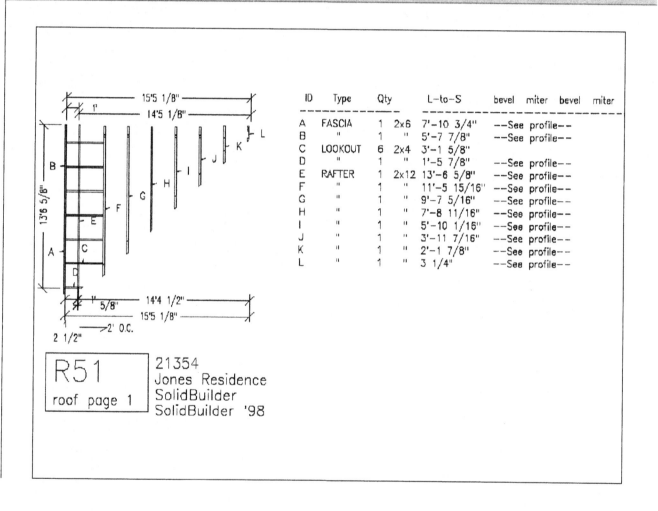

ID	Type	Qty		L—to—S	bevel	miter	bevel	miter
A	FASCIA	1	2x6	7'-10 3/4"	--See profile--			
B	"	1	"	5'-7 7/8"	--See profile--			
C	LOOKOUT	6	2x4	3'-1 5/8"				
D	"	1	"	1'-5 7/8"	--See profile--			
E	RAFTER	1	2x12	13'-6 5/8"	--See profile--			
F	"	1	"	11'-5 15/16"	--See profile--			
G	"	1	"	9'-7 5/16"	--See profile--			
H	"	1	"	7'-8 11/16"	--See profile--			
I	"	1	"	5'-10 1/16"	--See profile--			
J	"	1	"	3'-11 7/16"	--See profile--			
K	"	1	"	2'-1 7/8"	--See profile--			
L	"	1	"	3 1/4"	--See profile--			

R51
roof page 1

21354
Jones Residence
SolidBuilder
SolidBuilder '98

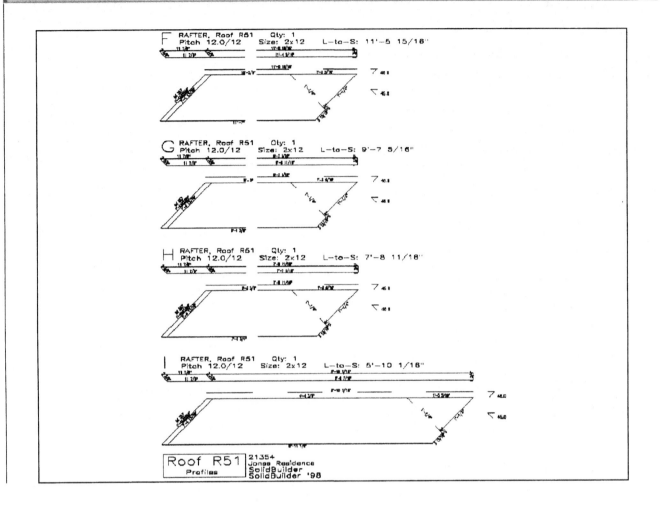

Chapter Seven

Advanced Framing: Stairs

S tairs are one of the more difficult parts of framing. Although cutting and putting them together is basic framing work, figuring them out takes some concentrated thinking. It's easy to make a mistake and difficult to correct one once it's made. This chapter has two parts. The first is a review of the aspects of stair building that you will want to check to make sure your framers are building them correctly. The second part describes the steps involved in building a circular set of stairs.

Contents

Key Stair Elements

The following are important items to go over with your framers to make sure they end up with a good set of stairs.

- Check the code maximum and minimum widths, depths, and heights.

- Remember to review the floor finish on the top, the bottom, and any midway decks for different thickness in the finish floor material. For example, if there is going to be lightweight concrete on the floor sheathing, or if a carpet stair ends on a concrete slab, then the last tread height would have to be adjusted. It is important to stay within the 3/8" height variance (specified in the codes) from most to least between all the risers.

- If you have a midway deck in the stairs, make sure you check the height. Figure the height and measure from the top or bottom of the stairs and then check by figuring the height and measuring from the opposite of top or bottom. If you figured right, your marks should align. (See illustration below.)

- It is not uncommon for a set of plans to be drawn up with the stair headroom to be less than the 6'–8" to finish that the code requires. To check the headroom before you frame the stairs, you need to find the

Deck Height Measures Up and Down

point that is plumb down from the lowest point above the stairs and then measure to the line in a plane with the nosing of your stair treads. Since the stairs are not built yet, the hardest part is finding that nosing plane. You can either work off the plans, if framing has not started, or work with the framing if the frame is ready for the stairs. To find this plumb point on the nosing plane, start from the first nosing, count the number of risers and multiply that number by the riser height; then add the partial riser. To get the partial riser height you just multiply the partial tread length by the riser percent, which is the riser height, divided by the tread length. Once you have found this length, you can measure either up or down, depending on which direction you used, to see if you have enough headroom.

Circular Stairs

Circular stairs are not as difficult as they seem the first time you think about doing them. They do, however, take some thinking and careful work. There

Headroom Calculations for Straight and Circular Stairs

Checking Headroom Height for Stairs
1. Plumb down from lowest headroom point.
2. Count the number of full risers from the end of the stair to the headroom plumb line.
3. Find the partial riser height by multiplying the partial tread length by the riser percent.
4. Height at lowest headroom location equals full riser heights plus partial riser height.

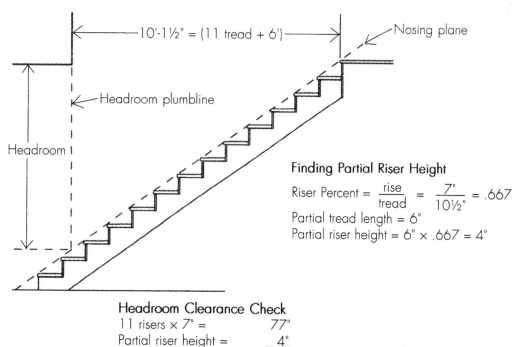

Finding Partial Riser Height

Riser Percent = $\dfrac{rise}{tread}$ = $\dfrac{7"}{10\frac{1}{2}"}$ = .667

Partial tread length = 6"
Partial riser height = 6" × .667 = 4"

Headroom Clearance Check
11 risers × 7" =   77"
Partial riser height =   4"
Headroom at plumbline = 81" = OK minimum to finish is 80"

is no particular way that curved stairs need to be built, as long as they are strong enough to bear the traffic. The method that follows is commonly used. First of all, unlike straight stairs, we will not use stringers. Instead, each tread will be supported independently, by either a wall or a header. The header method allows for space to be usable under the stairs. The system outlined here uses a header to create what are called *tread walls*.

8 Steps for Building Circular Stairs

1) Finding Riser Height

To get started, you first need to find your riser height. Quite often it is given on the plans, in which case you want to check it to make sure it works with the actual floor heights. If the height is not given on the plans, consider the following points when figuring the riser height.

- You want the steps to feel comfortable.

- When walking up steps, a person's mind determines the height of the riser based on the first step. Make sure all risers are equal, so the stairs will not cause people to trip and fall.

- The lower the riser, the longer the tread needs to be to feel comfortable.

- Common dimensions for riser and tread on straight stairs are 7" for the riser and 10½" for the tread.

- For circular stairs, the tread width varies and so it is more difficult to figure the riser and tread dimensions.

- The comfortable range for circular stairs is harder to determine than the range for straight stairs because of the varying tread width. The code for residential buildings requires a minimum of 6" at the narrow end and 11" at a point 12" out from the narrow end. For other buildings, the code requires a minimum of 10" at the narrow end and 11" at a point 12" out from the narrow end. Because most of the length of the tread is greater than 11", the rise will typically feel more comfortable if it is less than a comparable straight stair.

2) Marking the Circumference Lines

With the rise figured out and the number of treads known, you can start marking your circumference lines. The best way to start is by making the stair footprint on the floor in the position where the stairs are going to be built. If the plans show a radius dimension and location, then you can use the plans to locate the radius center point. To make your circumference lines (which represent your stairs and the walls on the sides of the stairs), set a nail part-way at the located radius center point. Then hook your tape to the nail and mark your circumference lines by swinging your tape around the nail and holding your pencil on the required dimension (see "Drawing the Circumference Lines" illustration). Most tape measures have a slot in the hooking end for a nail head (see "End of Tape" illustration).

Drawing the Circumference Lines

End of Tape

If the radius or the radius center point is not given, you will need to find it. You can vary the radius length, but make sure you can maintain the following four requirements.

- 6" minimum tread width at the narrow end of the tread, 10" in non-residential.
- 11" tread width at a point 12" in from the narrow end.
- A minimum stair width of 36" in clear to finish.
- In non-residential buildings, the smaller radius should not be less than twice the width of the stairway.

The first thing you need to do to find your radius is to establish two points on the circumference opposite each other. They can be any two points. Look on the plans for points that are already established. If there are no established points, then select points that fit with the location of the stairs. Once you have established two points, it is merely a matter of bisecting the line between these points, finding the radius origin, and drawing your circumference lines from the radius origin. (See the "Bisecting a Line to Establish the Radius Origin" illustration.)

3) Marking the Tread on the Footprint

Now that you have your circumference lines, you need your tread lines. Since you have figured your riser height, you know the number of treads that you will have. Knowing the number of treads, you can find the exact tread point along your stair circumference. To do this, divide the stair circumference in half, and then divide those halves in half again and again until you are down to single treads. (See "Divide Circumference for Treads" later in this chapter.)

If your stair has an uneven number of treads, then you have to subtract one tread before you begin dividing into halves. To subtract one tread, you first have to know the width. The width will be equal to the total stair circumference length divided by the number of treads. It is difficult to measure the stair circumference, and so your one tread will probably not be exact. Therefore when you are done marking all the other treads, remark the tread you measured first. Once you have all your division points for the treads, then chalk lines from the radius center point through the division points to the longest circumference line, and those lines will make your tread footprint. (See "Tread Footprint" illustration later in this chapter.)

4) Cut Bottom Plate

The bottom plate of the tread walls will not be parallel to the top plate as it would be in a straight stair. The bottom plate will follow the circumference and serve as the bottom plate for all the tread walls. A good way to make the bottom plate is to use two pieces of ¾" plywood. If the radius is not too small, you can cut the plywood with a circular saw. To mark on the plywood, set a nail anywhere and mark the plywood with a pencil and a tape measure. Use the dimensions from the stair footprint to get the radius length.

5) Nail Bottom Plate in Place

To build the stairs, start by nailing the bottom plates in place. (See "Bottom Plate Nailed in Place" later in this chapter.)

6) Build the Tread Walls

The walls supporting the treads will be built as header walls. Built this way, they will provide the riser and allow space for storage below the stairs. The wall will consist of a 2 × 12 single header that will serve as the riser, a top plate, a double plate, trimmers for under the 2 × 12 header, and king studs next to the trimmer. A ledger to support the tread below will be nailed onto the header. (See "Section of Tread Wall from End" later in this chapter.)

Each tread wall should be higher than the one below it by the riser height. The height of the first step will have to be figured separately to equal one riser height, adjusted for any difference in floor covering. The top step might also have to be adjusted for a difference in floor height.

Bisecting a Line to Establish the Radius Origin

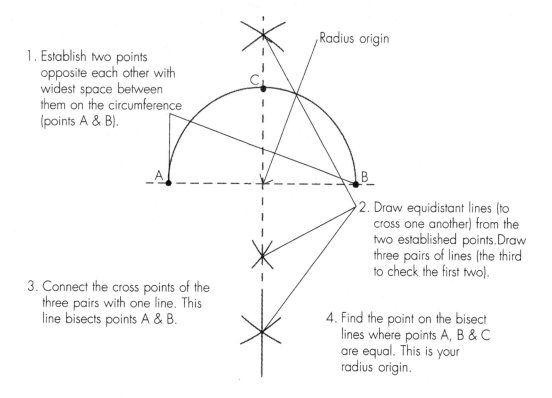

Radius origin

1. Establish two points opposite each other with widest space between them on the circumference (points A & B).

2. Draw equidistant lines (to cross one another) from the two established points. Draw three pairs of lines (the third to check the first two).

3. Connect the cross points of the three pairs with one line. This line bisects points A & B.

4. Find the point on the bisect lines where points A, B & C are equal. This is your radius origin.

7) Install the Tread Walls

Nail the tread walls in place using the footprint lines. The bottom of the studs will be toenailed into the bottom plate already in place. (See "Tread Walls Nailed in Place" illustration.)

8) Cut and Nail Treads

The treads should all be the same. They will be nailed onto the top of the tread walls and the ledgers. An equal nosing should be maintained the full length of the tread. Make sure the walls stay plumb both ways. Glue each tread to prevent squeaks. (See "Treads Halfway Up Stairs" illustration.)

Divide Circumference for Treads

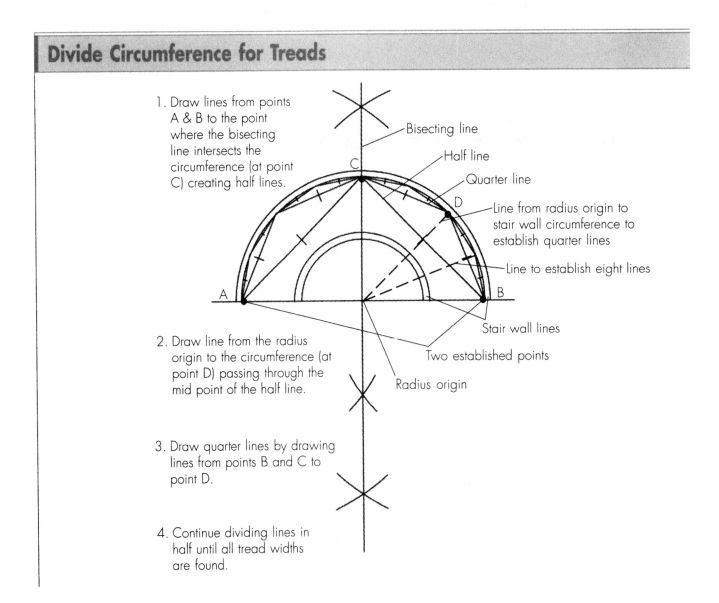

1. Draw lines from points A & B to the point where the bisecting line intersects the circumference (at point C) creating half lines.

2. Draw line from the radius origin to the circumference (at point D) passing through the mid point of the half line.

3. Draw quarter lines by drawing lines from points B and C to point D.

4. Continue dividing lines in half until all tread widths are found.

Bisecting line
Half line
Quarter line
Line from radius origin to stair wall circumference to establish quarter lines
Line to establish eight lines
Stair wall lines
Two established points
Radius origin

Tread Footprint

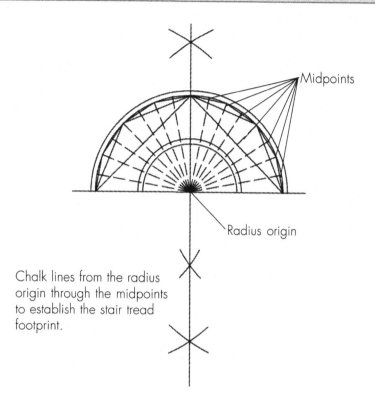

Midpoints

Radius origin

Chalk lines from the radius origin through the midpoints to establish the stair tread footprint.

Cutting Curved Bottom Plate

Bottom Plate Nailed in Place

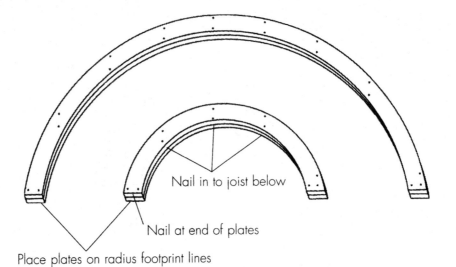

Nail in to joist below

Nail at end of plates

Place plates on radius footprint lines

Section of Treadwall from End

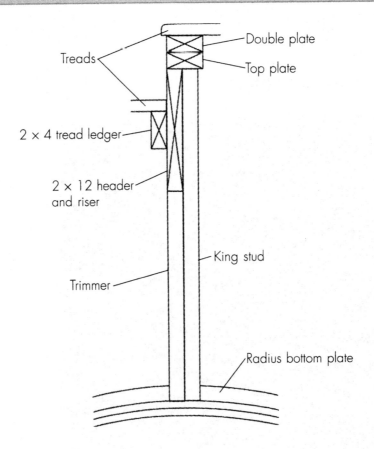

Treads

Double plate

Top plate

2 × 4 tread ledger

2 × 12 header and riser

King stud

Trimmer

Radius bottom plate

Tread Walls Nailed in Place

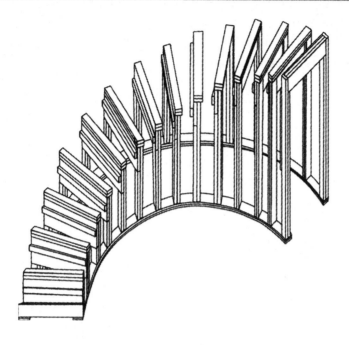

Tread Halfway Up Stairs

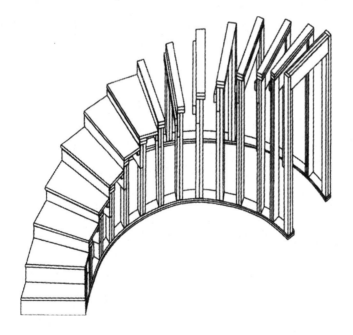

Conclusion

Once you have the circular stair concept in your head, the building of circular stairs becomes a standard framing operation. Remember, when you or your crew are building circular stairs as well as straight stairs, go through the stair building checklist presented in the first part of this chapter.

Chapter Eight

Advanced Framing: Rake Walls

Rake walls (sometimes referred to as *gable end walls*) typically start at the height of the standard wall and go up to the ridge of the roof. The challenge of building rake walls is figuring the heights of the studs and making sure the wall is built square. Lifting the assembled rake wall into place can also be a challenge. This chapter will cover four ways to figure stud heights and build rake walls efficiently—using methods that will make your work easier.

Contents

There are four common ways to figure stud heights and build rake walls.

1. Chalk lines on the floor.

2. Figure lengths on paper.

3. Build and chalk lines.

4. Stick frame.

Each has its own advantages. With all these methods, you must use the pitch given in the plans to determine the wall height. The pitch is generally shown on the elevation sheet just above the roof slope.

1. Chalk Lines on the Floor

The first method is to chalk out a duplicate on the floor, if you have the space. Then you can measure and cut the studs and plates right from your chalk lines.

To Chalk the Lines:

To chalk the lines, you need to know the heights of your low point and your high point. You must also ensure that the wall is square. To find the height, you can use the *Chalk the Actual Dimensions* system. The pitch on the plans gives you the relationship of the rise to the run. For example, a $6\frac{12}{}$ pitch means that for every 12 units of run, there are 6 units of rise. To find the high point on the wall, go out 12 units of run, then up square 6 units. Mark this reference point and chalk a line from the low point of the wall through this point and extend it as far as necesary to reach the high point in the wall. The closer you make the reference point to the high point in the wall, the more accurate your line will be.

To find the rake wall stud heights using the Chalk the Actual Dimensions method, follow these steps:

1. Chalk a Bottom Plate Line (1). Usually you can use the chalk line for your wall. (See "Chalk the Actual Dimensions" illustration next page.)

2. Chalk the Short Stud Line (2). Make sure it's square (perpendicular) with the bottom plate line (1). You can use the 3-4-5 triangle to square the line. (Explained in "To Square the Wall" and "3-4-5 Triangle" later in chapter.)

3. Chalk a Parallel Line (3) with the bottom plate line (1) that aligns with the top of the short stud. Extend this line out toward the long stud (5).

4. Chalk a Square Line (4) to the parallel line that is close to the long stud line (5), but convenient for figuring its length. The length of the square line (4) will be in a relationship to the parallel line (3), depending on the pitch of the rake wall. If, for example, the pitch is 6/12 and the parallel line is 12, the square line will be 6.

5. Chalk a line square (4) with the bottom plate line (1) where the long stud line (5) should be.

6. Chalk a line from the short point of the short stud (2) through the top of the square line (4) and on past the long stud line (5). This will be your Bottom of Top Plate Line (6).

7. Once you have these lines, you will be able to fill in all the remaining studs.

To Square the Wall:

- Draw a straight line where you want to place your bottom plate, then make a perpendicular line at the high point of your wall.

- Use a 3-4-5 triangle to double check that the line is exactly perpendicular or square. (See "3-4-5 Triangle" illustration later in chapter, and in Chapter 3.)

A 3-4-5 triangle will help you establish that two lines are square or at right angles to each other. To establish square, just follow these steps:

1. Start with the line you want to square from; this will be the 4-unit line— also referred to as the *run*.

2. Measure a line perpendicular to the run line at 3 units in length, called the *rise*.

3. Measure the diagonal from the outside of the 4-unit line (run) and the 3-unit line (rise), and adjust the 3-unit line so that the diagonal (hypotenuse) is exactly 5 units.

Chalk the Actual Dimensions

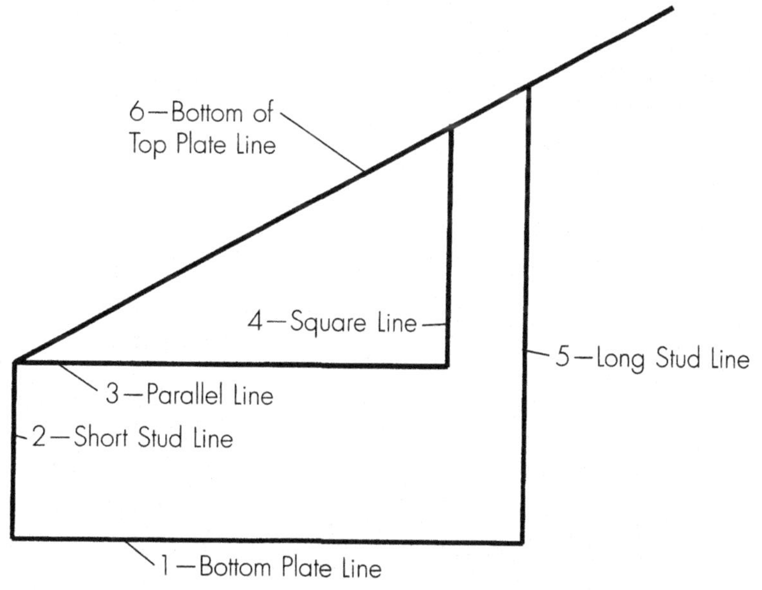

6—Bottom of Top Plate Line
4—Square Line
5—Long Stud Line
3—Parallel Line
2—Short Stud Line
1—Bottom Plate Line

The units can be anything as long as they are in the same ratio, for example they could be 3 feet, 4 feet, and 5 feet, or they could be 15 feet, 20 feet, and 25 feet. The longer the units, the more accurate your measurement will be.

The advantage to using this method is that it is quick, easy, and accurate and doesn't require a lot of math. However if you don't have the space on the floor, if it's raining and you can't chalk lines, or you have a lot of rake walls in the building, it is probably best to use one of the other methods suggested.

2. Figure Lengths on Paper

With this method you figure the stud heights, plate lengths, and layout anywhere you want—whether in the office, at home, or on the job site. All you need is a set of plans. Once you have the heights and lengths figured, you can build the wall anywhere, then move it into position.

Use the "Rake Wall Stud Heights" form on the next page to figure the stud heights, the plate lengths, and the layout points. Give the completed form with all needed information to whoever is framing the wall.

A construction calculator such as Construction Master IV® can be used to figure lengths accurately. With a construction calculator, you can work in feet and inches and use a memory function for repetitive calculations.

To use the Rake Wall Stud Heights form, just fill in the blanks and find the stud heights. D represents the distance on the bottom plate from the start of the rake wall to the short point on the stud. There is less confusion if you always use the short point on the studs. It is also easier to cut the short point than the long point when using a worm drive saw.

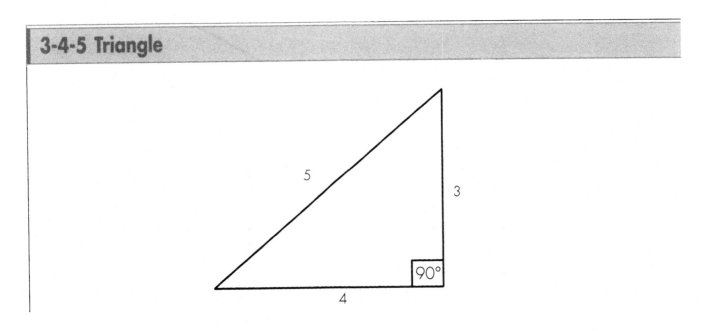

3-4-5 Triangle

116

Rake Wall Stud Heights—Example

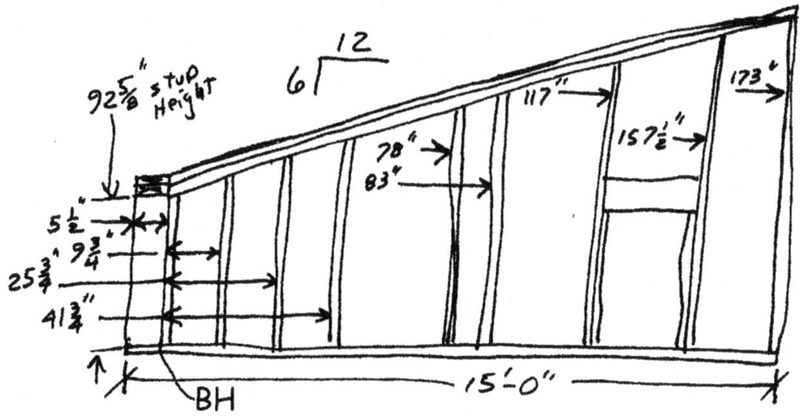

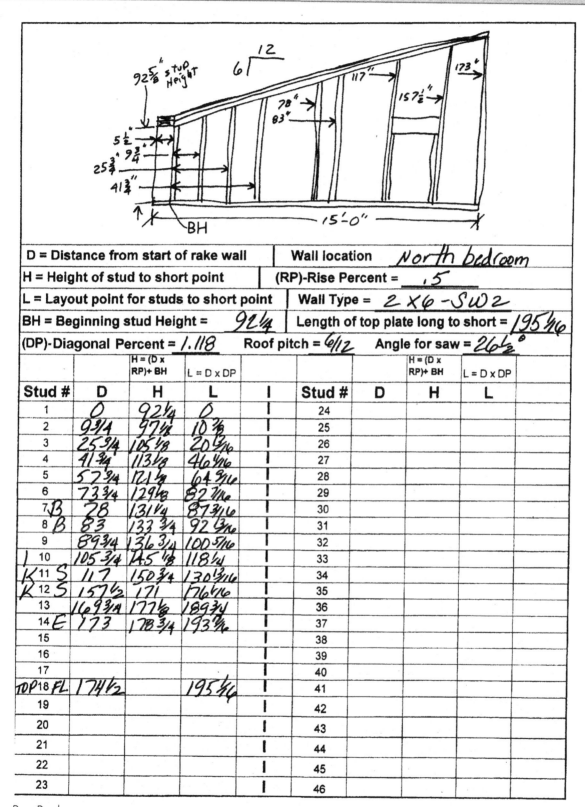

D = Distance from start of rake wall	Wall location North bedroom
H = Height of stud to short point	(RP)-Rise Percent = .5
L = Layout point for studs to short point	Wall Type = 2 X 6 - SW 2
BH = Beginning stud Height = 92 1/4	Length of top plate long to short = 195 1/16
(DP)-Diagonal Percent = 1.118 Roof pitch = 6/12	Angle for saw = 26 1/2°

		H = (D x RP)+ BH	L = D x DP					H = (D x RP)+ BH	L = D x DP	
Stud #	**D**	**H**	**L**		**I**	**Stud #**	**D**	**H**	**L**	
1	0	92 1/4	0		I	24				
2	9 3/4	97 1/8	10 7/8		I	25				
3	25 3/4	105 1/8	20 13/16		I	26				
4	41 3/4	113 1/8	46 11/16		I	27				
5	57 3/4	121 1/8	64 9/16		I	28				
6	73 3/4	129 1/8	82 7/16		I	29				
7 B	78	131 1/4	87 3/16		I	30				
8 B	83	133 3/4	92 13/16		I	31				
9	89 3/4	136 3/4	100 5/16		I	32				
I 10	105 3/4	145 1/8	118 1/4		I	33				
K 11 S	117	150 3/4	130 13/16		I	34				
K 12 S	157 1/2	171	176 1/16		I	35				
13	169 3/4	177 1/8	189 3/4		I	36				
14 E	173	178 3/4	193 7/16		I	37				
15					I	38				
16					I	39				
17					I	40				
TOP 18 PL	174 1/2		195 1/16		I	41				
19					I	42				
20					I	43				
21					I	44				
22					I	45				
23					I	46				

B = Backer
KS = King Stud
Top PL = Top Plate

D = Distance from start of rake wall	Wall location _____
H = Height of stud to short point	(RP)-Rise Percent = _____
L = Layout point for studs to short point	Wall Type = _____
BH = Beginning stud Height = _____	Length of top plate long to short = _____
(DP)-Diagonal Percent = _____	Roof pitch = _____ Angle for saw = _____

Stud #	D	H H = (D x RP)+ BH	L L = D x DP	I	Stud #	D	H H = (D x RP)+ BH	L L = D x DP
1				I	24			
2				I	25			
3				I	26			
4				I	27			
5				I	28			
6				I	29			
7				I	30			
8				I	31			
9				I	32			
10				I	33			
11				I	34			
12				I	35			
13				I	36			
14				I	37			
15				I	38			
16				I	39			
17				I	40			
18				I	41			
19				I	42			
20				I	43			
21				I	44			
22				I	45			
23				I	46			

B = Backer
KS = King Stud
Top PL = Top Plate

The **stud height** to the short point is found by using the formula $((D \times RP) + BH)$. **RP** is the **R**ise **P**ercent, or the relationship between the **R**ise and the **Run**. The relationship gives you the height increase of the studs per increase in the **D**istance of the plate. This relationship is illustrated in the filled-in version of the Rake Wall Stud Heights form. The formula for finding **RP** is also shown, in the "Rise and Diagonal Percent" illustration later in chapter.

The "Rake Wall, RP, DP, Saw Angle" illustration provides the Rise Percent for common roof pitches. The **BH** from the formula is the Beginning Stud Height. **BH** is a constant and is the height of the first stud at the lowest point. This height can vary depending on how the rafter or lookouts rest on the rake wall. A typical beginning height would be slightly lower than the adjoining wall as shown in "Rake Wall Beginning Stud Height." Here the beginning stud height is only 3/8" less than the adjoining wall stud height because the plates on the rake are thicker on a slope than they are when flat.

To find the **layout points** for the studs and the **length of the plates,** use the formula **D × DP.** **DP** is the **D**iagonal **P**ercent, or the relationship between the **D**iagonal and the **Run**. This relationship tells you the length increase of the top plate or layout point per increase in the **D**istance of the bottom plate. This relationship is shown in the "Rise Percent and Diagonal Percent" illustration, which also provides the formula for finding **DP.** The drawing gives the Diagonal Percents for the common roof pitches and the **Saw Angles**—the different angles at which you can set your saw to cut the top of the studs and the ends of the top plate and double plate.

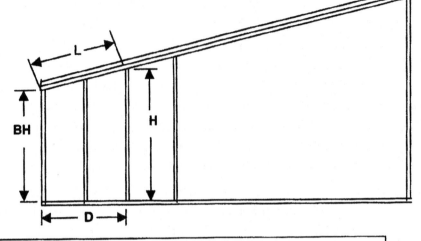

D = Distance from start of rake wall
H = Height of stud to short point
L = Layout point for studs to short point
BH = Beginning height of rake wall

H = (D x RP) + BH   L = D x DP

PITCH	RP-Rise Percent	DP-Diagonal Percent	SAW ANGLE
1/12	0.08	1.00	4.50
2/12	0.17	1.01	9.50
3/12	0.25	1.03	14.00
4/12	0.33	1.05	18.50
5/12	0.42	1.08	22.50
6/12	0.50	1.12	26.50
7/12	0.58	1.16	30.25
8/12	0.67	1.20	33.75
9/12	0.75	1.25	37.00
10/12	0.83	1.30	40.00
11/12	0.92	1.36	42.50
12/12	1.00	1.41	45.00

Rake Wall Beginning Stud Height

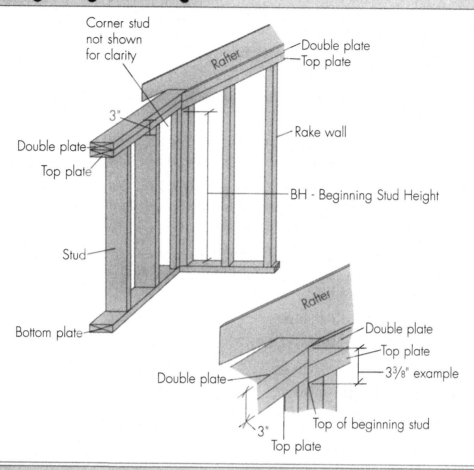

Corner stud not shown for clarity

Rafter

Double plate

Top plate

Rake wall

3"

Double plate

Top plate

BH - Beginning Stud Height

Stud

Bottom plate

Rafter

Double plate

Top plate

3⅜" example

Double plate

Top of beginning stud

3"

Top plate

Rise and Diagonal Percent

Rise Percent

RP = **R**ise **P**ercent = Rise divided by Run = Rise/Run

Rise

Run

Diagonal Percent

DP = **D**iagonal **P**ercent = Diagonal divided by Run = Diagonal/Run

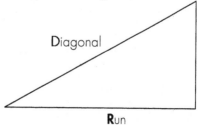

Diagonal

Run

3. Build and Chalk Lines

This method is possibly the quickest way to figure stud heights and build rake walls. Here is how it is done:

- First lay out the bottom plate in the same way you would if you were going to frame an ordinary wall.
- Spread your studs, making sure that they are long enough to reach the top of the rake wall.
- Toenail the bottom plate from the inside of the plate so that when the wall is lifted, the nail will function as a pivot point on the layout line.
- Cut the length of the beginning stud to match the adjoining wall. Take into consideration the location of the rafters if the look-outs rest on the rake wall, and the thickness of the plates on the rake.
- Set the beginning stud square with the bottom plate.
- Use the Rise Percent to find the length of the longest stud. (See "Rake Wall, RP, DP, Saw Angle" illustration.)
- Set that stud square with the bottom plate.
- Nail the rest of the studs to the bottom plate.
- Block the wall where required.
- Position all the studs so they are square.
- Chalk a line along the top of the studs.
- Cut each stud.
- Measure and cut the top plate and double plate.
- Nail the top plate to the studs, and the double plate to the top plate.

4. Stick Frame

With this method, you are framing the wall in place.

- Find the beginning stud and the longest stud heights in the same way you would with the other methods.
- Nail the bottom plates to the floor and brace the beginning stud and the longest studs in place.
- Make sure that the studs are plumb before continuing.
- Measure, cut, and nail the top plate onto the studs.
- Lay out the top plate using the "Figure Lengths on Paper" method, or plumb up from the bottom plate. Measure, cut, and nail the remaining studs in place.

Chapter Nine

Wind and Earthquake Framing

Buildings are naturally affected by the forces of nature and also by artificial forces. Elements such as gravity, wind, snow, earthquakes, retained soil, water, impact by an object, and mudslides can all have negative effects on a building.

This chapter will give you a basic understanding of the forces that affect buildings, and some helpful information on the framing methods used to resist those forces.

Although as a framer you are not responsible for designing structural requirements for buildings, it is important to have some understanding of a building's structural loads. When you are aware of the reasons behind the decisions engineers and architects make, it is easier to interpret the plans, and to make sure that the structure is built accordingly.

Contents

The Strength of Good Framing

The forces of nature can have devastating effects on buildings. The photo below shows an example of how destructive the elements can be. This photo is quite dramatic: you can see that the ground literally fell out from under the house. But the photo also shows the strength of good framing—the house stayed together even though the ground fell out from under it.

Understanding Structural Loads

As the forces of nature hit a building, they travel throughout seeking a weak link. Ultimately, if a weak link is not found, the force or energy will be transferred to the ground, which will absorb the force. Each component of the building must be strong enough to transfer the load in a path to the ground. The components are:

- Walls
- Floors

The House Stayed Together Even as the Ground Fell from Under It

Source: APA, The Engineered Wood Association

- Roofs
- Connections

To achieve the strength needed, a building's walls, floors, and roof must work together as a unit. The vertical elements that are used to resist forces are commonly called **shear walls,** and the horizontal elements (like floors and roofs) are called **diaphragms.** The path of energy to the ground is called the **load path.** The diagram below shows the load path for transferring the forces to the ground.

Building Code Load Requirements

Conventional and *nonconventional* codes regulate the strength needed in the walls, floors, roofs, and connections to resist the forces on buildings. The conventional code describes a *prescriptive* standard to resist the forces. The standard applies to simple buildings using common construction methods.

Load Path

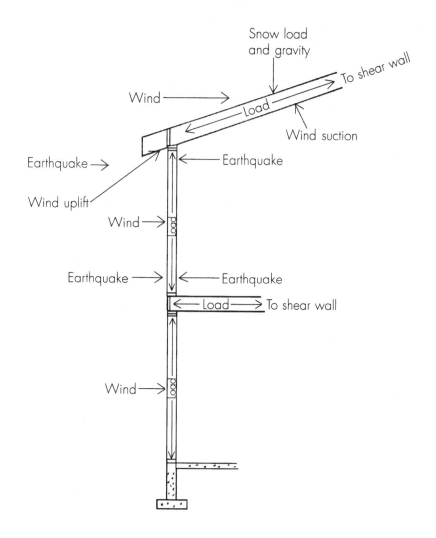

The nonconventional code is a performance-rated system and provides *non-prescriptive* engineering guidelines that can be applied to more unusual or more difficult buildings.

Prescriptive Format

The prescriptive format has specific requirements such as the size of studs needed or the type of wall bracing. If you build the structure following these requirements, then the building meets the minimum code standards for a safe building. The prescriptive codes are covered in more detail in Chapter 11.

Framers meet prescriptive code requirements on a regular basis, sometimes without even knowing it. As they brace their walls, block and nail their floor system, nail their walls to the floors, and bolt the building to the foundation, they are creating a load path that transfers the forces of nature to the ground—in ways that are prescribed by the code.

Non-Prescriptive Code

The performance, or non-prescriptive, code provides for free design, as long as it stays within certain code standards. Performance designing is different for each building, and the engineer or architect must specify and detail all aspects of the design.

A special design might be needed because a building is in a high-earthquake or a high-wind zone, because it requires large open spaces or window walls or to resist other forces. The most common forces affecting buildings are shown in the illustration, "Forces on Buildings."

Regional Considerations

Different forces affect buildings in the various parts of the country. Builders have to worry about earthquakes in California, high winds in Florida, and snowload in Colorado. It's easier to understand the architect's or engineer's plans if you are aware of these factors. The following maps give you an idea some of the areas of the country that suffer most from the effects of earthquakes, winds, and snowloads.

Framing Details

The most common framing details can be broken down into three categories.

1. Shear wall construction
2. Diaphragm construction
3. Connections

Wind Map

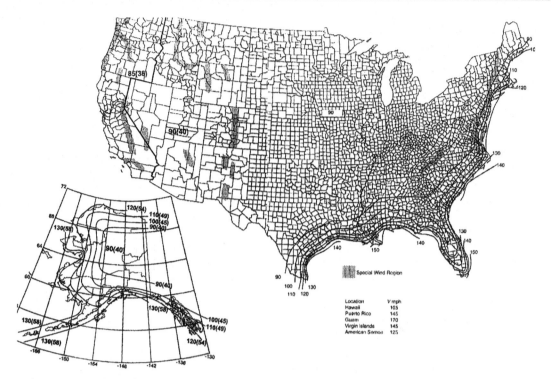

Snow Map

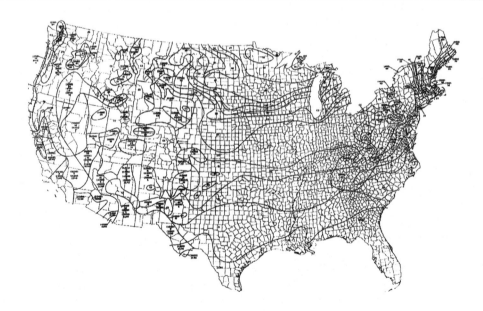

Forces on Buildings

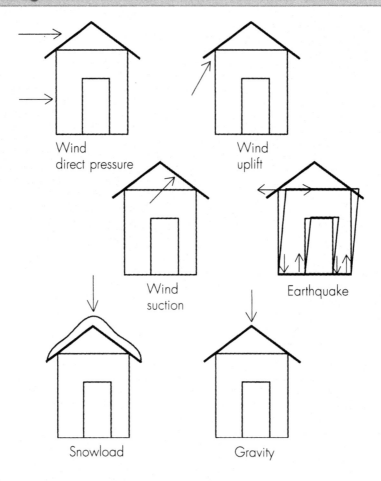

Wind
direct pressure

Wind
uplift

Wind
suction

Earthquake

Snowload

Gravity

Seismic Map of Continental U.S.

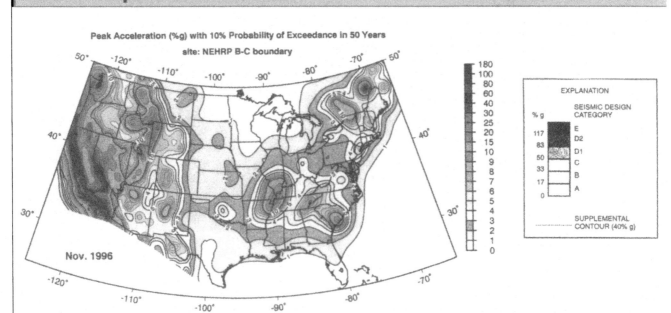

Peak Acceleration (%g) with 10% Probability of Exceedance in 50 Years

site: NEHRP B-C boundary

Nov. 1996

Source: U.S. Geological Survey National Seismic Hazard Mapping Project

Seismic Map of Alaska

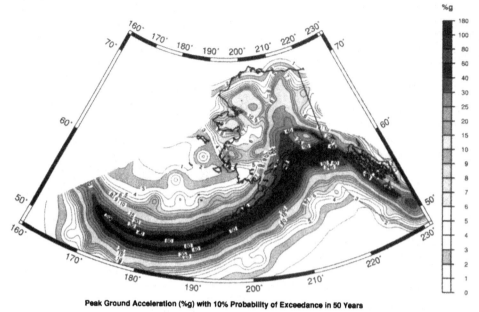

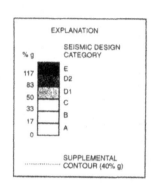

Peak Ground Acceleration (%g) with 10% Probability of Exceedance in 50 Years

Source: U.S. Geological National Seismic Hazard Mapping Project

Seismic Map of Hawaii

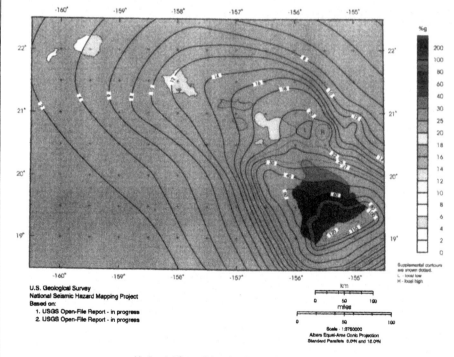

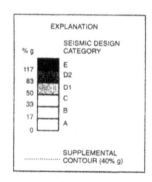

U.S. Geological Survey
National Seismic Hazard Mapping Project
Based on:
1. USGS Open-File Report - in progress
2. USGS Open-File Report - in progress

Horizontal Ground Acceleration (%g)
With 10% Probability of Exceedance in 50 Years
Firm Rock - 760 m/sec shear wave velocity

Source: U.S. Geological Survey National Seismic Hazard Mapping Project

Each of these categories is covered in this section, including important points for framing.

Shear Wall Construction

The factors that affect the strength of any shear wall are:

- The size and type of material used for the plates and studs.
- The size and type of material used for the sheathing.
- Whether one side or both sides have sheathing.
- The nail sizes and patterns.
- Whether or not there is blocking for all the edges of the sheathing.

Engineers and architects are free to use any system they prefer, as long as they can prove that it meets the minimum strength requirements. The easiest and most common method is using the code book tables that provide accepted values for walls with given resistance capabilities. (Table 2306.4.1 in the *2000 International Building Code (IBC)* shows these values.)

If there are many shear walls in a building, the engineer usually creates a schedule from a code table to show the wall requirements. Unfortunately, there is no standard for labeling shear walls, so the schedules made by the engineers may all be different. They do, however, usually have common components. You will need to study the shear wall schedule on the plans to understand all the components that apply to framing.

The table below is a typical shear wall schedule. It is an easy one to use because the labels also identify the nailing pattern and the type of sheathing.

Important Points for Shear Wall Framing

1. **Stud sizes**—Specified nailing patterns may require changes in the stud sizes. There are three conditions in which 3x studs are required for nailing adjoining sheathing edges:
   - If the edge nailing is 2" O.C. or less.

Shear Wall Schedule

Wall Type	Sheathing Minimum Thickness	Stud at Edge	Edge Nailing	Plate Nailing	Anchor bolt to concrete
P6	15/32" ply one side	2x	6"	12d 6" O.C.	5/8" A.B. 72" O.C.
P4	15/32" ply one side	3x	4"	12d 4" O.C.	5/8" A.B. 48" O.C.
P3	15/32" ply one side	3x	3"	12d 3" O.C.	5/8" A.B. 32" O.C.
2P3	15/32" ply both sides	3x	3"	12d 1½" O.C.	5/8" A.B. 18" O.C.

- If there is sheathing on both sides of the wall, the adjoining sheathing edges fall on the same stud on both sides of the wall, and the nailing pattern is less than 6" O.C.
- If 10d nails are used with more than 1½" penetration, and they are spaced 3" or less O.C.

2. **Penetration**—It is very important that the nail does not penetrate the outside veneer of the sheathing (see "Nail Penetration" illustration). A pressure regulator or nail-depth gage can be used to make sure this doesn't happen (see "Nail Regulator and Flush Nailer" illustration). The top of the nail should be flush with the surface of the sheathing.

3. **Nail size**—The nail size may change from wall to wall. Check the specified thickness and length of the nails.

4. **Nail spacing**—The pattern for nailing the sheathing to the intermediate framing members is usually the standard 12" on center. It is the edge nailing that changes to increase the strength. If 3x studs are required, then the pattern must be staggered. Make sure that the nails are at least ⅜" away from the edge of the sheathing.

5. **Blocking**—The details or shear wall schedule should specify whether blocking is required for panel edges. If the wall is less than 8', you can

Nail Penetration

⅜" minimum from nail to edge of sheathing

⅛" minimum gap

Top of nail head flush with sheathing

Nail Regulator and Flush Nailer

Pressure regulator

Nail depth gage

Staggered Nailing

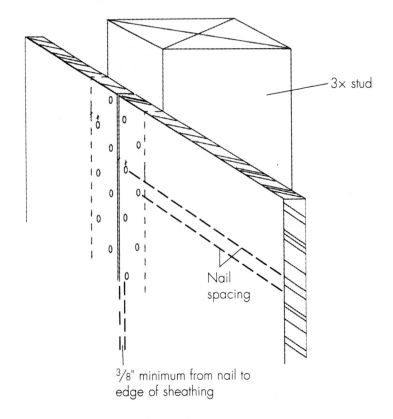

3× stud

Nail
spacing

3/8" minimum from nail to
edge of sheathing

usually satisfy this requirement by running the plywood vertically, so that all the panel edges have backing.

Diaphragm Construction

The strength of diaphragms is affected by these factors:

- The size and type of material used for the joists or rafters.
- The size and type of material used for the sheathing.
- The direction of the sheathing in relation to the members it is attached to.
- The nail sizes and patterns.
- Any blocks, bridging, or stiffeners.

Building codes provide tables for diaphragms similar to those for shear walls. The variables used to increase the strength of the diaphragm are the thickness of the sheathing, the size of the nails, the width of the framing member, the nail spacing, and whether or not the diaphragm is blocked.

Diaphragm Framing Tasks of Particular Concern:

- **Nail spacing**—The nailing pattern for nailing the sheathing to the intermediate framing members is usually the standard 12" O.C. It is the edge nailing that changes to increase the strength.
- **Penetration**—The nail must not penetrate the sheathing's outside veneer.
- **Nail size**—The nail sizes will vary based on the engineer's design, or code requirements. Check the specified thickness and length.
- **Blocking**—It is common to have blocking in the joist space that runs parallel to the exterior walls. It will be detailed on the plans if it is required. Blocking can also used on the edges of the sheathing.

Connections

"Connectors" can refer to beams or other construction elements, but in most cases, connectors are hardware specifically designed for common framing connections. As part of the load path, connections have to be strong enough to transfer the forces of nature.

In the prescriptive code, the connections are made with anchor bolts to the foundation and with nails to connect floor joists to the plates below them, wall bottom plates to floors, and rafters or trusses to wall plates.

In non-prescriptive design, there are many ways to achieve the required force transfer between the shear walls, diaphragms, and foundation. The most common method involves metal connectors, which are produced by many companies. The Simpson Strong-Tie Company, because of its work in developing, testing, and cataloging connectors, is often referenced in building plans. Simpson Strong-Tie connector catalog numbers will be used in the balance of this book. Please note that substitutes with equivalent strength are available.

There are connectors made for just about every type of connection you can think of. As the framer in charge, however, it is not your job to decide on the type of connector, but rather to use correctly the connector that is specified. The best way to do this is to read the specifications in the connector catalog. Following is a page from a Simpson Strong-Tie Catalog, and a good example of instructions for installing hold-downs.

There are different connectors for the variety of different framing details, but only four common areas of connection:

- Foundation
- Wall-to-wall
- Roof-to-wall
- Foundation-to-top-of-the-top-wall

Important Points for Connection Framing

- Install all connectors per catalog instructions.
- Drill holes no more than $1/16$" bigger than bolts.
- Use washers next to wood.
- Fill all nail holes unless using catalog specifications.
- Know that the connection is only as strong as the weakest side. Make sure to space and nail each side the same. See "Equal Nailing" illustration.
- Be aware that some connectors have different-shaped nail holes. The different shaped holes have different meaning as illustrated in "Nail Hole Shapes" later in this chapter.

Hold-Downs

Hold-downs are connections commonly used for foundations, wall-to-wall connections, wall-to-concrete connections, and wall or floor-to-drag strut. Hold-downs are also called *anchor downs* and *tie-downs*. They can be difficult to install, but if you plan ahead and install as you go, the job is more manageable. Hold-downs that attach walls to the concrete foundation are typically attached to bolts already in the concrete. These bolts are generally set in place by the foundation crew. Sometimes they won't be set in the right place.

You will want to locate the hold-down as close to the end of the shear wall as possible. If the bolt is already in the concrete, you will have to locate a hold-down on either side of the bolt. When considering the location, be aware of how it relates to what is on the floor above it; you don't want, for example, the hold-down coming up in a door or window. You should also allow enough space to install and tighten nuts and bolts.

HDA/HD HOLDOWNS

SIMPSON Strong-Tie® CONNECTORS

Holdowns are used to transfer tension loads between floors, to tie purlins to masonry or concrete, etc. Use HDAs and HDs for overturning requirements and other applications to transfer tension loads. **All HDAs and the HD15 are self-jigging, ensuring code-required minimum 7 bolt diameter spacing from the end of the wood member to the center of the first bolt hole.**

HD6A, HD8A, HD10A and HD14A's seat design allows greater installation adjustability. An overall width of 3¼" for the HD6A, HD8A and HD10A, and 3½" for the HD14A provides an easy fit in a standard 4x wall.

HDA SPECIAL FEATURES:
- Single piece non-welded design results in higher capacity.
- Load Transfer Plate eliminates the need for a seat washer.
- Fewer inspection problems.

MATERIAL: See table

FINISH: HD2A, 5A, 6A, 8A, 10A—galvanized. HD8A may be ordered HDG; check with factory. HD14A, HD15, HD20A—Simpson gray paint

INSTALLATION: • Use all specified fasteners. See General Notes.
- For an improved connection, use a steel nylon locking nut or a thread adhesive on the anchor bolt.
- Bolt holes shall be a minimum of ¹⁄₃₂" to a maximum of ¹⁄₁₆" larger than the bolt diameter (per 1997 NDS, section 8.1.2.1.).
- Standard washers are required between the base plate and anchor nut (HD15 only), and on stud bolt nuts against the wood. The Load Transfer Plate is an integral part of the HDA Holdown and no washer is required. See page 10 for BP/LBP Bearing Plates.
- See SSTB Anchor Bolts, Simpson's Anchoring Systems and Additional Anchorage Designs for anchorage options. The design engineer may specify any alternate anchorage calculated to resist the tension load for a specific job.
- Locate on wood member to maintain a minimum distance of seven bolt diameters, distance is automatically maintained when end of wood member is flush with the bottom of the holdown.
- To tie double 2x members together, the designer must determine the fasteners required to bind members to act as one unit without splitting.
- **For holdowns, anchor bolt nuts should be finger-tight plus ⅓ to ½ turn with a wrench, with consideration given to possible future wood shrinkage. Care should be taken to not over-torque the nut.**
- Stud bolts should be snugly tightened (1997 NDS, section 8.1.2.4).
- For additional information, request T-HD.

CODES: BOCA, ICBO, SBCCI NER-393, NER-469; City of L.A. RR 24818, RR 25158 and RR 25293. HD6A and HD14A are not NER listed.

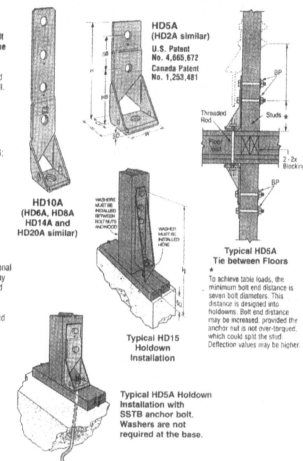

HD5A (HD2A similar)
U.S. Patent No. 4,665,672
Canada Patent No. 1,253,481

HD10A (HD6A, HD8A HD14A and HD20A similar)

Typical HD15 Holdown Installation

Typical HD5A Tie between Floors

* To achieve table loads, the minimum bolt end distance is seven bolt diameters. This distance is designed into holdowns. Bolt end distance may be increased, provided the anchor nut is not over-torqued, which could split the stud. Deflection values may be higher.

Typical HD5A Holdown Installation with SSTB anchor bolt. Washers are not required at the base.

Model No.	Material		Dimensions							Fasteners			Avg Ult	Allowable Tension Loads[1,7,8,10] (133)						Holdown[11] Deflection at Highest Allowable Design Load
	Base Ga	Body Ga	HB[4]	SB	W	H	B	SO	CL	Anchor Dia[5,9]	Stud Bolts			Length of Bolt[2,3] in Vertical Wood Member (DF/SP)						
											Qty	Dia		1½	2	2½	3	3½	5½	
HD2A	7	12	4⁹⁄₁₆	2½	2¾	8	2⁵⁄₁₆	⅞	1¼	⅝	2	⅝	12150	1555	2055	2565	2775	2775	2760	0.058
HD5A	3	10	5½	3	3½	9⁷⁄₁₆	3⁵⁄₁₆	½	2³⁄₁₆	⅝ or ¾	2	¾	20767	1870	2485	3095	3705	4010	3980	0.067
HD6A	¾	7	6¾₁₆	3½	3¼	11¼₁₆	3¾₁₆	⅝	2¼	⅞	2	⅞	27333	2275	2980	3665	4405	5105	5510	0.041
HD8A	¾	7	6¾₁₆	3½	3¼	14⅝₁₆	3¾₁₆	⅝	2¼	⅞	3	⅞	28667	3220	4350	5415	6465	7460	7910	0.111
HD10A	¾	7	6¾₁₆	3½	3¼	18⅝	3¾₁₆	⅝	2¼	⅞	4	⅞	28667	3945	5540	6935	8310	9540	9300	0.269
HD14A	⅝	3	7	4	3½	20⅝₁₆	3½	⅝	2¾₁₆	1	4	1	38167	—	—	—	—	11080	13380	0.215
HD20A	⅝	3	7	4	4½	20⁹⁄₁₆	4½	⅞	2⅝	1¼	4	1	51333	—	—	—	—	11080	13380	0.250
HD15	⅝	3	7	4	3½	24½	4⁷⁄₁₆	3⅜	2⅜	1¼	5	1	55333	—	—	—	—	—	15305	0.082

1. Allowable loads have been increased 33% for earthquake or wind loading with no further increase allowed; reduce where other loads govern.
2. HD15 requires a minimum 6x6 nominal post. Minimum post size is required to ensure the load carrying capacity of the critical net section meets the holdown capacity.
3. Use a minimum 4x6 nominal post for the HD14A and the HD20A. Minimum post size is required to ensure the load carrying capacity of the critical net section meets the holdown capacity.
4. HB is the required minimum distance from the end of the stud to the center of the first bolt hole. End distance may be increased as necessary for installation.
5. The designer must specify anchor bolt type, length and embedment. See SSTB Anchor Bolts and Additional Anchor Designs.
6. See page 32 for anchor bolt retrofit.
7. Lag bolts will not develop the listed loads.
8. Holdowns installed raised off the mudsill have larger deflection values. Consult Simpson for info.
9. Full tension loads apply when HD5A is used with a ⅝" anchor bolt.
10. See pgs 6, 7 for testing and other important information.
11. Deflection at Highest Allowable Design Load: The deflection of a holdown measured between the anchor bolt and the strap portion of the holdown when loaded to the highest allowable load listed in the catalog table. This movement is strictly due to the holdown deformation under a static load test conducted on a steel jig.
12. For Hem Fir values request T-HEMFIR.

Courtesy of Simpson Strong-Tie Company

Equal Nailing

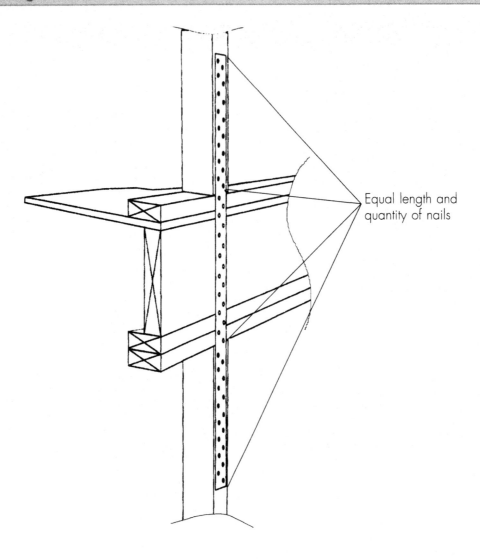

Equal length and quantity of nails

Nail Hole Shapes

Hexagonal Holes
Used for concrete
or masonry screw
applications.

Obround Holes
Used to provide easier
nailing access in tight
locations.
Fasteners may be
installed at an angle.

Diamond Holes
Optional holes
to temporarily
secure connectors
to the member
during installation.

Triangle Holes
Provided on some
products in addition to
round holes. Round and
triangle holes must be
filled to achieve the
published maximum
load value.

Courtesy of Simpson Strong-Tie Company

Although it is common to wait until the building is framed to install the hold-downs, waiting can also present problems, such as studs that are already nailed in place where you want to install the hold-downs, sheathing that is hard to nail because it may be on the exterior of a second to fifth floor, and possible pipes or wires running in the stud cavity.

It is helpful to install the hold-down studs as you build the walls. The layout framer should detail the hold-down studs while detailing the wall plates, and should also drill the plates for the anchor bolt or the threaded rods. If an upper floor is involved, he should also drill down through the subfloor sheathing and the top and double plate of the wall on the floor below. The wall builder should drill the studs before nailing them into the wall. When the wall sheathing is installed, make sure it is nailed to the hold-down studs using the same nailing pattern that was used for edge nailing. (See "Hold-Down Nailing" illustration.)

Install the hold-downs and bolts, and washers and nuts as soon as possible. Note, too, that when installing hold-downs after the walls are built, it is more productive to do an entire floor at one time. If the anchor bolts in the concrete do not extend high enough, a coupler nut can be used to extend the length. (See the "Coupler Nuts Can Extend Anchor Bolts," illustration later in this chapter.)

As noted previously, the holes drilled for the bolts attaching the hold-down to the studs should not be more than $1/16"$ bigger than the bolts. However, it is acceptable to oversize the holes you drill for the threaded rod that passes between the floors. This will make it easier for installation without affecting strength. (See "Drill Hole Size for Hold-Downs" illustrations later in this chapter.)

With all nail-on connection hardware, it is important to use the right size nail. Hardware manufacturer's catalogs indicate nail size appropriate for each piece of hardware. Most catalogs also give some options for nail use.

Conclusion

Quality of installation is probably the most important part of framing to withstand the forces of nature. APA (The Engineered Wood Association) confirmed this fact when it conducted a study of the construction failures in the aftermath of Hurricane Andrew. In the houses they investigated, roof failures were the most common. Those roof systems most often failed due to lack of sheathing nailing.

Wind and earthquake-resistant framing is an important skill for lead framers, and essential to those in susceptible parts of the country. Building codes, along with the designs architects and engineers create to meet code requirements, specify the framing for wind and earthquake resistance. The lead framer must take that information, along with data from connector manufacturers, and ensure that those requirements are met.

Hold-Down Nailing

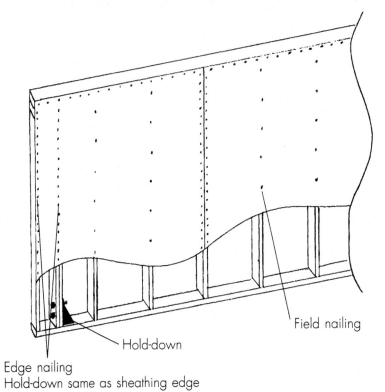

Field nailing

Hold-down

Edge nailing
Hold-down same as sheathing edge

Coupler Nuts Can Extend Anchor Bolts

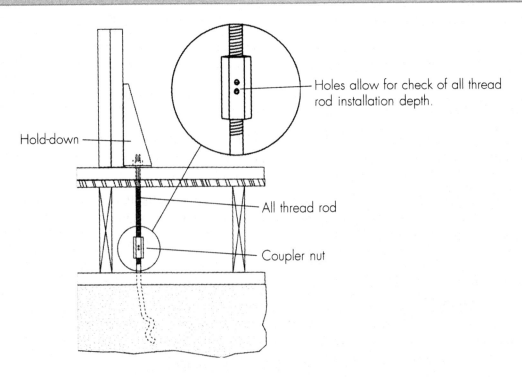

Holes allow for check of all thread rod installation depth.

Hold-down

All thread rod

Coupler nut

Drill Hole Size for Hold-Downs

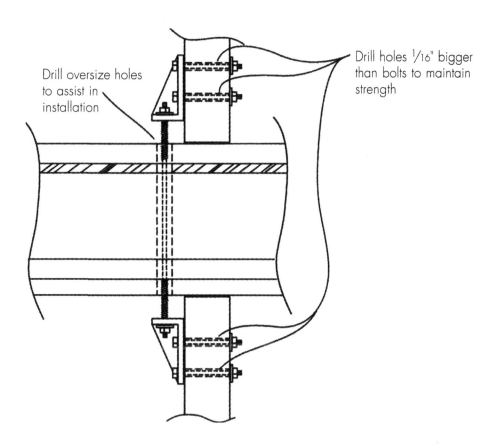

Drill oversize holes to assist in installation

Drill holes 1/16" bigger than bolts to maintain strength

Roof Failure as a Result of Hurricane Andrew

Source: APA, The Engineered Wood Products Association

Chapter Ten

Engineered Wood Products

Engineered Wood Products have been around for years, particularly in the form of plywood, glu-lam beams, and metal-plate-connected wood trusses. I-joists are more recent, as are LVLs (Laminated Veneer Lumber), PSLs (Parallel Strand Lumber), and LSLs (Laminated Strand Lumber).

It is not the intent of this chapter to explain everything there is to know about engineered wood products, but rather to make you familiar with this category of materials, and give you a sense of what to look out for when you are working with them.

Contents

Engineered Wood Products (EWP) fit into two general categories, **Engineered Panel Products (EPP)** and **Engineered Lumber Products (ELP)**. The first group includes plywood, oriented strand board (OSB), waferboard, and composite and structural particleboard.

The second group includes I-joists, glu-lam beams, metal-plate-connected wood trusses, and structural composite lumber (LVLs, PSLs, and LSLs).

Engineered Panel Products

Engineered Panel Products are so common that their uses are defined in the building codes. Specific applications vary from job to job, and from manufacturer to manufacturer.

Plywood

The earliest form of plywood was used 3,500 years ago by the pharaohs of Egypt. Thin sheets of wood were cross-laminated and glued in decorative objects and furniture. Not until the early 1900s did modern plywood begin to be widely used. Today, plywood installation is specifically covered in the building codes.

Oriented Strand Board and Waferboard

Oriented strand board and waferboard are made out of flakes, strands, or wafers that are sliced from small wood logs bonded under heat with a waterproof and boil-proof resin binder. Waferboard was the first to be widely used. Oriented strand board evolved from waferboard and made its way into the market in the late 1970s. The strength of both products comes from uninterrupted wood fiber, which is interwoven with long strands or

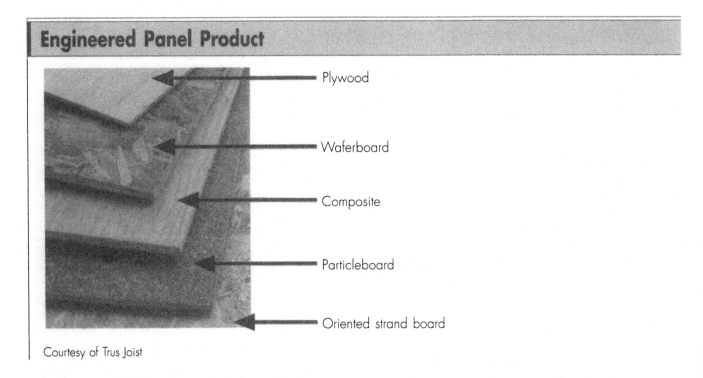

Engineered Panel Product

- Plywood
- Waferboard
- Composite
- Particleboard
- Oriented strand board

Courtesy of Trus Joist

wafers. Most building codes recognize oriented strand board and waferboard for the same uses as plywood, as long as the thicknesses match.

Particleboard

Particleboard is made out of wood particles bonded by an adhesive under a hot pressing, and formed into a solid, three-layered panel with two surface layers. Sheet thickness and size are similar to plywood and waferboard. Unlike plywood, particleboard is not used as a structural member. Because of its density, it is generally used as an underlayment. There is no specific grain to the sheet, so it does not matter which direction a sheet is placed in relation to the direction of the floor joists.

Working with Engineered Panel Products

When working with any engineered panel products, keep the following guidelines in mind:

1. On floors and roofs, run the face grain perpendicular to the supports (except with particleboard, which has no grain). See "Using Enginneered Panel Products" illustration below.

Using Engineered Panel Products

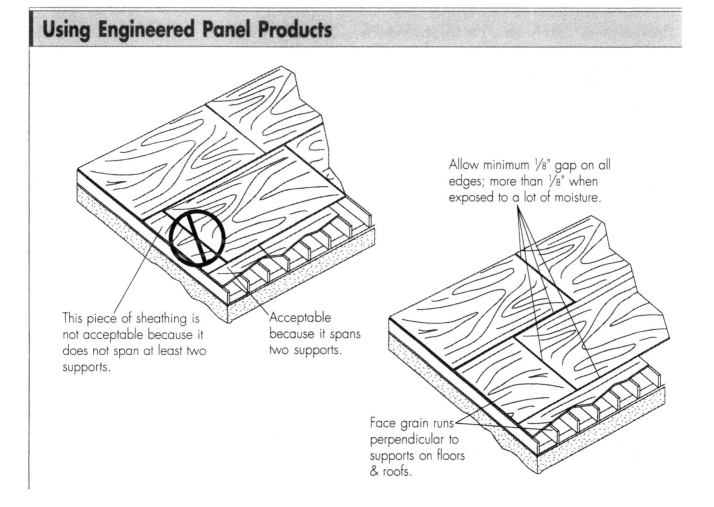

This piece of sheathing is not acceptable because it does not span at least two supports.

Acceptable because it spans two supports.

Allow minimum ⅛" gap on all edges; more than ⅛" when exposed to a lot of moisture.

Face grain runs perpendicular to supports on floors & roofs.

2. Do not use any piece that does not span at least two supports for floors and roofs.

3. Allow a gap of at least ⅛" on all edges, and a gap of more than ⅛" if the piece will be exposed to a lot of moisture. Note that this also applies to walls.

4. Follow manufacturers' recommended installation directions.

Engineered Lumber Products

I-Joists

I-joists were introduced in 1968 by the Trus Joist Corporation. Although use of this product has grown rapidly over the years, there is still no industry standard for its manufacture and installation. And while the Engineered Wood Association ("APA") has established a standard for its members, not all manufacturers are members of APA. Because there is no universal standard, it's important to use the installation instructions that come in the I-joist package. The I-joist package is generally prepared by a manufacturer's representative working with the architect or designer.

The I-joist package should include installation plans for the building. These plans will be specific to the building you are working on, and will include a material list and accessories. Accessories can include web stiffeners, blocking panels, joist hangers, rim boards, and beams. The plans typically include a sheet of standard details (see "Material List" next page).

Initially, the plans might look like a big puzzle and seem overwhelming, but once you become familiar with the language in them, everything should come together. You will notice that there are differences among I-joists, but most of them share common elements.

Below is a list of elements you'll find in most I-joists, and some items to consider when installing them:

1. Minimum **bearing** is 1¾". (See "Solid Blocking & I-Joist Minimum Bearing" illustration later in chapter.)

2. Closure is required at the end of I-joist by rim-board, rim-joist, or blocking. This closure also serves to transfer vertical and lateral loads, as well as providing for deck attachment, and fireblocking if required. Do not use dimensional lumber such as 2 × 10 because it is typically 9¼" instead of 9½." It shrinks much more than the I-joists and will leave the I-joists supporting the load.

3. Interior bearing walls below I-joists require blocking panels or squash blocks when load-bearing walls are above.

4. Rim boards are required to be a minimum of 1¼" in thickness.

5. Make sure **squash blocks,** which are used to support point loads (like the load created by a post) are 1/16" taller than the joists, so that they will properly support the load. (See "Squash Blocks" illustration later in the chapter.)

Engineered Lumber Product

Courtesy of Trus Joist

Material List

TJI Material List

QTY.	TYPE	DEPTH	SERIES	C. LENGTH	LINEAL FT
11	T38.5	9 1/2"	15 DF.	38'-6"	423.5
10	T33			33'-0"	330
12	T25.5			25'-6"	306
138	T24			24'-0"	3312
4	T20.5			20'-6"	82
6	T19.5			19'-6"	117
20	T19			19'-0"	380
10	T18			18'-0"	180
23	T15			15'-0"	345
41	T14			14'-0"	574
43	T13.5			13'-6"	580.5
41	T11			11'-0"	451
72	T10.5			10'-6"	756
7	T9			9'-0"	63
32	T4.5			4'-6"	144
470				TOTAL	8046
4	J20	9 1/2"	25 DF.	20'-0"	80
12	J18			18'-0"	216
11	J14.5			14'-6"	159.5
5	J13.5			13'-6"	67.5
23	J12.5			12'-6"	287.5
6	J11			11'-0"	66
5	J8.5			8'-6"	42.5
10	J5.5			5'-6"	55
76				TOTAL	974

Paralam Material List

QTY.	TYPE	SIZE	SERIES	C. LENGTH	LINEAL FT
2	A9	3 1/2"x9 1/2"	PSL.	9'-0"	18
9	A6			6'-0"	54
11				TOTAL	72
4	B15	2 11/16"x9 1/2"	PSL.	15'-0"	60
6	B5			5'-0"	30
10				TOTAL	90
4	D13.5	5 1/4"x9 1/2"	PSL.	13'-6"	54

HANGERS

SERIES	QTY.	TYPE	MAX. LOAD
①	76	ITT29.5	1005
②	22	HUSC410	1800
③	10	MIT29.5-2	2500
④	20	LSSU125	1305
⑤	10	ITT49.5	1200
⑥	38	ITT9.5	995
⑦	36	IUT29	1005

BLOCKING PANELS

QTY.	DEPTH	JOIST SERIES	LENGTH
650	9 1/2"	PRO	14 1/4"

WEB STIFFENERS

QTY.	DEPTH	JOIST SERIES	DETAIL
40	9 1/2"	25 DF.	

LSL RIM

QTY.	DEPTH	LENGTH

JOB NAME: BALLARD MIXED-USE BLDG.
ADDRESS: 6300 32nd AVE. N.W.
CITY: SEATTLE
STATE: WA.
IDENTIFICATION: THIRD FLOOR

SHEET 1 OF 2

6. **Web stiffeners,** which are sometimes required at bearing and/or point loads, should be at least ⅛" shorter than the web. Install web stiffeners tight against the flange that supports the load. If the load comes from a wall above, install the web stiffener tight against the top of the flange. If the load comes from a wall below, the stiffener should go tight against the bottom.

7. Use **filler blocking** between the webs of adjacent I-joists to provide load sharing between the joists.

8. **Backer blocking** is attached on one side of the web to provide a surface for attachment of items like face mount hangers. (See "Filler Blocking and Backer Blocking" illustration.)

9. I-joists are permitted to **cantilever** with very specific limitations and additional reinforcement. If the I-joists are supporting a bearing wall, the maximum cantilever distance with additional reinforcement is 2'. If the I-joists are not supporting a bearing wall, the maximum cantilever is 4'. Check plans for specifics on the cantilever.

10. **Top-flange hangers** are most commonly used for I-joists. They come with the I-joist package, but you can also get them from a construction supply store. When installing top flange hangers, make sure that the bottom of the hanger is tight against the backer block or the header. (See "Top Flange Hanger Tight" illustration.)

    When nailing the hanger into the bottom of the joist, be sure to use the correct length nails. Nails that are too long can go through the bottom flange and force the joist up. (See "Use Right Nail" illustration.)

    When installing hangers on wood plates that rest on steel beams, the hanger should not touch the steel. The distance it can be held away from the steel depends on the plate thickness. Note that hangers rubbing against the steel can cause squeaks. (See "Top Flange Hanger Spacing" illustration.)

11. **Face-mount hangers** can be used. Make sure that the hangers are tall enough to support the top flanges of the hangers. Otherwise use web stiffeners. (See "Face-Mount Hangers" illustration.) Be sure to use the correct length and diameter of nail.

12. **The bottom flange cannot be cut or notched** except for a bird's mouth. At a bird's mouth, the flange cut should not overhang the edge of the top plate. (See "Bottom Flange I-Joist" illustration.)

13. Leave a ¹⁄₁₆" gap between I-joists and the supporting member when I-joists are placed in hangers. (See "Gap Between I-Joists and Support" illustration.)

14. The **top flange** can be notched or cut only over the top of the bearing and should not extend beyond the width of the bearing. (See "Top Flange I-Joist" illustration.)

Solid Blocking and I-Joist Minimum Bearing

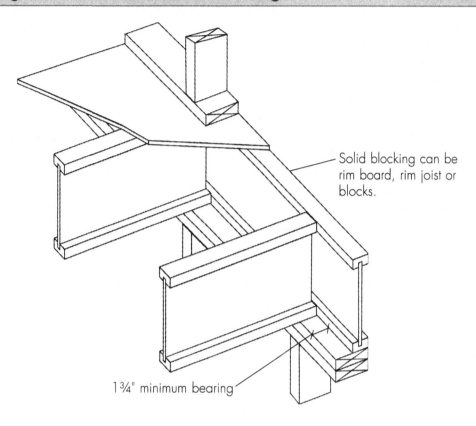

Solid blocking can be rim board, rim joist or blocks.

1¾" minimum bearing

Interior Bearing Wall Blocking Panel

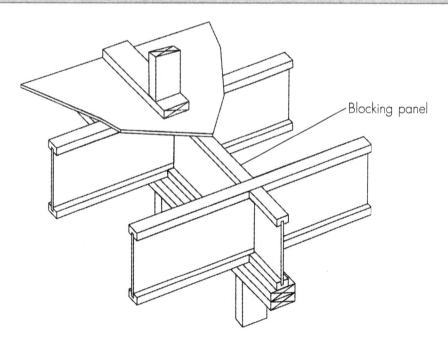

Blocking panel

Squash Blocks

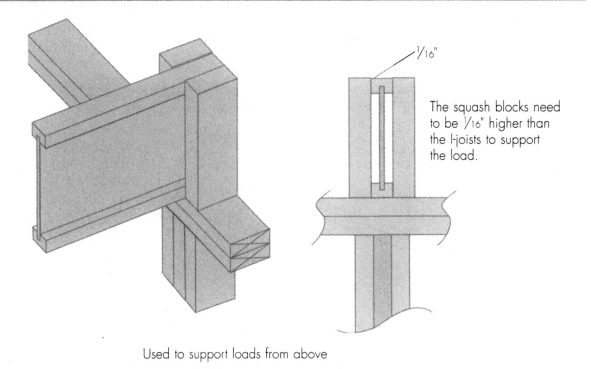

1/16"

The squash blocks need to be 1/16" higher than the I-joists to support the load.

Used to support loads from above

Web Stiffener

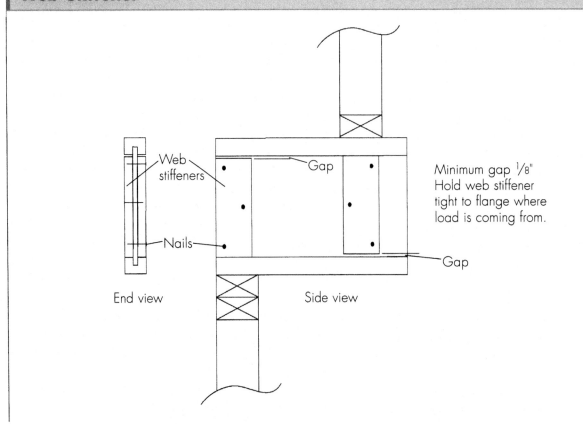

Web stiffeners

Gap

Nails

End view

Side view

Gap

Minimum gap 1/8"
Hold web stiffener tight to flange where load is coming from.

Filler Blocking and Backer Blocking

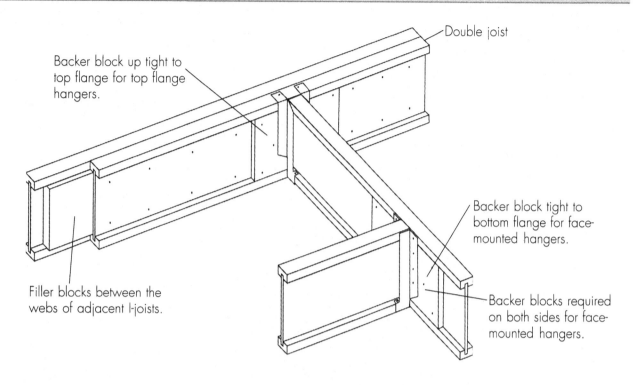

Backer block up tight to top flange for top flange hangers.

Double joist

Filler blocks between the webs of adjacent I-joists.

Backer block tight to bottom flange for face-mounted hangers.

Backer blocks required on both sides for face-mounted hangers.

Top Flange Hanger Tight

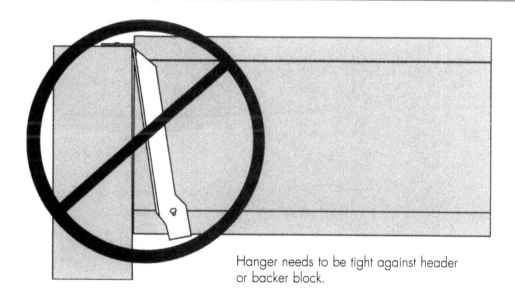

Hanger needs to be tight against header or backer block.

Use Right Nail

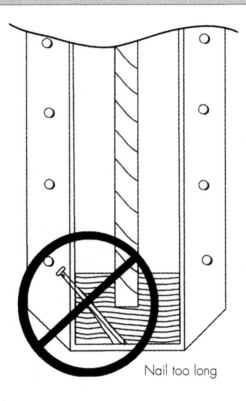

Nail too long

Top Flange Hanger Spacing

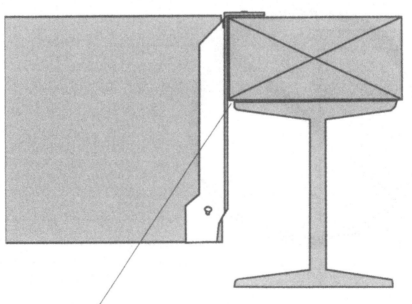

To prevent squeaks, hold hanger away from steel, but
generally not more than ¼" away (distance depends
on plate thickness).

Face-Mount Hangers

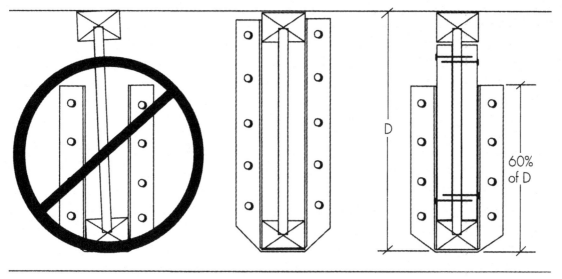

Incorrect: No support   Hanger supports top flange   Web stiffeners support I-joist

Bottom Flange I-Joist

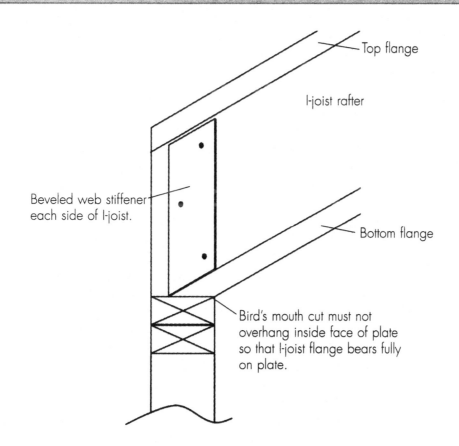

Top flange

I-joist rafter

Beveled web stiffener each side of I-joist.

Bottom flange

Bird's mouth cut must not overhang inside face of plate so that I-joist flange bears fully on plate.

15. **The web can have round or square holes.** Check the information provided with the I-joist package. Typically the center of the span requires the least strength and can have the biggest holes. The closer to the bearing point, the smaller the hole should be.

16. **When I-joists are used on sloped roofs,** they must be supported at the peak by a beam. This is different from dimensional lumber where rafters may not require such a beam.

There may be times when you want to lay out for I-joists so you can prepare for delivery. If you have not yet received the I-joists or the information that comes with them, you will need to know the flange width of the I-joist to lay it out. The following chart gives you the flange widths for the most common I-joists. (See "I-Joist Sizes" chart.)

In working with residential I-joists, you should be aware that the APA has developed a standard for residential I-joists called "Performance Rated I-joists" (PRI). This standard shows the span and spacing for various uses for marked I-joists. (See "APA Performance Rated I-Joists".)

Gap Between I-Joist and Support

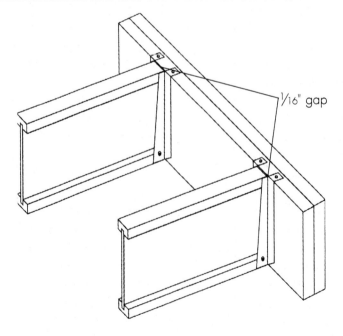

1/16" gap

Top Flange I-Joists

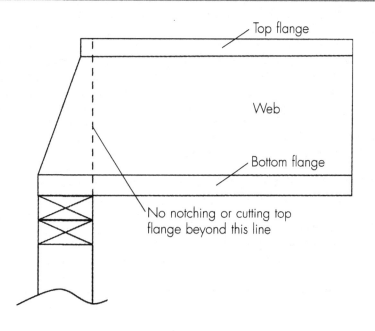

Top flange

Web

Bottom flange

No notching or cutting top
flange beyond this line

I-Joist Sizes

TJI	D	FW
TJI®/Pro ™ 100TS	9.5", 11.875",	1.75"
TJI®/Pro ™ 130TS	9.5", 11.875, " 14, " 16"	2-5/16"
TJI®/Pro ™ 150	9.5", 11.875"	1.5"
TJI®/Pro ™ 250	9.5", 11.875," 14, " 16"	1.75"
TJI®/Pro ™ 350	11.875," 14, " 16"	2-5/16"
TJI®/Pro ™ 550	11.875," 14, " 16"	3.5"

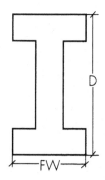

Glu-lam Beams

Glu-lam beams are used when extra strength and greater spans are needed. They are usually big, heavy, expensive, and require hoisting equipment to set them in place. Most often glu-lam beams are engineered for particular jobs especially where long spans are required. Glu-lam beams are produced by gluing certain grades of dimensional lumber together in a specific order. Many times the pieces are glued together to create a specific shape or camber. If a camber is created, the top of the beam will be marked. Make sure your crew installs it right-side-up.

Advanced planning is needed before you install glu-lam beams. You must consider the weight of the glu-lam beams as well as the intended location and make sure there is adequate access for a mobile boom truck or crane.

The approximate weight of glu-lam beams can be determined by using the "Glu-lam Beam Weight Chart." Note that weights will vary based on the species of lumber and the moisture content.

The expense of glu-lam beams and the time required for replacing one makes it very important that they are cut correctly. It is good policy to have a second framer check measurements before cutting begins. This includes physically checking the measurement of the location where the glu-lam

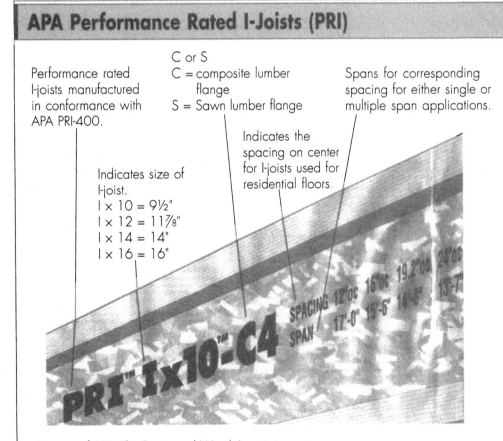

APA Performance Rated I-Joists (PRI)

Performance rated I-joists manufactured in conformance with APA PRI-400.

Indicates size of I-joist.
I × 10 = 9½"
I × 12 = 11⅞"
I × 14 = 14"
I × 16 = 16"

C or S
C = composite lumber flange
S = Sawn lumber flange

Indicates the spacing on center for I-joists used for residential floors.

Spans for corresponding spacing for either single or multiple span applications.

PRI™ 1x10-C4

SPACING 12"oc 16"oc 19.2"oc 24"oc
SPAN 17'-0" 15'-6" 14'-8" 13'-7"

Courtesy of APA, The Engineered Wood Association

beam will be installed and checking the plans to make sure that you have the right glu-lam beam for the location. It's easy for the first person measuring the glu-lam beam to explain the details to the person checking the measurement, but with any explanation, there is room for misunderstanding, and any mistake made by the first person could be passed on to the second. Make sure the framer doing the checking figures the measurements independent of the framer who set the measurements.

Notching and Drilling

The general rule for glu-lam beams is no notching or drilling without an engineer's direction. The engineer who determined the strength needed for the glu-lams is the person who will know how a notch or hole will affect the integrity of the glu-lam beam. Before checking with the engineer, you should have a basic understanding of the parts of the beam most important to its strength. The "Glu-lam Beam Strength" illustration gives you this information. The drilling or notching required to attach the connection hardware specified on the plans is pre-approved by an engineer.

How glu-lam beam connections are made can affect the strength and integrity of the beams. Following are examples of connections that show the correct and incorrect ways to connect glu-lam beams, and some tips for easy installation.

Glu-lam Beam Weight Chart

		Weight Per Lineal Foot					
GLB	Width	3-1/2"	5"	5-1/4"	7"	9"	11"
# of 2x's	GLB Depth						
4	6-1/2"	6.98	7.67	8.05	10.8	13.8	
5	8-1/8"	6.23	9.59	10.1	13.4	17.2	
6	9-3/4"	7.48	11.5	12.1	16.1	20.7	
7	11-3/8"	8.72	13.4	14.1	18.8	24.2	29.5
8	13"	9.97	15.3	16.1	21.5	27.6	33.8
9	14-5/8"	11.2	17.3	18.1	24.2	31.1	38
10	16-1/4"	12.5	19.4	20.1	26.8	34.5	42.2
11	17-7/8"	13.7	21.1	11.2	29.5	38	46.4
12	19-1/2"	15	23	24.2	32.2	41.4	50.6
13	21-1/8"		24.9	26.2	34.9	44.9	54.8
14	22-3/4"		26.9	28.2	37.6	48.3	59.1
15	24-3/8"		28.8	30.2	40.3	51.8	63.3
16	26"		30.7	32.2	43	55.2	67.5
17	27-7/8"		32.6	34.2	45.6	58.7	71.7
18	29-1/4"		34.6	36.2	48.3	62.1	75.9
19	30-7/8"		36.5	38.2	51	65.6	80.2
20	32-1/2"				53.7	69	84.4
21	34-1/8"				56.4	72.5	88.6
22	35-3/4"				59.1	75.9	92.8
23	37-3/8"				61.7	79.4	97
24	39"				64.4	82.8	101
25	40-5/8"				67.1	86.3	105
26	42-1/4"				69.8	89.7	110
27	43-7/8"					93.2	114
28	45-1/2"					96.6	118
29	47-1/8"					100.1	122
30	48-3/4"					103.6	127
31	50-3/8"					107	131
32	52"					110.4	135
33	53-5/8"					113.9	139

Tips for Installing Glu-lam Beams

- For glu-lam beams that are installed at a pitch and need to have the bottom cut to be level, make sure that the end of the bottom cut closest to the bearing edge receives full bearing. (See "Cut Edge Full Bearing" illustration.)

- Ends of beams should not be notched unless approved by the engineer. (See "No Notching End of Glu-lam Beam" illustration.)

- Glu-lam beams will shrink as they dry out. If the top of the beam is connected in a way that doesn't allow for shrinkage, the glu-lam beam will split. (See "Glu-lam Beam Shrinkage" illustration.)

- When a lateral support plate is used to connect two glu-lam beams, the holes should be slotted horizontally to prevent splitting. (See "Lateral Support Plate" illustration.)

- Glu-lams are also used for posts. It is important to keep them away from concrete, which contributes to their decay. Placing a steel shim under the beam will keep it from touching the concrete. (See "Decay Prevention Next to Concrete" illustration.)

- Hinge connectors should be installed so that they don't cause splitting of the glu-lam beams. This can be done by using a strap that is independent of the hinge connector, or by vertical slotting the holes in a strap that is connected to the hinge connector. (See "Hinge Connectors Slotted Holes" and "Hinge Connectors" illustrations.)

- Glu-lam beams rest on metal post caps that often have a weld or radius in the bottom corner. If you don't ease the bottom corners of the beam, the beam will sit up in the pocket. Often, the glu-lam beam's bottom corners are already rounded and won't need attention.

- In some cases, the sides of the metal post caps are bent in so that the beams will not slide in properly. Check all the sides of the metal post caps before they are installed, so you won't have a boom truck and crew standing around waiting while someone labors on top of a ladder to

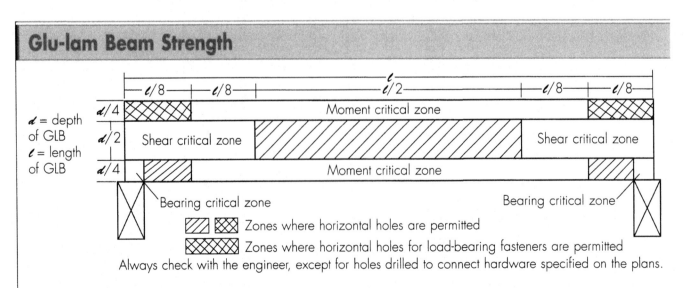

Glu-lam Beam Strength

d = depth of GLB
ℓ = length of GLB

$\ell/8$ — $\ell/8$ — $\ell/2$ — $\ell/8$ — $\ell/8$

Moment critical zone
Shear critical zone
Moment critical zone
Bearing critical zone

Zones where horizontal holes are permitted
Zones where horizontal holes for load-bearing fasteners are permitted
Always check with the engineer, except for holes drilled to connect hardware specified on the plans.

widen the sides of the post cap. (See "Boom Truck Setting Glu-lam Beams" illustration.)

- Glu-lam beams are often attached to metal caps with bolts. The holes can be drilled either before or after setting the glu-lam beams. If the holes are drilled after the beams are set, use a drill with a clutch. It's easy to break a wrist or get thrown from a ladder when a ½" drill motor without a clutch gets caught on the metal.

Metal Plate-Connected Wood Trusses

Metal plate-connected (MPC) wood trusses were first used in the early 1950s. Today they are used in more than 75% of all new residential roofs. Basically they are dimension lumber engineered and connected with metal plates. Less expensive than alternative roof systems, these trusses can also span longer distances. The "Pitched Truss Parts" illustration shows the parts of a single pitched truss.

Because MPC trusses are engineered products, they should never be cut, notched, spliced, or drilled without first checking with the designing engineer.

Building codes require that a truss design drawing be delivered to the job site. The drawings must show, among other things, the layout locations

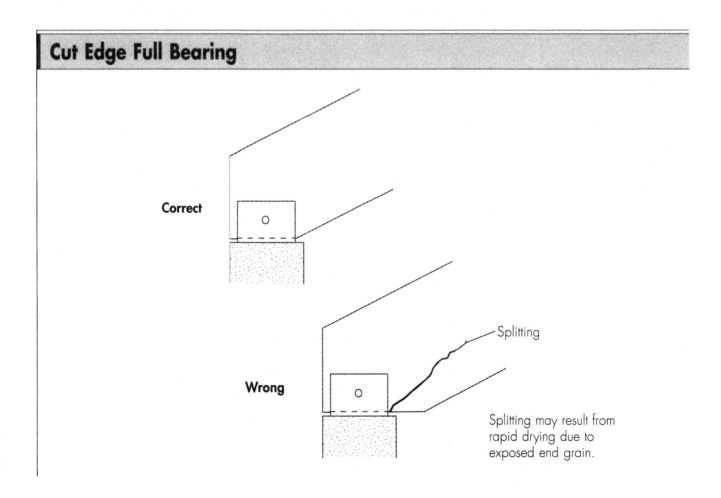

Cut Edge Full Bearing

Correct

Wrong

Splitting

Splitting may result from rapid drying due to exposed end grain.

and bracing details. Note that these drawings are typically not made with framers in mind, so it might take some study time to figure out where the engineer wants the braces. The bracing details often show the braces as small rectangles running laterally between the trusses. See "Lateral Truss Bracing."

When flying trusses you should attach the cables around the panel points. When the trusses are greater than 30', a spreader bar should be used. The cables should toe inward to prevent the truss from buckling. If the truss is longer than 60' you will need a strongback temporarily attached to the truss to stabilize it. (See "Flying Trusses" illustration.)

If you have multiple trusses, you can build a subassembly of several trusses on the ground with cross braces and sheathing, then erect them together.

When trusses sit on the ground, on the building, or in place for any length of time, keep them as straight as possible. They are more difficult to set in place and to straighten if they have not been stored properly on site.

Structural Composite Lumber (SCL)

Structural composite lumber (SCL) is an engineered wood product that combines veneer sheets, strands, or small wood elements with exterior

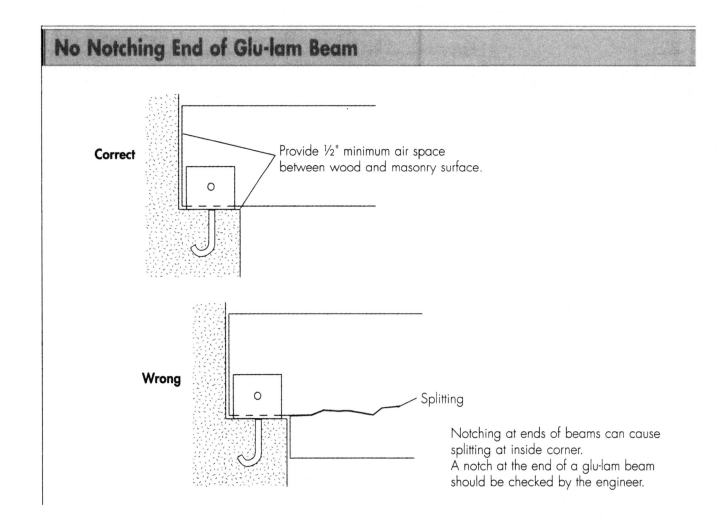

No Notching End of Glu-lam Beam

Correct

Provide ½" minimum air space between wood and masonry surface.

Wrong

Splitting

Notching at ends of beams can cause splitting at inside corner.
A notch at the end of a glu-lam beam should be checked by the engineer.

structural adhesives. The most common of these products are laminated veneer lumber (LVL), parallel strand lumber (PSL), and laminated strand lumber (LSL). Their names pretty well describe the differences between them.

Like other engineered products, structural composite lumber requires that you follow the engineered specifications that will appear on the plans. Sometimes the specifications simply indicate the use of a particular piece of SCL in a particular location. For larger jobs, you will find the SCL requirements called out in the shop drawings or the structural plans.

Because these are engineered products, you must consult the design engineer before you can drill or notch. Some manufacturers provide guidelines for drilling and notching, but this is not typical.

SCL has the advantages of dimensional consistency, stability, and availability of various sizes. It is important to note, however, that where dimensional lumber 4 × 10s, 4 × 12s, etc. can shrink significantly, SCLs have minimal shrinkage. The engineer should allow for this in the design so that you will not have to consider this factor when using SCLs as the plans specify.

Note that SCL studs are becoming common in building tall walls. They provide a degree of straightness that dimensional lumber does not. Although they are heavy and, as a result, not so easy to work with, they make nice, straight walls.

Conclusion

Engineered wood products come in a variety of forms. Becoming familiar with these products is important if you plan to work with them. Always be sure to follow manufacturers' directions, and always consult an engineer if you plan to cut, notch, or drill engineered wood product components.

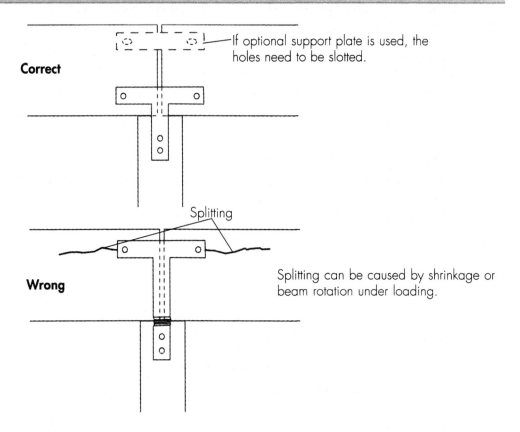

Correct

If optional support plate is used, the holes need to be slotted.

Splitting

Wrong

Splitting can be caused by shrinkage or beam rotation under loading.

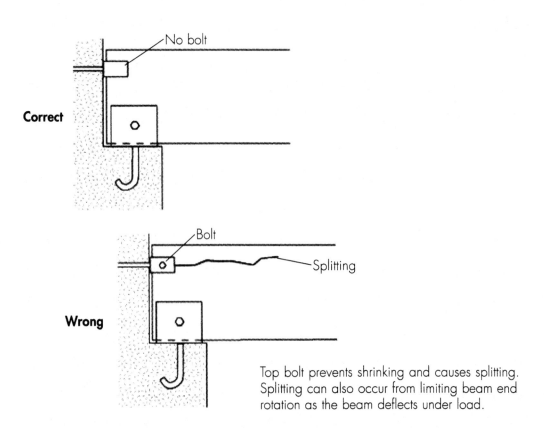

No bolt

Correct

Bolt

Splitting

Wrong

Top bolt prevents shrinking and causes splitting. Splitting can also occur from limiting beam end rotation as the beam deflects under load.

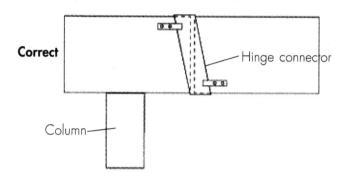

Correct

Hinge connector

Column

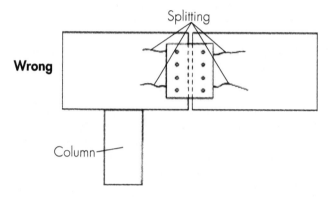

Splitting

Wrong

Column

Splitting can be caused by shrinkage on large splice plates.

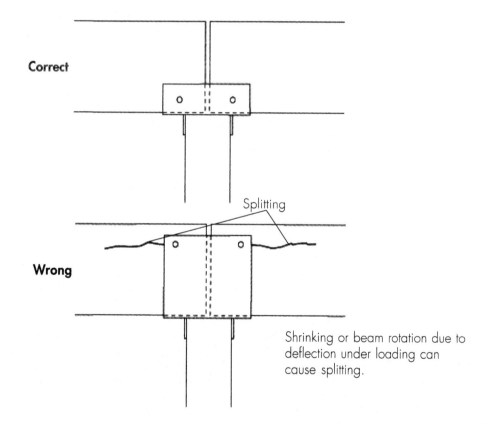

Correct

Splitting

Wrong

Shrinking or beam rotation due to deflection under loading can cause splitting.

Lateral Support Plate

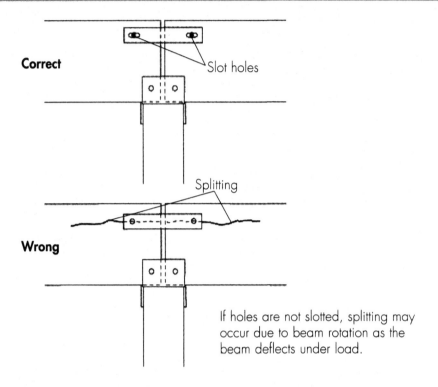

Correct

Slot holes

Splitting

Wrong

If holes are not slotted, splitting may occur due to beam rotation as the beam deflects under load.

Decay Prevention Next to Concrete

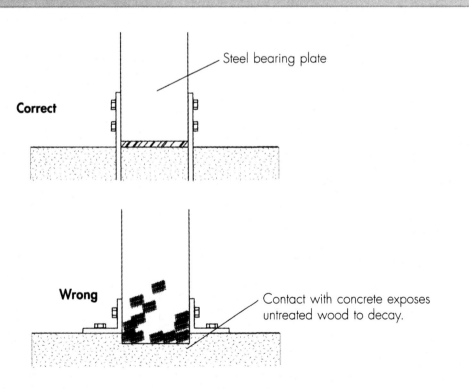

Steel bearing plate

Correct

Wrong

Contact with concrete exposes untreated wood to decay.

Hinge Connector Slotted Holes

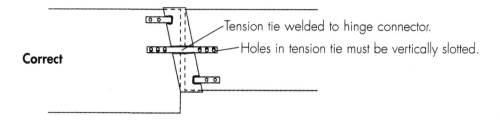

Correct

Tension tie welded to hinge connector.

Holes in tension tie must be vertically slotted.

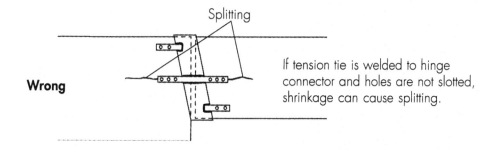

Splitting

Wrong

If tension tie is welded to hinge connector and holes are not slotted, shrinkage can cause splitting.

Hinge Connectors

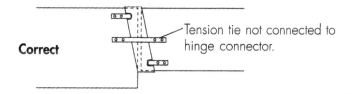

Correct

Tension tie not connected to hinge connector.

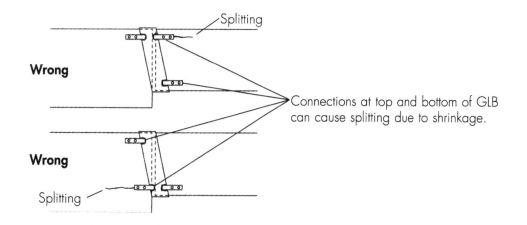

Splitting

Wrong

Connections at top and bottom of GLB can cause splitting due to shrinkage.

Wrong

Splitting

Boom Truck Setting Glu-lam Beams

Pitched Truss Parts

Peak

Top chord

Panel point

Tail

Heel

Bottom chord

Splice

Webs

Lateral Truss Bracing

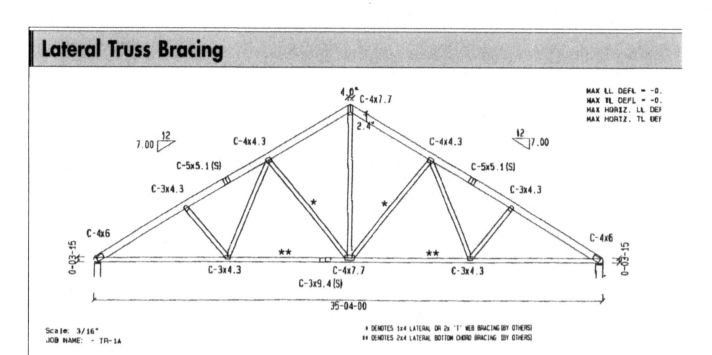

MAX LL DEFL = -0.
MAX TL DEFL = -0.
MAX HORIZ. LL DEF
MAX HORIZ. TL DEF

Scale: 3/16"
JOB NAME: - TR-1A

* DENOTES 1x4 LATERAL OR 2x 'T' WEB BRACING (BY OTHERS)
** DENOTES 2x4 LATERAL BOTTOM CHORD BRACING (BY OTHERS)

Flying Trusses

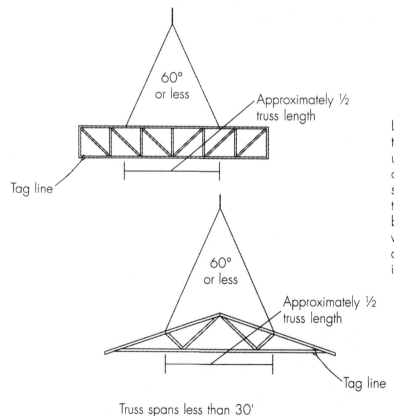

60°
or less

Approximately ½ truss length

Tag line

60°
or less

Approximately ½ truss length

Tag line

Truss spans less than 30'

Lifting devices should be connected to the truss top chord with a closed-loop attachment utilizing materials such as slings, chains, cables, nylon strapping, etc. of sufficient strength to carry the weight of the truss. Each truss should be set in proper position per the building designer's framing plan and held with the lifting device until the ends of the truss are securely fastened and temporary bracing is installed.

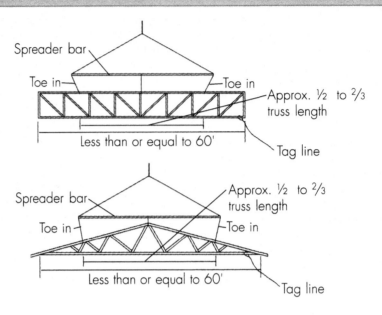

Spreader bar

Toe in — — Toe in

Approx. ½ to ⅔ truss length

Tag line

Less than or equal to 60'

Spreader bar

Approx. ½ to ⅔ truss length

Toe in — — Toe in

Less than or equal to 60'

Tag line

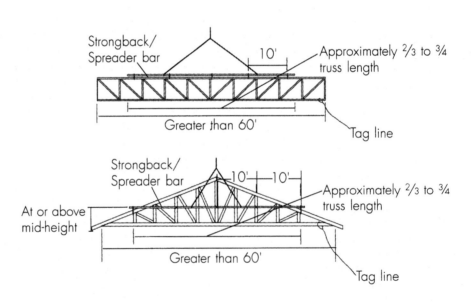

Strongback/ Spreader bar

10'

Approximately ⅔ to ¾ truss length

Tag line

Greater than 60'

Strongback/ Spreader bar

10' — 10'

Approximately ⅔ to ¾ truss length

At or above mid-height

Greater than 60'

Tag line

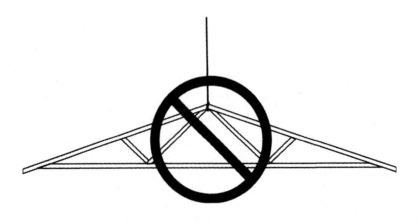

Chapter Eleven

Building Code Requirements

F ramers, builders, architects, engineers, and building inspectors alike have contributed to the system of building codes we use today. As a framer, you should be aware of the codes that apply to the part of the country you are working in, as well as the important features of those codes. This chapter will discuss what you should know about building code requirements.

Contents

The Evolution of Building Codes

Although carpentry is one of the oldest professions, framing as we know it today didn't start until 1832 when a man named George Snow wanted to build a warehouse in Chicago. It was difficult to obtain enough large timbers to build the structure using the traditional post and beam method. Being creative (as all good builders and lead framers must be), he cut up the small timbers he had growing on his property into pieces similar to 2 x 4s. He placed them in a repetitive manner, thus creating the first 2 x 4 style walls.

Since then, architects, engineers, builders, building inspectors, and framers have all contributed to the system we use today. Along the way, builders constructed buildings in the way they saw fit. Although this "every man for himself" approach to building gave us structures to live and work in, it did not guarantee that such buildings would last a lifetime or stand up against earthquakes and hurricanes.

It wasn't until 1915 that a group of building officials decided they needed a standard. That year the Building Officials & Code Administrators International (BOCA) was established to bring some uniformity to the systems being used.

The IBC

Two other building code agencies appeared not long after: the International Conference of Building Officials (ICBO), and the Southern Building Code Congress International (SBCCI). All three organizations worked to meet the particular needs of their regions of the country.

In the year 2000, these agencies combined their codes to create one common code that would cover the entire country. This code is divided into two books: the *International Residential Code (IRC)*, which covers all one- and two-family dwellings and multiple single-family dwellings (townhouses) not more than three stories in height, and the *International Building Code (IBC)* which covers all buildings. Separating the code in this way makes it easier to find the information you need. If you are building only houses, duplexes, or townhouses, you would go straight to the IRC.

There are two ways to comply with code. The prescriptive method, most commonly used, gives specific requirements (such as how many inches on center to space the framing lumber) to build walls that are acceptable. The **performance method** tells us how a person can determine the strength of a wall using properly stamped, graded lumber, and if that strength meets the minimum code requirements.

Because the prescriptive system is most commonly used, it is the one we'll cover here. It applies to conventional construction otherwise known as *platform* or *balloon* framing, which has been developed over the years on job sites, and has been tested and standardized. Prescriptive code requires no "engineering" design by a registered professional, as long as the project is built in compliance with the *International Residential Code* (IRC) or *International Building Code* (IBC).

(Note that with a performance-rated system, you will have a set of plans that you must follow to the letter. These plans come with structural components that must be used exclusively with the plans. Performance-rated codes require design by a registered professional who must specify in accordance with the IRC or IBC.)

A Framer's Code Responsibility

Although it may seem that the codes are written for lawyers instead of framers, framers must be sure that their work complies to code. Note that some areas of the country may not be covered by a statewide, town, city, or county code. (Counties have historically been the jurisdictions controlling code establishment and enforcement.) Note, too, that code-writing organizations are not government agencies, so codes are not enforceable until or unless a government jurisdiction accepts the codes and makes them part of local law.

Code Revisions and Time Delays

Code Revisions: Revisions are important to keep in mind when working with codes. Codes are normally updated annually, and revised versions are published every three years. Typically the revisions are not major, but it is important to know which code you must comply with. On some jobs the plans will indicate which codes apply. This information can usually be found on the cover page or with the general specifications in the plans. If the applicable code is not shown on the plans, ask the builder, owner, or whoever acquired the building permit about the code.

Time Delays: Another thing to keep in mind is the time that may elapse between when the code writing organizations publish a revised code and when that code edition becomes the ruling code on the job you are framing. There are delays between when the code agencies certify the new codes and when the local government agencies review and approve the new codes. There can also be delays between the date the permit is issued and the date the job is framed. It is not unusual to be working on plans that are three or four years or more behind the current building code. Although you have to comply with the code that is specified on the plans or that was used when the building permit was approved, you should also understand the current code because, in general, additions to the codes are improvements, or ways that contribute to making a building stronger. After every major earthquake or hurricane, codes have been adjusted and upgraded. By using the latest code, you can feel confident that you are framing with the latest construction knowledge.

Latest Code Used in This Book

This book uses the 2000 edition of the IBC and IRC to explain the major features of codes related to framing. These features include life safety issues, structural requirements, and the spreading of fire. Although the code books look pretty big and intimidating when you first see them, the number of pages that deal with framing are relatively few.

The IBC IRC Framing Index chart categorizes the IBC and IRC sections on framing. In the IRC, the framing information can be found primarily in 4 of the total 43 chapters. In the IBC, 3 of the total 35 chapters deal with framing. The IRC framing chapters are Chapters 3, 5, 6, and 8. The IBC chapters containing framing information are 10, 12, and 23.

Important Code Features and Points

What follows are key features of the code, and illustrations presented in a framer-friendly way. If you do a lot of framing, it's a good idea to have a copy of the code book available for reference.

Here are the three major categories used in the IBC:

Use and Occupancy Classification:

A — Assembly group

B — Business group

E — Educational group

F — Factory group

H — High-hazard group

I — Institutional group

M — Mercantile group

R — Residential group

S — Storage group

U — Utility and Miscellaneous group

Fire-Resistance-Rated Construction Classification:

Type I— Noncombustible material.

Type II— Noncombustible material.

Type III— Exterior walls noncombustible and interior, any material permitted by code.

Type IV— Exterior walls noncombustible, and interior, solid or laminated wood without concealed spaces. (Heavy Timber)

Type V— Any material permitted by code.

Seismic Design Categories:

In the IRC, these categories are A, B, C, D1, D2, and E. They relate to the potential for earthquake damage risk. "A" represents the lowest risk, and "E" represents the highest risk.

IBC IRC Framing Index

Framing code	IRC #	IRC page	IBC#	IBC page	Table-Fig.
Floor Framing					
Double joists under bearing partitions	R502.4	79	2308.8.4	572	
Bearing	R503.6	79	2308.7	569	
Bearing			2308.8.1	572	
Minimum lap	R502.6.1	79	2308.8.2	572	
Joist support	R502.6.2	79	2308.8.2	572	
Lateral support	R502.7	84	2308.8.2	572	
Bridging	R502.7.1	84	2308.8.5	572	
Drilling and notching	R502.8	84	2308.8.2	572	
Framing around openings	R502.1	86	2308.8.3	572	
Framing around openings - seismic			2308.11.3.3	591	
Wall Framing					
Stud size, height and spacing	R602.3	103	2308.9.1	573	IBC-2308.9.1
Stud size, height and spacing					R602.3(5)
Cripple wall stud size	R602.9	112	2308.9.4	577	
Cripple wall connection			2308.11.3.2	591	IBC-2308.11.3.2
Double and top plate overlap	R602.3.2	103	2308.9.2.1	573	
Drilling and notching	R602.6	112	2308.9.10	580	IRC-602.6(1)&(2)
Drilling and notching			2308.9.11	580	IRC-602.7.2
Headers	R602.7	112			IRC-502.5(1)&(2)
Headers			2308.9.5	577	IBC-2308.9.5&6
Fireblocking	R602.8	112	716.2	115	
Wall bracing	R602.10-11.3	112-121			R602.10.3&5&11
Wall bracing					R602.11.3
Wall bracing			2308.9.3	573	IBC-2308.9.3(1)
Braced wall lines			2308.3	569	
Anchor bolts			2308.3.3	569	
Anchor bolts			2308.6	569	
Plate washers			2308.12.8	596	
Rafter Framing					
Ridge board and hip & valley rafters	R802.3	213	2308.10.4	589	
Rafter bearing	R802.6	217			
Drilling and notching	R802.7	217	2308.10.4.2	589	
Lateral support	R802.8	235	2308.10.6	589	
framing around openings	R802.9	235	2308.10.4.3	589	
Roof tie downs & wind uplift	R802.11	236	2308.10.1	580	
Rafter connections	R802.3.1	213	2308.10.4.1	589	
Ceiling Framing					
Ceiling heights	R305.1	43	1207.2	261	
Ceiling joist lapped	R802.3.2	213			
Ceiling joists bearing	R802.6	217			
Ceiling joist connectors			2308.10.4.1	589	

Source: The *International Residential Code*, copyright © 2000, with the permission of the publisher, the International Conference of Building Officials, under license from the International Code Council. The 2000 *International Residential Code* is a copyrighted work of the International Code Council.

Framing code	IRC #	IRC page	IBC#	IBC page	Table-Fig.
Ceiling framing			2308.1	568	
Truss Framing					
Truss bracing	R802.10.3	236	2308.10.7.2	589	
Truss alterations	R802.10.4	236	2308.10.7.3	589	
Attic Access					
Attic spaces			1208.2	262	
Attic access	R807.1	249			
Stair & Ramp Framing					
Stair landings	R312.1	47	1003.3.3.4	226	
Stair width	R314.1	48	1003.3.3.1	225	
Stair treads & risers	R314.2	48	1003.3.3.3	225	
Stair headroom	R314.3	48	1003.3.3.2	225	
Spiral stairs	R314.5	48	1003.3.3.9	227	
Circular stairs	R314.6	48	1003.3.3.7	227	
Handrails	R315	49			
Ramps	R313	48	1.003.3.4	228	
Ventilation					
Attic			1202.3	259	
Under floor			1202.4	260	
Roof	R806	249			
Nailing					
Nailing table			2304.9.1	547	2304.9.1
Sheathing nailing			2304.9.2	550	
Sheathing nailing			2305.1.2.1	553	
Prevention of Decay					
Decay map					IRC-R301.2(7)
Pressure treated	R322	52			
Pressure treated joists, girders & subfloor			2304.11.2.1	551	
Pressure treated framing			2304.11.2.2	551	
Pressure treated sleepers & sills			2304.11.2.3	551	
Girder ends at masonry			2304.11.2.4	551	
Pressure treated post & columns			2304.11.2.6	551	
Pressure treated post & columns			2304.11.4.1	552	
Pressure treated laminated timbers			2304.11.3	551	
Pressure treated wood contact with ground			2304.11.4	552	
Pressure treated wood structural members			2304.11.4.2	552	
Pressure treated wood structural members			2304.11.5	552	
Termite protection					
Termite protection			2304.11.6	552	
Miscellaneous					
Wind excess of 90 MPH	R301.2.1.1	21			

In the IBC, the seismic design categories are based on their seismic use group. The categories are A, B, C, D, D[a], E, and F. Although they are similar to the categories in the IRC, there are some differences.

Floor Framing

The list below shows the code requirements and instructions related to floor framing (see the "Floor Joist Framing" illustration, also below):

- Double joists are required under parallel bearing walls.
- If pipes penetrate floors where double joists are required, the joists must be separated and have full-depth, solid blocks at least every 4' along their length.
- Bearing for joists must be 1½" minimum on wood or steel, and a minimum of 3" on concrete or masonry.
- Where joists lap, there must be a minimum lap of 3" or a wood or metal splice of equal strength.
- The ends of joists shall be kept from turning by using 1½" full-depth solid blocking or by being attached to a header, band, rim joist, or adjoining stud.

Floor Joist Framing

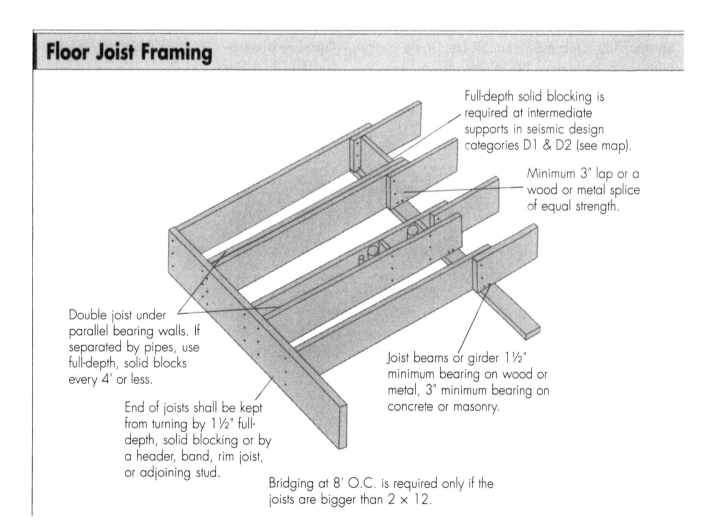

Full-depth solid blocking is required at intermediate supports in seismic design categories D1 & D2 (see map).

Minimum 3" lap or a wood or metal splice of equal strength.

Double joist under parallel bearing walls. If separated by pipes, use full-depth, solid blocks every 4' or less.

Joist beams or girder 1½" minimum bearing on wood or metal, 3" minimum bearing on concrete or masonry.

End of joists shall be kept from turning by 1½" full-depth, solid blocking or by a header, band, rim joist, or adjoining stud.

Bridging at 8' O.C. is required only if the joists are bigger than 2 × 12.

- Full-depth solid blocking is required at intermediate supports in IRC seismic design categories D1, D2, and E. (See seismic maps in Chapter 9.)
- Bridging at 8' O.C. is required only with joists larger than 2 × 12.

"Floor Joists–Anchor or Ledger" shows how joists framing into girders must be supported by framing anchors or a 2 × 2 or larger ledger.

"Floor Joists–Drilling and Notching" shows requirements for allowable drilling and notching of joists. Engineered wood products such as I-joists can be notched according to the manufacturer's specifications. (See Chapter 10 on engineered wood products.)

The "Framing Floor Openings" illustration, later in the chapter, shows the following code requirements and instructions related to framing around openings in floors.

- If the header joists are more than 4', the header joists and trimmer joists should be doubled.
- If the distance from the bearing point of a trimmer joist to the header joist is more than 3', the trimmer joists should be doubled.
- If header joist is greater than 6', hangers must be used on the header joists.
- If the tail joists are more than 12', use framing anchors or a 2 × 2 ledger.

"Seismic Floor Opening Framing", later in the chapter, illustrates what to do if you are building in IRC seismic design categories B, C, D, or E and the opening is greater than 4' perpendicular to the joists. In such cases, you must provide blocking beyond the headers, and metal ties must be used to connect the headers with the blocks.

Floor Joists—Anchor or Ledger

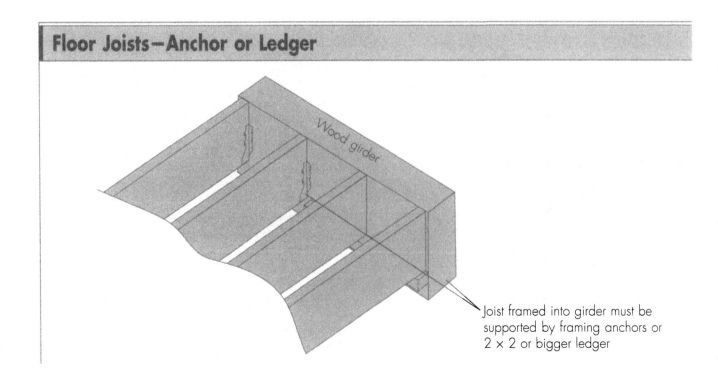

Joist framed into girder must be supported by framing anchors or 2 × 2 or bigger ledger

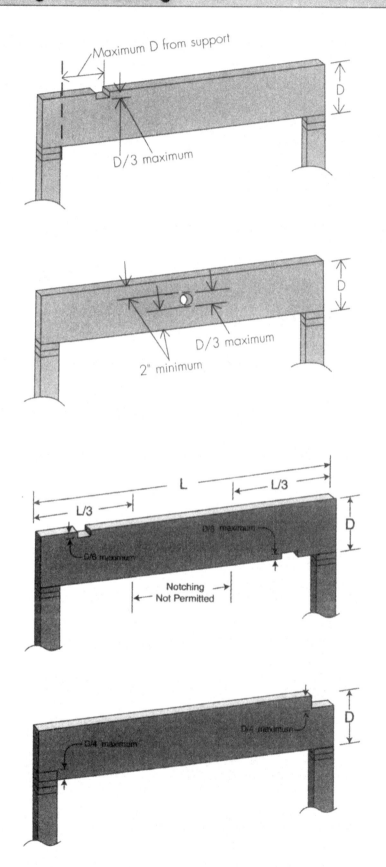

Framing Floor Openings

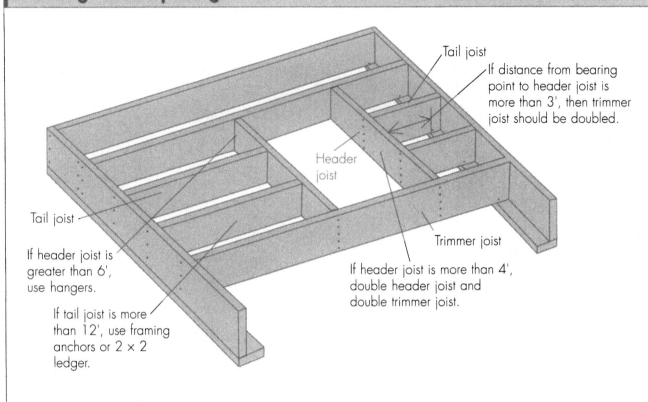

Tail joist

If distance from bearing point to header joist is more than 3', then trimmer joist should be doubled.

Header joist

Tail joist

If header joist is greater than 6', use hangers.

If tail joist is more than 12', use framing anchors or 2 × 2 ledger.

Trimmer joist

If header joist is more than 4', double header joist and double trimmer joist.

Seismic Floor Opening Framing

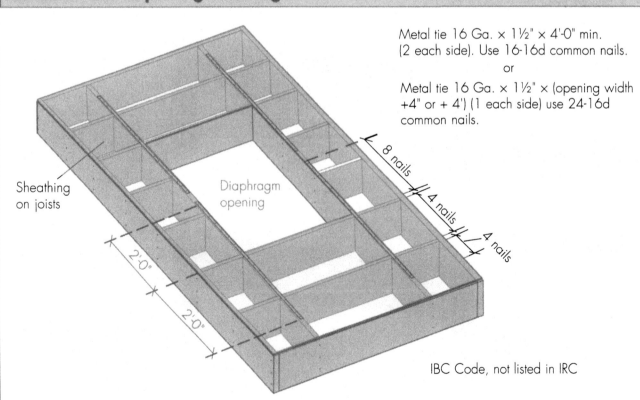

Sheathing on joists

Diaphragm opening

2'-0"

2'-0"

8 nails

4 nails

4 nails

Metal tie 16 Ga. × 1½" × 4'-0" min. (2 each side). Use 16-16d common nails.

or

Metal tie 16 Ga. × 1½" × (opening width +4" or + 4') (1 each side) use 24-16d common nails.

IBC Code, not listed in IRC

Wall Framing

Stud spacing should be shown on the plans, but it is still good to be familiar with the code limitations. For 2 × 4 studs less than 10 feet tall, the maximum stud spacing is 24" O.C., provided the wall is supporting one floor or a roof and ceiling only. For the support of one floor, a roof, and ceiling, 16" O.C. is the maximum. To support two floors, a roof, and a ceiling with a maximum spacing of 16" O.C. and height of 10', a minimum of 3 × 4 studs must be used. If studs are 2 × 6, a wall can support one floor, a roof, and ceiling at 24" O.C. or two floors, a roof, and ceiling at 16" O.C. Again, this stud spacing only applies to walls that don't exceed 10 feet in height. (See "Stud—Spacing and Size" illustration.)

Cripple walls less than 4' in height should be framed with studs at least as big as those used in the walls above them. If the cripple walls are higher than 4', then the studs need to be at least the size required for supporting an additional floor level (as described in previous paragraph). (See "Foundation Cripple Walls" illustration.)

Double plates are needed on top plates for bearing and exterior walls. The end joints of the top plates and double plates should be offset by at least 48". The IRC allows a 24" offset at nonstructural interior walls. The end joints need to be nailed with at least eight 16d nails or twelve 3" × 0.131" nails on each side of the joint. A single top plate may be used if the plates are tied together at the joints, intersecting walls, and corners with 3" × 6" galvanized steel plates or the equivalent, and all rafters, joists, or trusses are centered over the studs. (See "Walls, Top and Double Plate" illustration.)

Allowable **drilling** and **notching** is different for bearing or exterior walls, and for interior *non-bearing* or interior walls. Bearing or exterior walls can be notched up to 25% of the width of the stud and drilled up to 40% of the stud provided that the hole is at least ⅝" away from the edge. With interior *non-bearing* walls, the percentages are 40% for notches and 60% for drilling. (See "Drilling and Notching Studs, Exterior and Bearing Walls" and "Drilling and Notching Studs, Interior Non-Bearing Walls" illustrations later in this chapter.)

Header sizes for exterior and bearing walls should be specified on the plans. For *non-bearing* walls, a flat 2 × 4 may be used as a header for a maximum of up to 8' span where the height above the header to the top plate is 24" or less. (See "Header for Non-Bearing Walls" illustration later in this chapter.)

Fireblocking refers to material you install to prevent flames from traveling through concealed spaces between areas of a building. The location of fireblocks is sometimes difficult to understand. It helps to think of where flames would be able to go. A 1½" thick piece of wood can create a fireblock. If you place a row of these blocks in a wall, you create a deterent for the vertical spread of fire. Vertical and horizontal fireblocks are required in walls at least every 10 feet. (See "Fireblocking Vertical" and "Fireblocking Horizontal" illustrations.)

Stud—Spacing and Size

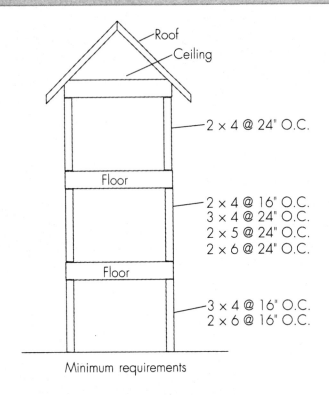

Roof
Ceiling

2 x 4 @ 24" O.C.

Floor

2 x 4 @ 16" O.C.
3 x 4 @ 24" O.C.
2 x 5 @ 24" O.C.
2 x 6 @ 24" O.C.

Floor

3 x 4 @ 16" O.C.
2 x 6 @ 16" O.C.

Minimum requirements

Foundation Cripple Walls

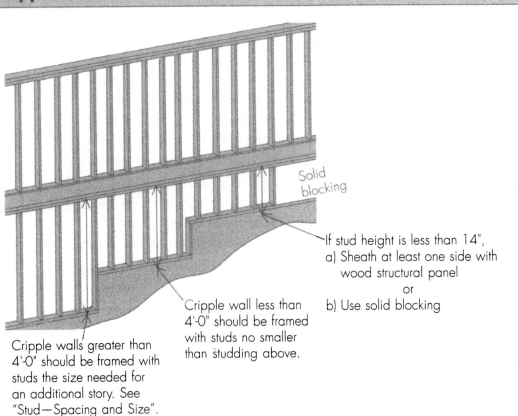

Solid blocking

If stud height is less than 14",
a) Sheath at least one side with
wood structural panel
or
b) Use solid blocking

Cripple wall less than
4'-0" should be framed
with studs no smaller
than studding above.

Cripple walls greater than
4'-0" should be framed with
studs the size needed for
an additional story. See
"Stud—Spacing and Size".

In a party wall construction where you have two walls next to each other, you can create a fireblock by installing a stud in the space between the studs in the two adjoining walls. This creates a vertical fireblock. Note that ½" gypsum board can also be used to create this type of fireblock.

Fireblocking is required between walls, floors, ceilings, and roofs. Typically, the drywall covering creates this fireblock. If it doesn't, then fireblocking is needed. This situation, in which fireblocking is required behind the ledger, can occur at the interconnections of any concealed vertical and horizontal space like that which occurs at soffits, drop ceilings, or cove ceilings. (See "Fireblocking at Interconnections" illustration later in this chapter.)

Stair stringers must be fireblocked at the top and bottom of each run and between studs along the stair stringers if the walls below the stairs are unfinished.

Walls, Top and Double Plate

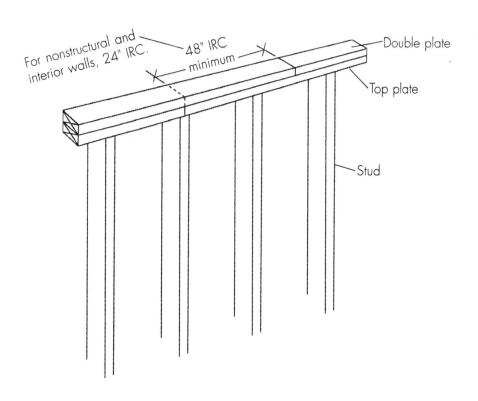

Bored holes and notches may not be in same cross section

Bored holes cannot be bigger than 40% of stud width.
For 2 x 4 = 1⅜" maximum
For 2 x 6 = 2³/₁₆ maximum

⅝" minimum between hole and edge of stud

Notch cannot be bigger than 25% of stud depth
For 2 x 4 = ⅞" maximum
For 2 x 6 = 1⅜" maximum

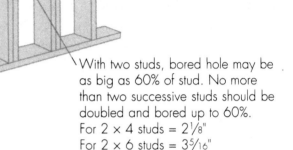

With two studs, bored hole may be as big as 60% of stud. No more than two successive studs should be doubled and bored up to 60%.
For 2 x 4 studs = 2⅛"
For 2 x 6 studs = 3⁵/₁₆"

Drilling and Notching, Studs, Interior Non-Bearing Walls

Bored holes and notches may not be in same cross section

Bored holes cannot be bigger than 60% of stud depth
For 2 x 4 = 2⅛" maximum
For 2 x 6 = 3⁵/₁₆" maximum

⅝" minimum between hole and edge of stud

Notch cannot be bigger than 40% of stud depth
For 2 x 4 = 1⅜" maximum
For 2 x 6 = 3⁵/₁₆" maximum

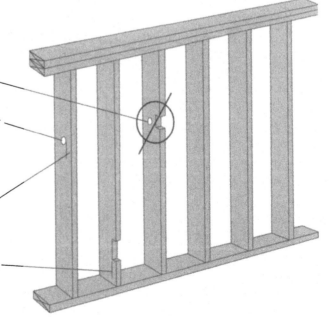

Header for Non-Bearing Walls

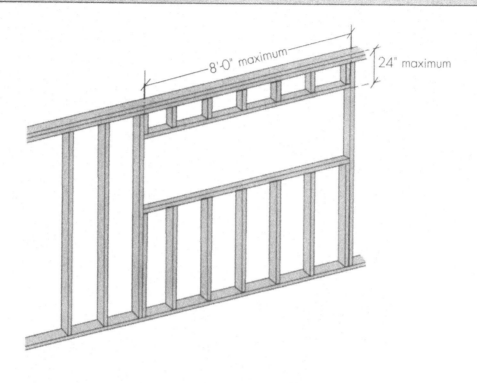

8'-0" maximum

24" maximum

Fireblocking Vertical

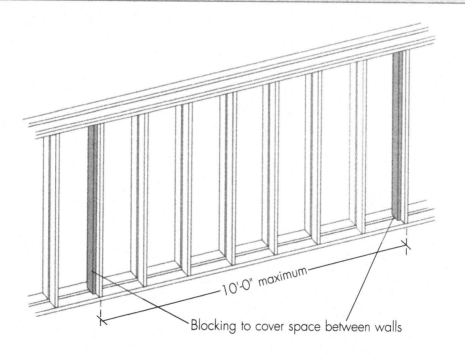

10'-0" maximum

Blocking to cover space between walls

Fireblocking Horizontal

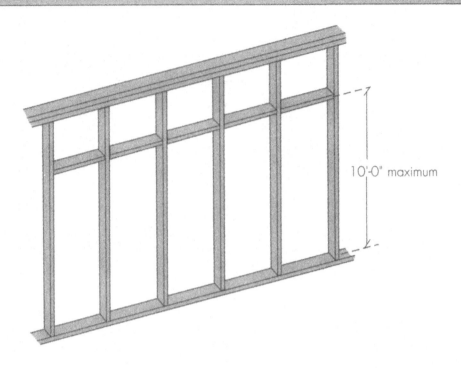

10'-0" maximum

Fireblocking at Interconnections

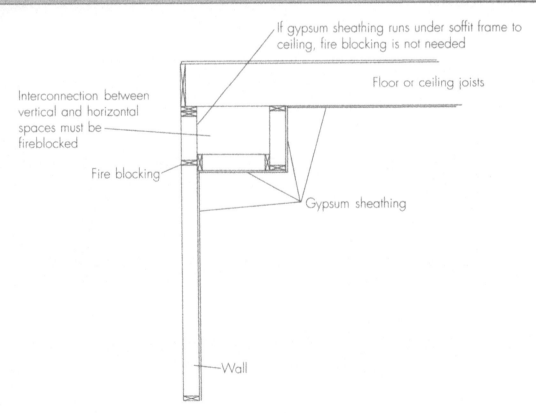

If gypsum sheathing runs under soffit frame to ceiling, fire blocking is not needed

Floor or ceiling joists

Interconnection between vertical and horizontal spaces must be fireblocked

Fire blocking

Gypsum sheathing

Wall

Wall bracing is needed to keep buildings from falling. Sheathing the exterior walls is a typical way to provide bracing. The architect, engineer, or whoever creates the plans will specify when any special bracing is needed. Although you don't need to know everything about wall bracing, it is good to have a basic understanding of it.

The eight basic construction methods for braced wall panels are as follows:

1. A 1 x 4 let-in, or metal strap diagonal braces

2. Wood boards diagonally applied

3. Wood structural panel sheathing

4. Structural fiberboard sheathing

5. Gypsum board sheathing

6. Particleboard sheathing

7. Portland cement plaster

8. Hardboard panel siding

Two common exceptions to these methods are: (1) the short wall often used for garages, and (2) the 24" wide corner wall. Note that cripple walls have their own requirements.

The IBC states that braced wall panels must be clearly indicated on the plans. However, this is not always the case in the real world. Although shear walls are usually marked on the plans, braced wall panels often are not.

The IBC and IRC contain a table that shows braced wall panel limitations and requirements. The limitations are related to the seismic design category, and to how many stories are built on top of the walls.

Where braced wall lines rest on concrete or masonry foundations, they must have **anchor bolts** that are not less than ½" in diameter or a code-approved anchor strap. The anchor bolts or straps should be spaced not more than 6' (or not more than 4' apart if the building is over two stories).

Each piece of wall plate must contain at least two bolts or straps. There must be one between 4" and 12" from each end of each piece. A nut and washer must be tightened on each bolt. In IBC seismic design categories D, E, and F, engineered shear walls require 2" x 2" x ³/₁₆" plate washers. In seismic design categories D1, D2, and E, braced walls require 2" x 2" x ¼" plate washers. (See "Anchor Bolts" illustration on following page.)

Rafter Framing

Ridge boards must be at least 1" nominal in width and must be as deep as the cut end of the rafter. Hip and valley rafters must be at least 2" nominal and must be as deep as the cut ends of the rafters connecting to the hip of the valley. **Gusset plates** as a tie between rafters may be used to replace a ridge board.

Rafters must have a bearing surface similar to that of joists at their end supports. Bearing needs to be 1½" on wood or metal and not less than 3" on masonry or concrete.

Drilling and **notching** have the same limitations for rafters as they do for floor joists. (See "Rafter Drilling and Notching" illustration.)

To prevent rotation of rafter framing members, **lateral support** or **blocking** must be provided for rafters and ceiling joists larger than 2 × 10s.

Bridging must be provided for roofs or ceilings larger than 2 × 12. The bridging may be solid blocking, diagonal bridging, or a continuous 1" × 3" wood strip nailed across the ceiling joists or rafters at intervals not greater than 8'. Bridging is not needed if the ceiling joists or rafters are held in line for the entire length with, for example, sheathing on one side and gypsum board on the other.

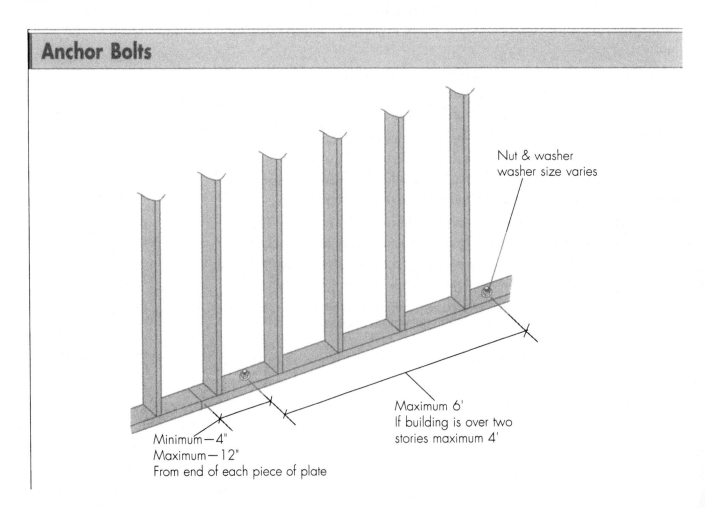

Anchor Bolts

Nut & washer
washer size varies

Minimum—4"
Maximum—12"
From end of each piece of plate

Maximum 6'
If building is over two
stories maximum 4'

Openings in the roof have the same requirements as the floor joists. (See "Framing of Openings in Roof" illustration.)

Rafter and **truss ties** or **hurricane clips** should be provided based on the wind uplift in your area. The plans should specify if and where the ties are needed.

When rafters are used to frame the roof, the walls that the rafters bear on must be tied together by a connection to keep them from being pushed out. If these walls are not tied together, then the ridge board must be supported by or framed as a beam in order to support the ridge. Ceiling joists are typically used to tie the walls together. The ceiling joists must be tied to the rafters, the walls, and any lapping ceiling joists. (See "Ceiling Joists" illustration on following page.)

Rafter Drilling & Notching

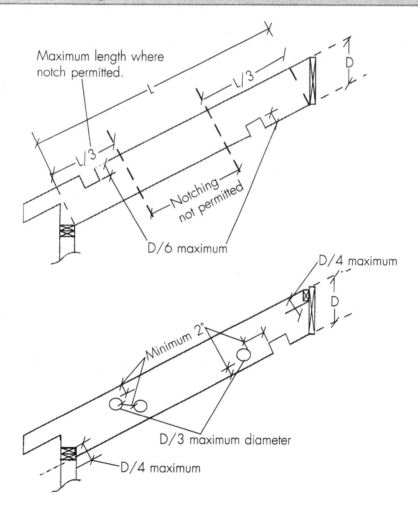

Framing of Openings in Roof

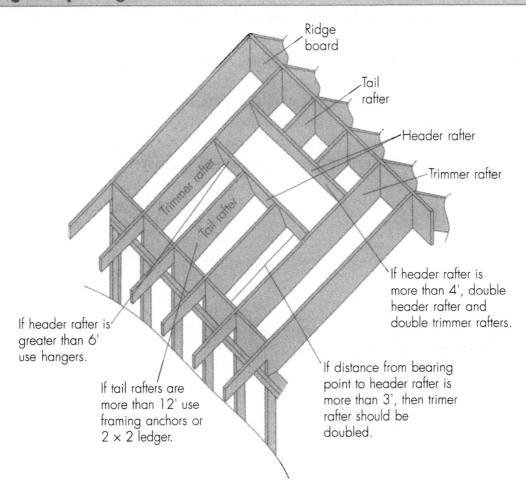

Ridge board

Tail rafter

Header rafter

Trimmer rafter

Trimmer rafter

Tail rafter

If header rafter is more than 4', double header rafter and double trimmer rafters.

If header rafter is greater than 6' use hangers.

If tail rafters are more than 12' use framing anchors or 2 × 2 ledger.

If distance from bearing point to header rafter is more than 3', then trimer rafter should be doubled.

Ceiling Joists

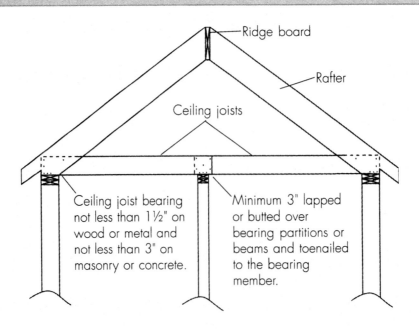

Ridge board

Rafter

Ceiling joists

Ceiling joist bearing not less than 1½" on wood or metal and not less than 3" on masonry or concrete.

Minimum 3" lapped or butted over bearing partitions or beams and toenailed to the bearing member.

Ceiling Framing

Ceiling joists must have **bearing support** similar to that of rafters. The bearing must be 1½" on wood or metal and not less than 3" on masonry or concrete.

The most important thing to remember about ceiling joists is that if they are used to tie the rafter-bearing walls at opposite ends of the building, then those joists must be **securely attached** to the walls, to the rafters, and to each other at the laps. If the ceiling joists do not run parallel with the rafters, an equivalent rafter tie must be installed to provide a continuous tie across the building.

The IRC calls for a **minimum ceiling clearance** of 7'-0". The IBC requires 7'-6" with the exception of bathrooms, kitchens, laundry, and storage rooms, where it can be 7'-0".

There are three exceptions to this rule. First, beams or girders can project 6" below the required ceiling height if they are spaced more than 4' apart. The second exception is for basements without habitable spaces. These may have a minimum height of 6'-8" and may have beams, girders, ducts, and other obstructions at 6'-4" in height. The third exception is for a sloped ceiling. Fifty percent of the sloped ceiling room area can be less than the minimum ceiling height. However, any portion of the room less than 5' in height cannot be included in figuring the room area. (See "Ceiling Heights" illustration.)

Truss Framing

Trusses are an engineered product. This means that an engineer or design professional must design them for each job to form a roof/ceiling system. Components and members of the trusses **should not be notched, cut, drilled, spliced,** or **altered** in any way without the approval of a registered design professional.

Attic Access

An attic access must be provided if the attic area exceeds 30 square feet, and the height is at least 30". This opening must be at least 22" × 30", and there must be a height of at least 30" at the access opening. (See "Attic Access" illustration later in this chapter.)

Stair and Ramp Framing

The **width** of stairs must be a minimum of 36" from finish to finish. Handrails may project into the 36" a maximum of 4½" on each side. If the occupant load is greater than 50, the width must be 44". (See "Stairs" illustration.)

Ceiling Heights

Habitable rooms, hallways, corridors, bathrooms, toilet rooms, laundry rooms and basements

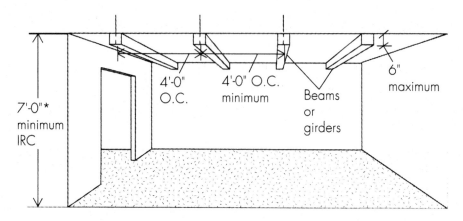

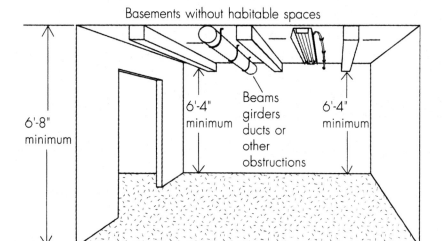

Basements without habitable spaces

Sloped ceiling

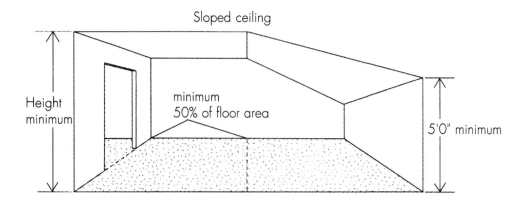

*7'-6" required by IBC for occupiable spaces, habital spaces, and corridor.
 7'-0" required for bathrooms, toilet rooms, kitchens, storage rooms, and laundry rooms.

Two sets of **tread** and **riser dimensions** apply to minimum and maximum requirement. One set is for Group R-3, Group R-2, and Group-U (houses, apartments, dormitories, non-transient housing). The other is for all other groups. The first set requires a maximum riser height of 7¾" and a minimum tread depth of 10", while the second requires a maximum riser height of 7", a minimum riser height of 4", and a minimum tread depth of 11".

The **variation** in riser height within any flight of stairs must not be more than ⅜" from finish tread to finish tread. The variation in tread depth within any flight of stairs cannot be more than ⅜" from the finish riser to the nose of the tread.

Headroom for stairways must have a minimum finish clearance of 6'-8", measured vertically from a line connecting the edge of the nosings.

Handrails for stairs must have a height of no less than 34" and no more than 38", measured vertically from a line created by joining the nosing on the treads.

Stairway **landings** must be provided for each stairway at the top and bottom. The width each way of the landing must not be less than the width of the stairway it serves. The landing's minimum dimension in the direction of travel cannot be less than 36", but does not need to be greater than 48" for a stair having a straight run. (See "Stair Landing" illustration.)

Circular stairways should have a minimum tread depth at a point 12" from the edge of the tread at its narrowest point of not less than 11". According to both the IRC and the IBC, the minimum depth at any point must be 6". (See "Circular Stairs" illustration.)

Attic Access

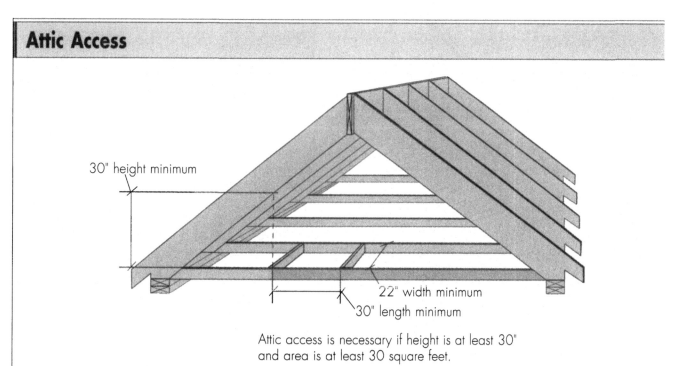

30" height minimum

22" width minimum

30" length minimum

Attic access is necessary if height is at least 30" and area is at least 30 square feet.

Spiral stairways must have a minimum width of 26". Each tread must have a minimum tread width of 7½" at a point 12" from the narrow edge of the tread. The rise must be no more than 9½". All treads must be identical. The headroom is a minimum of 6'-6". (See "Spiral Stairs" illustration.)

The maximum slope on a **ramp** is 12.5%, or one unit of rise for eight units of run. If the ramp is used as the means of egress, it cannot have a slope of more than 8%, or one unit of rise per 12 units of run. Handrails must be provided when the slope exceeds 8.33%, or one unit of rise and 12 units of run.

The **minimum headroom** on any part of a ramp is 6'-8".

A minimum 36" × 36" **landing** is required at the top and bottom of a ramp and where there is any door, or where the ramp changes direction. The actual minimum landing dimensions will depend on the building use and occupant capacity. This minimum does not apply to non-accessible housing.

The maximum **total rise** of any ramp cannot be more than 30" between level landings. (See "Ramps" illustration.)

Stairs

Not less than ¾" or more than 1¼".

IBC requires extension of 12" horizontal at top

Handrail

6'-8" minimum headroom (finish)

34" minimum 38" maximum

IBC requires extension of the depth of one riser at slope

7¾" maximum riser height—(R-3, R-2 & U)
7" max & 4" min—(other)

10" minimum tread depth—(R-3, R-2 & U)
11" minimum—(other)

36" minimum stair width above handrail—44" minimum occupant load 50 or more
31½" minimum stair width below handrail with handrail on one side
27" below handrail with handrail on both sides

The difference in the largest tread or riser cannot be more than ⅜" bigger than the smallest tread or riser.
Stairs with solid risers are required to have tread nosing not less than ¾" or more than 1¼"

Ventilation

Ventilation is required so that condensation does not occur on the structural wood, causing dry rot and the deterioration of the building. Cross ventilation is required in crawl spaces, attics, and in enclosed rafter spaces. In rafter spaces between the insulation and the roof sheathing there must be at least 1" clear space.

The **total area** of the space to be ventilated cannot be more than 150 times the size of the area of the venting. (Both are measured in square feet.)

Nailing

Nailing is one of the most important parts of framing. Table 2304.9.1, Fastening Schedule, is taken directly from the IBC 2000. This is the first year that alternate nails were included in the codes. The table shows use of the 3" × 0.131" nail, which is the most common nail gun nail used for framing. (See "IBC Nailing Table" later in chapter.)

Prevention of Decay

Moisture and warm air are catalysts of fungus, which causes dry rot that can destroy a building. In addition to calling for ventilation to control

Stair Landing

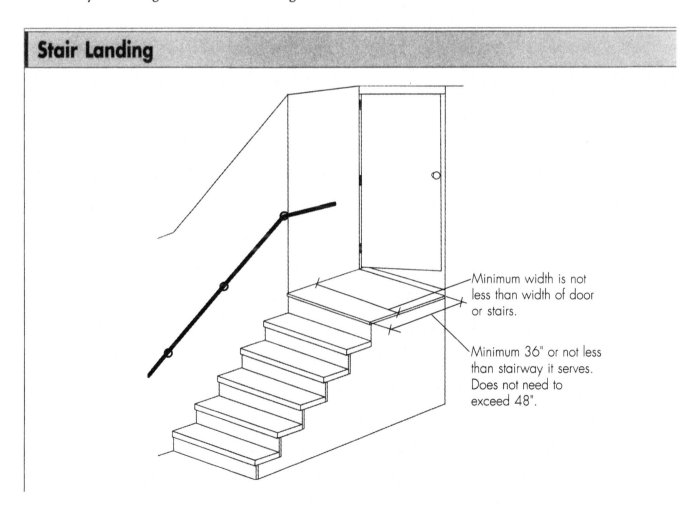

Minimum width is not less than width of door or stairs.

Minimum 36" or not less than stairway it serves. Does not need to exceed 48".

Circular Stairs

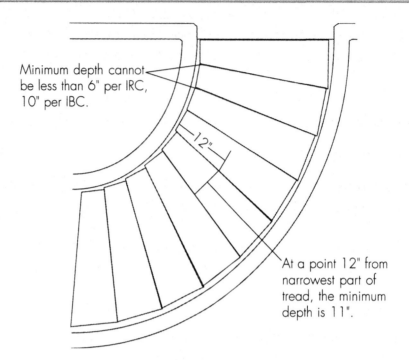

Minimum depth cannot be less than 6" per IRC, 10" per IBC.

12"

At a point 12" from narrowest part of tread, the minimum depth is 11".

Spiral Stairs

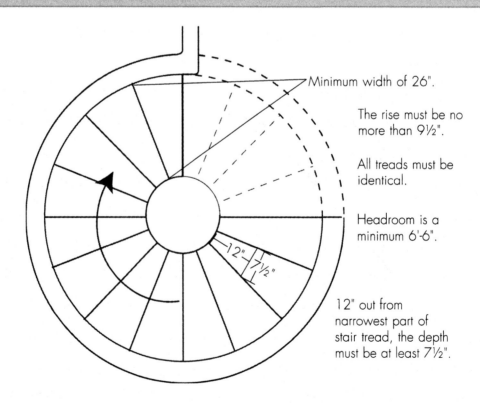

Minimum width of 26".

The rise must be no more than 9½".

All treads must be identical.

Headroom is a minimum 6'-6".

12" 7½"

12" out from narrowest part of stair tread, the depth must be at least 7½".

moisture, the code also requires decay-resistant wood wherever moisture can come in contact with structural wood. Some areas of the country are more conducive to decay than others. The "Decay Map" later in the chapter shows the areas most likely to have a decay problem.

The code requires naturally durable wood or preservative-treated wood in the following situations.

- Wood joist or the bottom of the wood floor structure if less than 18" from exposed ground. (See "Joists and Girder Protection" illustration.)

- Wood girders if closer than 12" from exposed ground.

- Wall plates, mudsills, or sheathing that rest on concrete or masonry exterior walls less than 8" from exposed ground. (See "Exterior Wall Decay Protection" illustration.)

- Sills or sleepers that rest on a concrete or masonry slab in direct contact with the ground, unless separated from the slab by an impervious moisture barrier. (See "Decay Protection from Slab" illustration.)

- The ends of wood girders entering exterior masonry or concrete walls having less than ½" clearance on tops, sides, and ends. (See "Ends of Girder in Masonry or Concrete" illustration.)

- Wood furring strips or framing members attached directly to the interior of exterior concrete or masonry walls below grade.

- Wood siding less than 6" from exposed ground.

- Posts or columns that support permanent structures and are themselves supported by a masonry concrete slab or footing in direct contact with the ground. (See "Post and Column Decay-Resistant Wood" illustration.)

Ramps

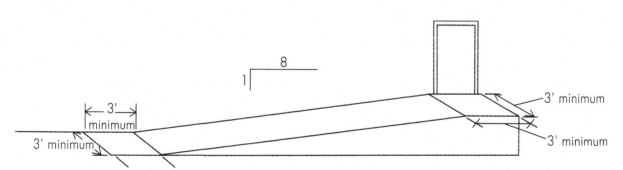

Maximum slope 1 unit of run in 8 units of rise (12.5%).
If ramp is used as a means of egress, the maximum slope is 1 unit of rise and 12 units of run.
Handrails are required for slopes greater than 1 unit rise in 12 units run (8.33%).

If the building's occupancy capacity is more than 50, then the minimum landing dimensions are 44". The actual minimum landing dimensions will depend on the building use and occupant capacity.

TABLE 2304.9.1
FASTENING SCHEDULE

CONNECTION	FASTENING[a, m]	LOCATION
1. Joist to sill or girder	3-8d common 3 - 3" × 0.131" nail 3 - 3" 14 gage staple	toenail
2. Bridging to joist	2-8d common 2 - 3" × 0.131" nail 2 - 3" 14 gage staple	toenail each end
3. 1" × 6" subfloor or less to each joist	2-8d common	face nail
4. Wider than 1" × 6" subfloor to each joist	3-8d common	face nail
5. 2" subfloor to joist or girder	2-16d common	blind and face nail
6. Sole plate to joist or blocking	16d at 16" o.c. 3" × 0.131" nail at 8" o.c. 3" 14 gage staple at 12" o.c.	typical face nail
Sole plate to joist or blocking at braced wall panel	3-16d per 16" 3" × 0.131" nail per 16" 3" 14 gage staple per 16"	braced wall panels
7. Top plate to stud	2-16d common 3 - 3" × 0.131" nail 3 - 3" 14 gage staple	end nail
8. Stud to sole plate	4-8d common 4 - 3" × 0.131" nail 3 - 3" 14 gage staple	toenail
	2-16d common 3 - 3" × 0.131" nail 3 - 3" 14 gage staple	end nail

TABLE 2304.9.1—continued
FASTENING SCHEDULE

CONNECTION	FASTENING[a, m]	LOCATION
9. Double studs	16d at 24" o.c. 3" × 0.131" nail at 8" o.c. 3" 14 gage staple at 8" o.c.	face nail
10. Double top plates	16d at 16" o.c. 3" × 0.131" nail at 12" o.c. 3" 14 gage staple at 12" o.c.	typical face nail
Double top plates	8-16d common 12 - 3" × 0.131" nail 12 - 3" 14 gage staple typical face nail	lap splice
11. Blocking between joists or rafters to top plate	3-8d common 3 - 3" × 0.131" nail 3 - 3" 14 gage staple	toenail
12. Rim joist to top plate	8d at 6" (152 mm) o.c. 3" × 0.131" nail at 6" o.c. 3" 14 gage staple at 6" o.c.	toenail
13. Top plates, laps and intersections	2-16d common 3 - 3" × 0.131" nail 3 - 3" 14 gage staple	face nail
14. Continuous header, two pieces	16d common	16" o.c. along edge
15. Ceiling joists to plate	3-8d common 5 - 3" × 0.131" nail 5 - 3" 14 gage staple	tocnail
16. Continuous header to stud	4-8d common	toenail
17. Ceiling joists, laps over partitions (See Section 2308.10.4.1, Table 2308.10.4.1)	3-16d common minimum, Table 2308.10.4.1 4 - 3" × 0.131" nail 4 - 3" 14 gage staple	face nail
18. Ceiling joists to parallel rafters (See Section 2308.10.4.1, Table 2308.10.4.1)	3-16d common minimum, Table 2308.10.4.1 4 - 3" × 0.131" nail 4 - 3" 14 gage staple	face nail
19. Rafter to plate (See Section 2308.10.1, Table 2308.10.1)	3-8d common 3 - 3" × 0.131" nail 3 - 3" 14 gage staple	toenail
20. 1" diagonal brace to each stud and plate	2-8d common 2 - 3" × 0.131" nail 2 - 3" 14 gage staple face nail	face nail
21. 1" × 8" sheathing to each bearing wall	2-8d common	face nail
22. Wider than 1" × 8" sheathing to each bearing	3-8d common	face nail
23. Build-up corner studs	16d common 3" × 0.131" nail 3" 14 gage staple	24" o.c. 16" o.c. 16" o.c.

(continued)

TABLE 2304.9.1—continued
FASTENING SCHEDULE

CONNECTION	FASTENING[a, m]		LOCATION

24. Built-up girder and beams	20d common 32" o.c.
	3" × 0.131" nail 24" o.c.
	3" 14 gage staple 24" o.c.
			face nail at
			  top and bottom staggered
			  on opposite sides

	2-20d common 3 - 3" × 0.131" nail 3 - 3" 14 gage staple		face nail at ends and at each splice
25. 2" planks	16d common		at each bearing
26. Collar tie to rafter	3-10d common 4 - 3" × 0.131" nail 4 - 3" 14 gage staple face nail		face nail
27. Jack rafter to hip	3-10d common 4 - 3" × 0.131" nail 4 - 3" 14 gage staple		toenail
	2-16d common 3 - 3" × 0.131" nail 3 - 3" 14 gage staple		face nail
28. Roof rafter to 2-by ridge beam	2-16d common 3 - 3" × 0.131" nail 3 - 3" 14 gage staple		toenail
	2-16d common 3 - 3" × 0.131" nail 3 - 3" 14 gage staple		face nail
29. Joist to band joist	3-16d common 5 - 3" × 0.131" nail 5 - 3" 14 gage staple		face nail
30. Ledger strip	3-16d common 4 - 3" × 0.131" nail 4 - 3" 14 gage staple		face nail
31. Wood structural panels and particleboard:[b] Subfloor, roof and wall sheathing (to framing):	$1/_2$" and less $19/_{32}$" to $3/_4$" $7/_8$" to 1"	6d[c, l] $23/_8$" × 0.113" nail[n] $13/_4$" 16 gage[o] 8d[d] or 6d[e] $23/_8$" × 0.113" nail[p] 2" 16 gage[p] 8d[c]	
Single Floor (combination subfloor- underlayment to framing):	$11/_8$" to $11/_4$" $3/_4$" and less $7/_8$" to 1" $11/_8$" to $11/_4$"	10d[d] or 8d[e] 6d[e] 8d[e] 10d[d] or 8d[e]	
32. Panel siding (to framing)	$1/_2$" or less $5/_8$"	6d[f] 8d[f]	
33. Fiberboard sheathing:[g]	$1/_2$" $25/_{32}$"	No. 11 gage roofing nail[h] 6d common nail No. 16 gage staple[i] No. 11 gage roofing nail[h] 8d common nail No. 16 gage staple[i]	
34. Interior paneling	$1/_4$" $3/_8$"		4d[j] 6d[k]

(continued)

NOTES TO TABLE 2304.9.1

For SI: 1 inch = 25.4 mm.

a. Common or box nails are permitted to be used except where otherwise stated.

b. Nails spaced at 6 inches on center at edges, 12 inches at intermediate supports except 6 inches at supports where spans are 48 inches or more. For nailing of wood structural panel and particleboard diaphragms and shear walls, refer to Section 2305. Nails for wall sheathing are permitted to be common, box or casing.

c. Common or deformed shank.

d. Common.

e. Deformed shank.

f. Corrosion-resistant siding or casing nail.

g. Fasteners spaced 3 inches on center at exterior edges and 6 inches on center at intermediate supports.

h. Corrosion-resistant roofing nails with $7/_{16}$-inch diameter head and $1^1/_2$ inch length for $1/_2$-inch sheathing and $1^3/_4$ inch length for $25/_{32}$-inch sheathing.

i. Corrosion-resistant staples with nominal $7/_{16}$-inch crown and $1^1/_8$ inch length for $1/_2$-inch sheathing and $1^1/_2$ inch length for $25/_{32}$-inch sheathing. Panel supports at 16 inches (20 inches if strength axis in the long direction of the panel, unless otherwise marked).

j. Casing or finish nails spaced 6 inches on panel edges, 12 inches at intermediate supports.

k. Panel supports at 24 inches. Casing or finish nails spaced 6 inches on panel edges, 12 inches at intermediate supports.

l. For roof sheathing applications, 8d nails are the minimum required for wood structural panels.

m. Staples shall have a minimum crown width of $7/_{16}$ inch.

n. For roof sheathing applications, fasteners spaced 4 inches on center at edges, 8 inches at intermediate supports.

o. Fasteners spaced 4 inches on center at edges, 8 inches at intermediate supports for subfloor and wall sheathing and 3 inches on center at edges, 6 inches at intermediate supports for roof sheathing.

p. Fasteners spaced 4 inches on center at edges, 8 inches at intermediate.

Termite Protection

Framers in certain areas of the country have to be concerned about protection against termites. Pressure preservative-treated wood or naturally termite-resistant wood or physical barriers can be used to prevent termite damage. The map at the end of this chapter shows termite infestation probability.

Conclusion

An important part of your job as a lead framer is being aware of the building codes that apply to framing in your part of the country. You should be aware of how to use the code and of any revisions to those codes. Although locating information you need in the code books is often the hardest part of using the codes, the "Framing Index" at the beginning of this chapter should make this easier for you. It's a good feeling to know that you have framed a building the way it's specified according to code.

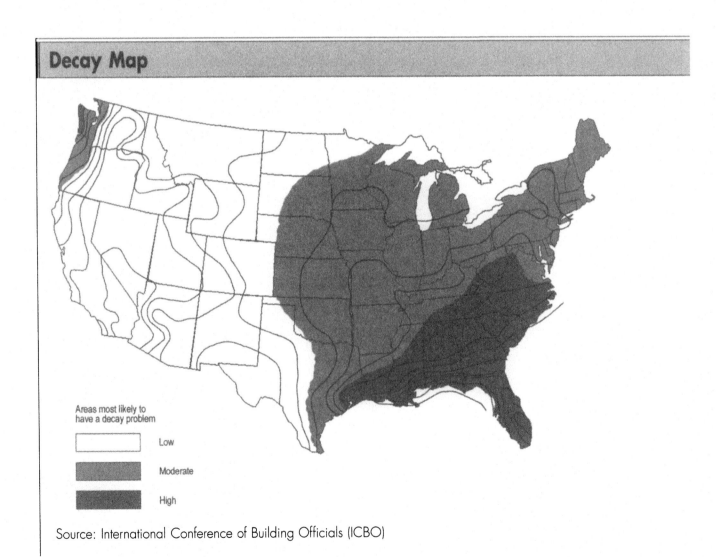

Decay Map

Areas most likely to have a decay problem

Low

Moderate

High

Source: International Conference of Building Officials (ICBO)

Joist & Girder Protection

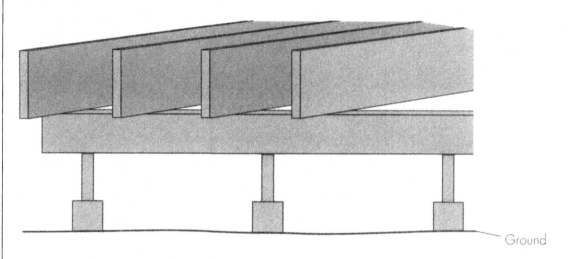

Decay resistant wood required if joists are less than 18" or girders less than 12" from the ground.

Exterior Wall Decay Protection

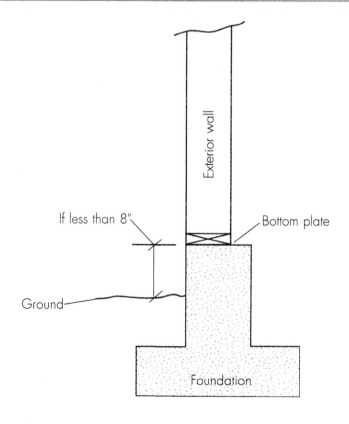

Exterior wall

If less than 8"

Bottom plate

Ground

Foundation

Decay Protection from Slab

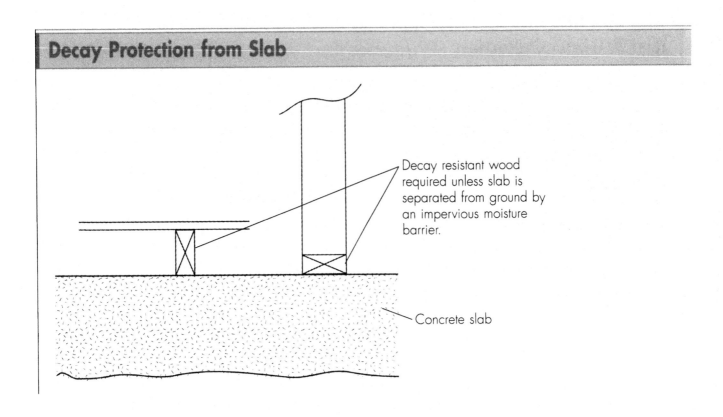

Decay resistant wood required unless slab is separated from ground by an impervious moisture barrier.

Concrete slab

Ends of Girders in Masonry or Concrete

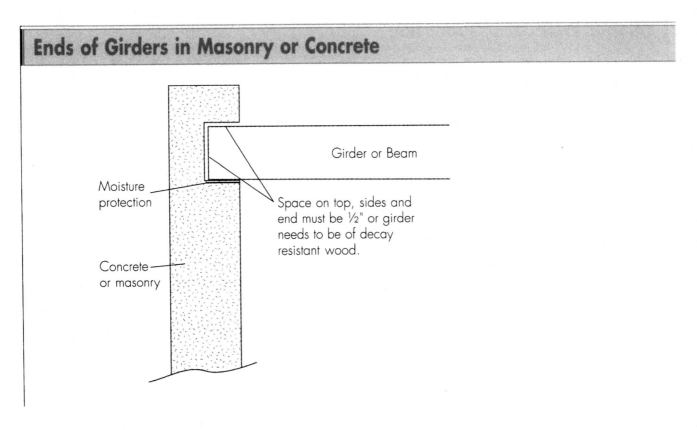

Girder or Beam

Moisture protection

Space on top, sides and end must be ½" or girder needs to be of decay resistant wood.

Concrete or masonry

Post and Column Decay Resistant Wood

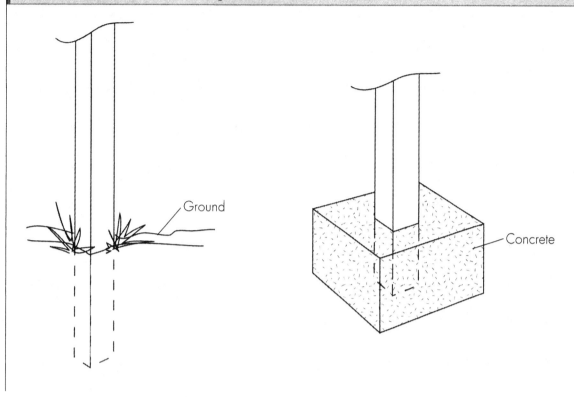

Ground

Concrete

Termite Infestation Probability

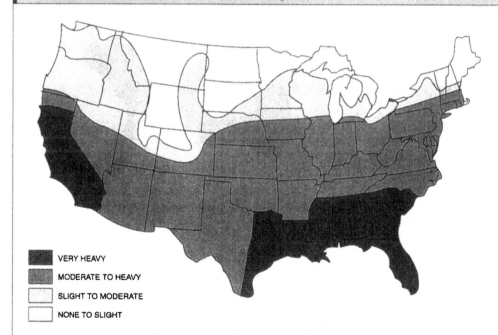

VERY HEAVY

MODERATE TO HEAVY

SLIGHT TO MODERATE

NONE TO SLIGHT

Note: Lines defining areas are approximate only. Local conditions may be more or less severe than indicated by the region classification.

Source: International Conference of Building Officials (ICBO)

Chapter Twelve

Safety

I f you have been framing long enough to understand advanced techniques or to be considering a career as a lead framer, you have probably seen enough accidents to make you aware of the importance of safety. Common sense will help guide you in knowing what is safe and what is not, but you must also be aware of the potential dangers. This information is usually acquired from the lead framer who taught you, from apprenticeship classes, and from weekly safety meetings, as well as state and federal regulations for the job site.

The safety topics presented in this chapter are not intended to be a complete list, but rather to cover the items you will come in contact with or have questions about most often.

Contents

Personal Protective Equipment

What we wear can either help prevent accidents or help cause them. Think about what you are going to do during the day, and prepare for it. It's a good idea to discuss personal protective equipment needed for specific tasks at your safety meetings. Keep an eye on new framers so you can detect any potential safety problems.

Hard hats are the symbol of the construction industry. Some jobs require that hard hats be worn. The Occupational Safety and Health Administration (OSHA) says that a hard hat needs to be worn if there is a possible danger of head injury from impact, or from falling or flying objects.

Eye protection is required by OSHA, when there is a reasonable probability of preventable injury when equipment such as a nail gun is used. Eye protection can be provided by safety glasses. Safety glasses can be found that are lightweight and also look good. They should always be worn when using power saws.

Ear protection is recommended when you are exposed to high levels of noise. High noise levels can cause hearing impairment and hearing loss, as well as physical and psychological stress. There is no cure for hearing loss caused by exposure to noise. Framers are exposed to these high levels at various times, not so much from their own work as from surrounding

Safety Glasses

operations. The easiest way to protect yourself from hearing impairment is to keep disposable earplugs handy. They are easy to use and once they are in, you barely notice them.

Foot protection can be provided by a pair of leather work shoes or boots with hard soles. The boots will help protect your ankles. Steel toes provide extra protection for your toes and can be useful as support for lumber you are cutting. Rubber boots are good in wet weather and provide an extra measure to prevent electric shock. (Also see ANSI Z41—1991, "American National Standard for Personal Protection Footwear.")

Pants and shirts should be fit for work. If they are too loose, there is the chance they can get caught in something like a drill and pull you into the drill bit, which might throw you off a ladder. If your pants are too loose or frayed at the bottoms, they can cause you to trip and fall. Be careful with other clothing, such as belts and coats, so that they don't hang loose and get caught.

"Oh, my aching back." Everybody has heard those words. In fact, back injuries are the most common type of injury in the workplace. Framing is lifting-intensive work—so measures to prevent back injuries deserve your attention. Stretching each morning and strengthening exercises are good for your back, but more important is making sure you lift properly. (See "Proper Lifting" photo.) Make it a point to use your legs to lift, and not

Proper Lifting

your back. When you are lifting walls, remind your crew to lift with their legs. When picking something up, bend your knees and keep your back straight. When carrying, keep objects close to your body, and avoid twisting and jerky motions.

Hand Tools

Nail guns are one of a framer's most commonly used tools. They are also one of the most dangerous. Most framers can show you a scar from having shot themselves with a nail gun. Fortunately, many of these injuries are not serious. However, there have been instances where serious injury or death has occurred. Following are some very basic guidelines that will help you operate a nail gun safely. (Always familiarize yourself with the manufacturer's complete operating instructions.)

- Wear safety glasses.
- Do not hold the trigger down unless you're nailing.
- Be careful when nailing close to the edge. The push lever at the nose of the gun can catch the wood and allow the gun to fire without the nail hitting the wood, allowing the nail to fly toward whatever is in line with the gun.
- Always keep your hand far enough away from the nose of the nail gun so that if the nail hits a knot or obstruction and bends, it will not hit your hand.
- Never point a nail gun at anyone.
- Disconnect the air hose before working on the gun.
- Use a gun hanger when working at heights, or secure your air hose so the gun does not get dragged off or fall. (See "Nail Gun and Hanger" photo.)
- When nailing off the roof or high floor sheathing, move in a forward, not a backward direction to prevent backing off the edge.
- Move from top to bottom on wall sheathing so you can use the weight of the gun to your advantage.

Trainees are the most vulnerable to nail gun accidents. Make sure that when you are training new recruits on nailing with a nail gun, you formally instruct them on nail gun safety and the potential for accidents.

Circular saws have cut off many fingers. A healthy respect for them is the first step toward safety. Follow these basic guidelines (and the manufacturer's operating instructions):

- Wear safety glasses when operating a circular saw.
- Always keep your fingers away from where the blade is going.

- Never remove or pin back the guard on the saw. The saw guard has a tendency to catch on many cuts, especially angle cuts, which makes it tempting to pin the guard back. Aside from the fact that it is an OSHA violation, a saw can become bound in a piece of wood, and "kick back." If the guard is pinned back, this can result in serious injury such as cuts to the thigh.

- Never use a dull blade. It will cause you to put excess directional force on the saw, which could cause it to go where you don't want it to.

- Disconnect from power if you are working on the saw.

- When you are cutting lumber, make sure that one end can fall free so that the blade does not bind and kick back.

As the teeth of a circular saw speed around at almost 140 miles per hour, it becomes very dangerous if not used properly.

Miscellaneous hand tools also need to be used properly for safety. The following guidelines apply to many hand tools.

- Make sure all safety guards are in place.

Nail Gun and Hanger

- Keep your finger off the trigger of power tools when you are carrying them to prevent accidental starting.

- Keep tools properly sharpened.

- Store tools in the locations provided.

- Before working on power tools, unplug them or take out the battery.

- Replace worn or broken tools immediately.

- Never leave tools in paths where they can become a tripping hazard.

To use a **powder-actuated tool,** you need to be trained by a certified trainer. Following are some of the basics that you will learn.

- You must wear safety glasses.

- Hard hats and hearing protection are recommended.

- Never point a powder-actuated nail gun at anyone.

- Before you fire make sure no one is on the other side of the material you are firing into.

- Do not load the firing cartridge until you are ready to use it.

- If there is a misfire, hold the tool against the work surface for at least 30 seconds; then try firing again. If the tool misfires a second time, hold it against the work surface again for 30 seconds; then remove the cartridge and inspect the gun. Soak the misfired cartridges in water in a safe location.

- Powder-actuated tools need to be placed firmly against the work, perpendicular to the work to avoid ricochet.

It's also a good idea to say "fire" just before you pull the trigger, so the shot noise will not startle the workers around you.

Ladders

Ladders are used so often in framing that it is easy to overlook basic safety guidelines. Always remember the following:

- The feet of the ladder need to be on a stable surface so the ladder will be level.

- When ladders are used to access an upper surface, make sure they extend at least three feet above the upper surface, and secure the top to prevent them from being knocked over. (See "Ladder Extension" photo on next page.)

- Do not use the top or top step of a step ladder.

- For straight or extension ladders, remember the 4 to 1 rule. For every four feet of height the ladder extends, it needs to be placed one foot out at the base.

- Check the ladder for defective parts, and remove any oil or grease on the steps.

- Never leave tools on the top step of a ladder.

Use common sense. If you are not sure that a ladder is safe, don't use it.

Fall Protection

OSHA provides that for unprotected sides and edges on walking or working surfaces, or for leading edges of six feet or more, framers must be protected from falls by the use of a guardrail system, a safety net system, or a personal fall arrest system. For leading edge work, if it can be demonstrated that these systems are not feasible or they create a greater hazard, then a plan may be developed and implemented to meet certain OSHA requirements.

The most commonly used fall protection systems in framing are the *personal fall arrest system* and the *guardrail system*. The guardrail system works well for a large flat deck. The fall arrest is better suited for pitched roofs.

Ladder Extension

Guardrails

Metal guardrail supports can be nailed to the outside of walls to support 2 × 4 railings. However, it is more common to see railing made out of 2 × 4 for the support and railings. These railings can be nailed on before the walls are raised. Following are some OSHA regulations on guardrails.

- The top edge of the top rail must be at least 42" (plus or minus 3") above the working level.
- Mid-rails shall be installed at a height midway between the top edge of the top rail and the working level.
- The top edge of the guardrail system must be able to withstand 200 pounds applied within 2 square feet in an outward or downward direction.
- The mid-rail must be able to withstand at least 150 pounds in an outward or downward direction.
- When access is provided in the guardrail system, a chain, gate, or removable guardrail sections should be placed across the opening when loading operations are not taking place.

Personal Fall Arrest Systems

These systems typically consist of a full body harness, a lanyard, a lifeline, and an anchor (See "Fall Arrest System" photo.) Each of these parts is available in many different types. Some of the OSHA regulations for these systems are listed below.

- Dee-rings, snaphooks, and carabiners must have a minimum tensile strength of 5,000 pounds.
- Lanyards and vertical lifelines shall have a minimum breaking strength of 5,000 pounds.
- Anchors must be capable of supporting at least 5,000 pounds per framer.
- The system must be rigged so that the framer cannot free-fall more than 6 feet.
- The attachment point for a body harness is to be located in the center of the wearer's back near the shoulder level or above the wearer's head.

If you have new framers who are not used to working with fall arrest systems, you will need to spend some time with them to help them become familiar and comfortable with this equipment.

Rough Terrain Forklift Safety

To operate a forklift, you need to be certified. To obtain certification, you need to be trained and actually operate a forklift. The points below are intended as a refresher for those who are already certified, and as an introduction to those intending to be certified.

- It is the weight of the forklift and the position of the tires that keep a forklift from turning over. There is an imaginary triangle between the front two tires and the space between the back two tires. This is called the *stability triangle*. The center of gravity for the forklift lies within this triangle. As the forks with weight extend out, the center of gravity moves. If the center of gravity goes outside the stability triangle, the forklift will tip. Getting the feel for the location of the center of gravity and the stability triangle is important to safe operation before you start working with a forklift. A good way to start is to lift a load of lumber and extend it out next to the ground until the back wheels start to come off the ground.

  The center of gravity is also changed when the forklift is on sloped ground. The situation is exaggerated greatly if there is a load on the forks and they are extended.

- If you are using a forklift and it starts to tip over, stay in the seat; do not jump out of the forklift.

- Before you operate any machine, be sure you are familiar with all the controls.

- Before you operate the forklift, do an inspection. Walk around the forklift checking for anything that does not look right, such as leaking fluids.

Fall Arrest System

Then get in the cab, start the engine, and check the gages and other controls.

- Never leave the forklift while the engine is running.
- Know the forklift hand signals. (See "Forklift Hand Signals" illustration.)
- Keep the forks close to the ground with or without a load.
- Always be looking for obstacles in your way like power lines overhead.

Forklift Center of Gravity

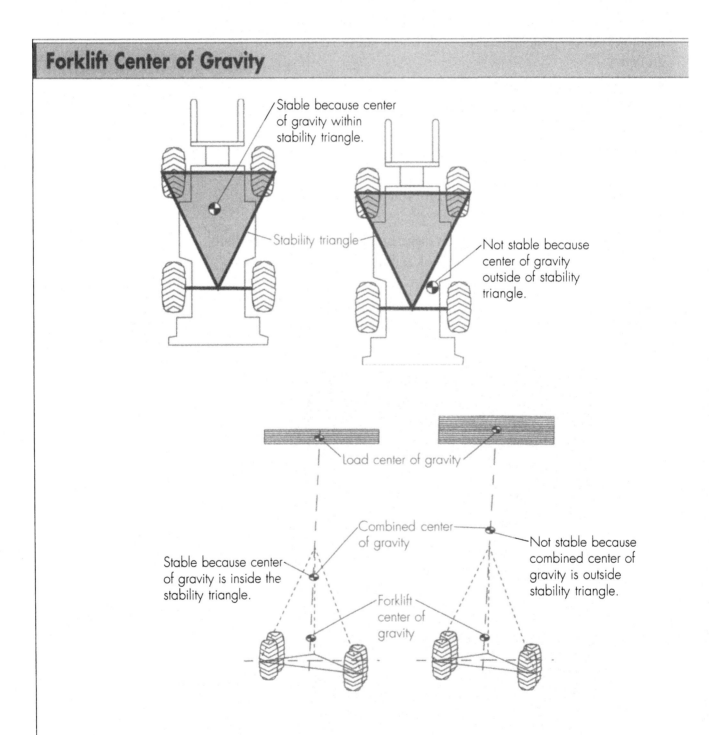

- Check the forklift load chart to make certain the forklift can handle the load you intend to move. The load capacity of a vehicle can be found on the identification plate and in the operator's manual. (See "Load Chart" photo.)

A forklift is a very big and heavy piece of machinery, capable of doing a great amount of damage. Make sure you treat it with respect.

Crane or Boom Truck Safety

When working with a crane or boom truck, the most important thing for a framer is to have good communication with the operator. Because you are typically out of audible range, you will need to use hand signals. You should use the industry-accepted standards shown in the "Crane and Boom Truck Hand Signals" illustration.

Housekeeping

Housekeeping is something we all grow up with. Some learn it better than others. On the job site, we all must practice good housekeeping because it

Forklift Hand Signals

Source: Mason Contractor's Association of America

affects safety and productivity. There are three main housekeeping issues: job site scraps, personnel debris, and tool organization.

Job site scraps are the cut-off ends of pieces of wood, lumber torn down that will not be used again, wrapping from lumber, empty nail boxes, and numerous other materials brought onto the job site that will not be used. You don't always want to take the time to attend to this debris at the moment it is made, but you do need to make sure that it is not left in a location that would pose a safety problem, such as in a walkway or at the bottom of a ladder. As you create the scraps, throw them in a scrap pile or at least in the direction of a scrap pile. Many cut-off pieces of lumber can be used for blocking and should be thrown in the direction of where they will be mass-cut later.

Whenever you have lumber with **nails** sticking out, pull the nails out if you are going to use the lumber again, or bend them if the lumber will be thrown away. It is easy to forget this, so attend to the nails while you are working with them and they are on your mind.

Personnel debris is the garbage individuals create personally, like lunch scraps and soda bottles. It makes it easier on your crew if you provide some sort of container near the lunch spot. You will be lucky if you don't have to keep reminding your crew that they are responsible for their own personal garbage.

Load Chart

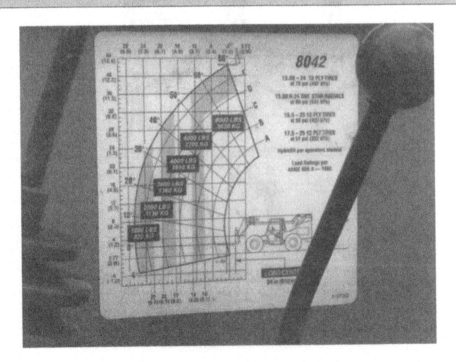

Mobile Crane and Boom Truck Hand Signals

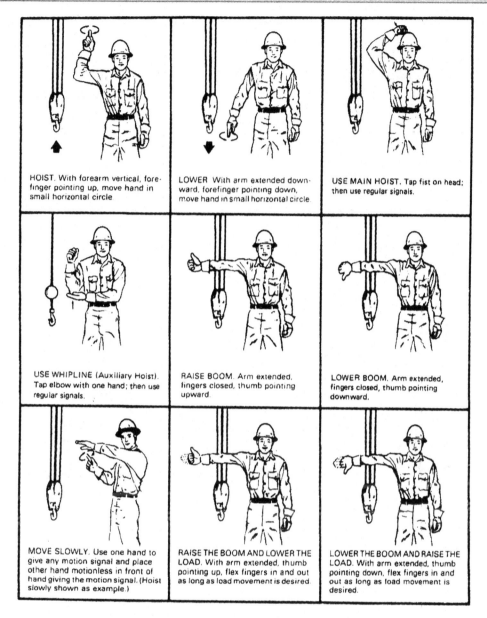

HOIST. With forearm vertical, fore-finger pointing up, move hand in small horizontal circle.

LOWER. With arm extended down-ward, forefinger pointing down, move hand in small horizontal circle.

USE MAIN HOIST. Tap fist on head; then use regular signals.

USE WHIPLINE (Auxiliary Hoist). Tap elbow with one hand; then use regular signals.

RAISE BOOM. Arm extended, fingers closed, thumb pointing upward.

LOWER BOOM. Arm extended, fingers closed, thumb pointing downward.

MOVE SLOWLY. Use one hand to give any motion signal and place other hand motionless in front of hand giving the motion signal. (Hoist slowly shown as example.)

RAISE THE BOOM AND LOWER THE LOAD. With arm extended, thumb pointing up, flex fingers in and out as long as load movement is desired.

LOWER THE BOOM AND RAISE THE LOAD. With arm extended, thumb pointing down, flex fingers in and out as long as load movement is desired.

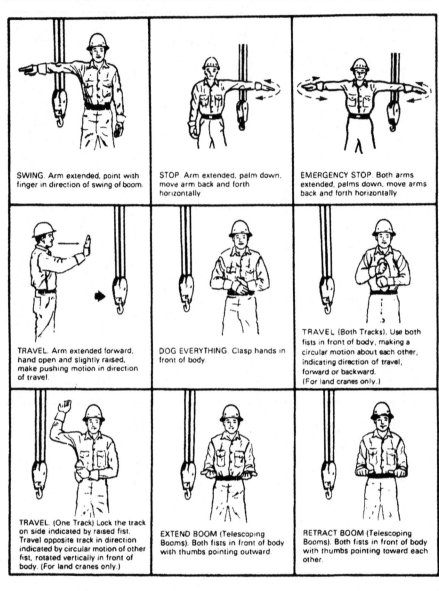

Source: Reprinted from ASME B30.5-2000 by permission of the American Society of Mechanical Engineers, all rights reserved.

Tool organization can save you time and a lot of aggravation. With tools that are in common use by the crew, it is important to return the tool to where it belongs. If tools are not stored in a location where other framers can expect them to be, a lot of time will be wasted looking for them. When rolling out your electric cords and air hoses, keep them organized. If you have to roll out in a walkway, try to stay to one side or the other. If you have to move your hose or cord, and it is rolled out underneath someone else's cord or hose, be careful that when you move yours, you don't drag theirs (and possibly their tools) along with you.

Housekeeping is sometimes difficult to organize, but getting it right can be a big asset for safety and productivity.

Conclusion

The safety topics in this chapter are just a small part of a total safety plan, but represent a good base. Remember, as a lead framer, you can't afford to forget about your own safety, not only for your own well-being, but because your framers will look to you to see how seriously you take it. It's easy to forget safety measures when you are in a rush on a job, but when you stop and think about it, the alternatives could be losing a finger or even risking death. It's not hard to see the importance of safety. With a little bit of effort, your jobs can be safe and productive.

Glossary

Anchor bolt

A device for connecting wood members to concrete or masonry.

Backer

Three studs nailed together in a U-shape to which a partition is attached.

Barge board

Board attached to a gable rafter to which a rake board is attached.

Beam

A large, horizontal structural member of wood or steel.

Bearing wall

A wall that supports the load of the structure above it.

Bevel

Any angle that is not 90°. Also, a tool for marking such an angle.

Bird's-mouth

The notch in a rafter that rests on the top plate of a wall.

Blocking

Small pieces of wood used to secure, join, or reinforce members, or to fill spaces between members.

Box nails

Nail similar to a common nail, but having a smaller diameter shank.

Bridging

Bracing installed in an X-shape between floor joists to stiffen the floor and distribute live loads. Also called *cross-bridging*.

Building line

The bottom measurement of a rafter's run, (the top being the ridge line); the plumb cut of the bird's-mouth.

Camber

A slight crown or arch in a horizontal structural member.

Cantilever

Any part of a structure that projects beyond its main support and is balanced on it.

Cant strip

A length of lumber with a triangular cross-section used around edges of roofs or decks to help waterproof.

Casing

A piece of wood or metal trim that finishes off the frame of a door or window.

Casing nail

A large finish nail with a cone-shaped head.

Chalk line

A string covered with chalk used for marking straight lines.

Check

A lengthwise crack across the grain in a piece of lumber.

Cheek cut

An angle cut that is made to bear against another rafter, hip, or valley.

Chord

Any principal member of a truss system. In a roof truss the top chord replaces a rafter, and the bottom chord replaces a ceiling joist.

Circumference

The boundary line of a circle.

Collar beam

A horizontal board that connects pairs of rafters on opposite roof slopes.

Column

A vertical structural member.

Common nail

Nail used in framing and rough carpentry having a flat head about twice the diameter of its shank.

Common rafter

A rafter running from a wall directly to a ridge board.

Connection angle

The angle at the end of a rafter needed to connect to other rafters, hips, valleys, or ridge boards.

Connectors

Beams, or construction hardware specifically designed for common framing connections.

Corner

Two studs nailed together in an L-shape, used to attach two walls and provide drywall backing.

Cornice

The horizontal projection of a roof overhang at the eaves, consisting of look-out, soffit, and fascia.

Crawl space

The area bounded by foundation walls, first-floor joists, and the ground in a house with no basement.

Cricket

A small, sloping structure built on a roof to divert water, usually away from a chimney. Also called a saddle.

Cripple

A short stud installed above or below a horizontal member in a wall opening.

Cripple jack rafter

A rafter that runs between a hip rafter and a valley rafter.

Crown

The high point of a piece of lumber that has a curve in it.

Cup

Warp across the grain.

d

Abbreviation for penny. The abbreviation comes from the Roman word *denarius*, meaning coin, which the English adapted to penny. It originally referred to the cost of a specific nail per 100. Today it refers only to nail size.

Dead load

The weight of all structures in place.

Diagonal

The distance between the far point on the run and the high point on the rise.

(Similar to hypotenuse in mathematical terms.)

Diagonal percent
The diagonal divided by the run (used when cutting rafters).

Dormer
A structure with its own roof projecting from a sloping roof.

Double cheek cut
A two-sided cut that forms a V at the end of some rafters, especially in hip and gambrel roofs.

Dry lines
A string line (as opposed to a chalk line) used to establish a straight line.

Eave
The part of a roof that projects beyond its supporting walls.

Engineered wood products (EWP)
Building framing, joists, and beams made from wood strands or fibers held together with a binder.

Face nailing
Nailing at right angles to the surface.

Face-mount hangers
Hangers that nail onto the face or vertical surfaces of their supporting members.

Fascia
A vertical board nailed to the lower ends of rafters that form part of a cornice.

Fireblock
A short piece of framing lumber nailed horizontally between joists or studs to partially block the flow of air and, thus, to slow the spread of fire.

Footings
The base, usually poured concrete, on which the foundation wall is built. The footing and foundation wall are often formed and poured as a single unit.

Footprint
The area that falls directly beneath and shares the same perimeter as the structure.

Form
A mold of metal or wood used to shape concrete until it has set.

Foundation
The building's structural support below the first-floor construction. It rests on the footing, and transfers the weight of the building to the soil.

Frame
The skeleton of a building. Also called *framing*.

Framer
A person who performs rough carpentry, building the frame of the structure to which sheathing and finish treatments will be attached.

Framing anchor
A metal device for connecting wood framing members that meet at right angles.

Framing point
The point where the center lines of connecting rafters, ridges, hips, or valleys meet.

Furring
Strips of wood fastened across studs or joists to a level or plumb nailing surface for finish wall or ceiling material, usually sheetrock. Also called *strapping*.

Gable
The triangular part of an end wall between the eaves and ridge of a house with a peaked roof.

Gable roof
A roof shape characterized by two sections of roof of constant slope that meet at a ridge; peaked roof.

Gambrel roof
A roof shape similar to a gable roof, but with two sections of roof on each side of the ridge, the lower section being steeper than the upper.

Girder
A primary horizontal beam of steel or wood.

Glu-lam beams
Structural beams created by gluing 2× dimensional lumber together in structurally ordered pattern.

Grade
1. A designation of quality, especially of lumber and plywood.
2. Ground level. Also the slope of the ground on a building site.

Gusset
A flat piece of plywood or metal attached to each side of two framing members to tie them together, or strengthen a joint.

Gusset plates
Plates that can be used to replace ridge board.

Header
Any structural wood member used across the ends of an opening to support the cut ends of shortened framing members in a floor, wall, or roof.

Hip
The outside angle where two adjacent sections of roof meet at a diagonal. The opposite of a valley.

Hip diagonal (or valley diagonal)
The distance between the far point on the hip or valley run and the high point on the hip or valley rise.

Hip rafter
The diagonal rafter, which forms a hip.

Hip roof
A roof shape characterized by four or more sections of constant slope, all of which run from a uniform eave height to the ridge.

Hip run (or valley run)
The horizontal distance below the hip or valley of a roof, from the outside corner of the wall to the center framing point.

Hip-Val diagonal percent
The hip or valley diagonal divided by the hip or valley run.

Hold-downs

Connections used to transfer tension loads between floors. Commonly used for foundations, wall-to-wall connections, wall-to-concrete connections, and wall or floor-to-drag strut. Also called anchor downs or tie-downs.

I-joist

An engineered wood product created with two flanges joined by a web and which develops certain structural capabilities. I-joists are also used for rafters.

International Building Code (IBC)

The Building code established in 2000 that covers all buildings other than one- and two-family dwellings and multiple single-family dwellings not more than three stories in height.

International Residential Code (IRC)

The Building code that covers all one- and two-family dwellings and multiple single-family dwellings not more than three stories in height.

Jack rafter

A short rafter, usually running between a top plate and a hip rafter, or between a ridge and a valley rafter.

Jack stud

A shortened stud supporting the header above a door or window. Also called a *trimmer* or *jamb stud*.

Jamb

The side of a window or door opening.

Joint

The line along which two pieces of material meet.

Joist

One of a parallel series of structural members used for supporting a floor or ceiling. Joists are supported by walls, beams, or girders.

Joist hanger

A metal framing anchor for holding joists in position against a rim joist, header or beam.

Kerf

The cut made by a saw blade.

King stud

A vertical support member that extends from the bottom to top plate alongside an opening for a door or window.

Kneewall

A short wall under a slope, usually in attic space.

Layout language

The written words and symbols the lead framer uses.

Lead framer

Foreman or leader of a crew

Ledger

A strip of lumber attached to the side of a girder near its bottom edge to support joists. Also, any similar supporting strip.

Level

Perfectly horizontal.

Lightweight plate

A plate that goes under the bottom plate to raise walls for lightweight concrete or gypcrete.

Live load

The total variable weight on a structure. It includes the weights of people, furnishings, snow, and wind.

Load path

The path that artificial and natural forces that affect a building take when they create a load exerted on the building.

Lookout

A horizontal framing member between a stud wall and the lower end of a rafter to which the soffit is attached.

Lumber

Wood cut at a sawmill into usable form.

Makeup

Parts of a wall, (such as backers, corners, headers, and stud trimmers) cut before the wall is spread.

Mansard roof

A type of roof with two slopes on each of four sides, the lower slope much steeper than the upper and ending at a constant eave height.

Mortise

A recess cut into wood.

Mudsill

The lowest plate in a frame wall. It rests on the foundation or slab.

Nail gun

A hand-operated tool powered by compressed air which drives nails.

Nominal size

The rounded-off, simplified dimensional name given to lumber, (For example, a piece of lumber whose actual size is 1½" × 3 ½" is given the more convenient, nominal designation of 2" × 4".)

Nonbearing

A dividing wall that supports none of the structure above it.

Nosing

The rounded front edge of a stair tread that extends over the riser.

On center (O.C.)

Layout spacing designation that refers to the distance from the center of one framing member to the center of another.

Oriented strand board (OSB)

Wood made out of flakes, strands, or wafers sliced from small wood logs bonded under heat with a waterproof and boil-proof resin binder.

Overhang

The part of a roof that extends beyond supporting walls.

Overhang diagonal

The distance between the far point on the overhang run and the high point on the overhang rise.

Overhang hip run

The horizontal distance below the hip or valley of a roof, from the outside corner of the wall to the center framing point.

Parallel

Extending in the same direction and equidistant at all points.

Parapet

A low wall or rail at the edge of a balcony or roof.

Particleboard, composite and structural

Engineered lumber made of wood particles bonded by an adhesive under a hot pressing, and formed into a solid, three-layered panel with two surface layers. (Usually used as an underlayment.)

Partition

An interior wall that divides a building into rooms or areas.

Party wall

A wall between two adjoining living quarters in a multi-family dwelling.

Penny

Word applied to nails to indicate size; abbreviated as "d".

Perpendicular

At right angles to a plane, or flat surface.

Pitch

The slope of a roof.

Pitch angle

The vertical angle on the end of a rafter that represents the pitch of a roof.

Plate

A horizontal framing member laid flat.

> **Bottom plate**
>
> The lowest plate in a wall in the platform framing system, resting on the subfloor, to which the lower ends of studs are nailed.
>
> **Double plate**
>
> The uppermost plate in a frame wall that has two plates at the top. Also called a *cap* or *rafter plate*.
>
> **Sill plate**
>
> The structural member, attached to the top of the foundation, that supports the floor structure. Also called a *sill* or *mudsill*.
>
> **Top plate**
>
> The framing member nailed across the upper ends of studs and beneath the double plate.

Platform framing

A method of construction in which wall framing is built on and attached to a finished box sill. Joists and studs are not fastened together as in balloon and braced framing.

Plumb

Straight up and down, perfectly vertical.

Plumb and line

The process of straightening all the walls so they are vertical and straight from end to end.

Plumb cut

Any cut in a piece of lumber, such as at the upper end of a common rafter, that will be plumb when the piece is in its final position.

Purlin

The horizontal framing members in a gambrel roof between upper and lower rafters.

Pythagorean theorem

The theorem that the sum of the squares of the lengths of the sides of a right triangle is equal to the square of the length of the hypotenuse.

Rabbet

A groove cut in or near the edge of a piece of lumber to receive the edge of another piece.

Rafter

One of a series of main structural members that form a roof.

Rake

The finish wood member running parallel to the roof slope at the gable end.

Rake Wall

Also called *gable end walls*. Any wall that is built with a slope.

Reveal

The surface left exposed when one board is fastened over another; the edge of the upper set slightly back from the edge of the lower.

Ridge

The horizontal board to which the top ends of rafters are attached.

Ridge end rafter

A rafter that runs from the end of a ridge.

Rim joist

A joist that forms the perimeter of a floor framing system.

Rise

1. In a roof, the vertical distance between the top of the double plate and the point where a line, drawn through the edge of the double plate and parallel to the roof's slope, intersects the center line of the ridgeboard.
2. In a stairway, the vertical height of the entire stairway measured from floor to floor.

Riser

The vertical board between two stair treads.

Roof sheathing

Material, usually plywood, laid flat on roof trusses or rafters to form the roof.

Rough opening (R.O.)

Any opening formed by the framing members to accommodate doors or windows.

Rout

To cut out by gouging.

Run

1. In a roof with a ridge, the horizontal distance between the edge of the rafter plate (building line) and the center line of the ridge board.

2. In a stairway, the horizontal distance between the top and bottom risers plus the width of one tread.

Scaffold

Any temporary working platform and the structure to support it.

Scribe

To mark for an irregular cut.

Seat cut

The horizontal cut in a bird's-mouth that rests on the double plate.

Sheathing

The covering (usually wood boards, plywood, or wallboards) placed over exterior studding or rafters of a building; provides a base for the application of exterior wall or roof cladding.

Shear wall

A wall that, in its own plane carries shear resulting from forces such as wind, blast, or earthquake.

Shed roof

A roof that slopes in only one direction.

Shim

A thin piece of material, often tapered (such as a wood shingle) inserted between building materials for the purpose of straightening or making their surfaces flush at a joint.

Sill

1. A sill plate.

2. The structural member forming the bottom of a rough opening for a door or window. Also, the bottom member of a door or window frame.

Single cheek cut

A bevel cut at the end of a rafter, especially in hip and gambrel roofs.

Sleeper

Lumber placed on a concrete floor as a nailing base for wood flooring.

Slope

The pitch of a roof, expressed as inches of rise per twelve inches of run.

Soffit

The underside of a projection, such as a cornice.

Solid bridging

Blocking between joists cut from the same lumber as the joists themselves and used to stiffen the floor.

Spacer

Any piece of material used to maintain a permanent space between two members.

Span

The distance between structural supports, measured horizontally (typically from the outside of two bearing walls).

Speed square

A triangle-shaped tool used for marking perpendicular and angled lines.

Squash blocks

A structural block used to support point loads.

Square

1. At 90° or a right angle.

2. The process of marking and cutting at a right angle.

3. Any of several tools for marking at right angles and for laying out structural members for cutting or positioning.

4. A measure of roofing and some siding materials equal to 100 square feet of coverage.

Stair

A single step.

Stair nuts

Two screw clamps that are attached to a framing square for marking stair stringers.

Stair stringer

An inclined board which supports the end of the treads. Also known as *stair jacks*.

Stairway

A flight of stairs, made up of stringers, risers, and treads.

Stairwell

The opening in a floor for a stairway.

Stickers

Strips of scrap wood used to create an air space between layers of lumber.

Stop

In general, any device or member that prevents movement.

Story pole

A length of wood marked off and used for repetitive layout or to accurately transfer measurements.

Stringer

In stairway construction, the diagonal member that supports treads and to which risers are attached.

Structural

Adjective generally synonymous with "framing."

Stud

The main vertical framing member in a wall to which finish material or other covering is attached.

Subfloor sheathing

The rough floor, usually plywood, laid across floor joists and under finish flooring.

Stick frame
Method of framing involving building one structural member at a time, e.g. nailing one stud at a time in place.

Tail
The part of a rafter that extends beyond the double plate.

Tail joist
A shortened joist that butts against a header.

Tape
A measure of coiled, flexible steel.

Template
A full-sized pattern.

Threshold
The framing member at the bottom of a door between the jambs.

Toenailing
Driving a nail at an angle to join two pieces of wood.

Tongue
The shorter and narrower of the two legs of a framing square.

Top-flange hangers
Hangers with flanges that attach to the top of supporting members.

Transit line
In surveying, any line or a survey traverse that is projected, either with or without measurement, by the use of a transit or similar device.

Tread
The horizontal platform of a stair.

Trimmer
The structural member on the side of a framed rough opening used to narrow or stiffen the opening. Also, the shortened stud (jack stud) that supports a header in a door or window opening.

Truss
An assembly for bridging a broad span, most commonly used in roof construction.

Trussed joist
A joist in the form of a truss.

Utility knife
A hand-held knife with a razor-like blade, commonly used to cut drywall, sharpen pencils, etc.

Valley
The inside angle where two adjacent sections of a roof meet at a diagonal. The opposite of a hip.

Valley rafter
A rafter at an inside corner of a roof that runs between and joins with jack rafters that bear on corner walls.

Wall puller
A tool used for aligning walls.

Wall sheathing
Material, usually plywood, attached to studs to form the outside wall and provide structural strength.

Wane
A defect in lumber caused at the mill by sawing too close to the outside edge of a log and leaving an edge either incomplete or covered with bark.

Warp
Any variation from straight in a piece of lumber; bow, cup, crook, or twist.

Web stiffeners
A piece of wood or composite wood used to provide additional strength for the webs of I-joists.

Western framing
Platform framing.

Worm-drive saw
A circular power saw turned by a worm-gear drive. It is somewhat heavier and produces more torque on the blade than a standard circular saw.

For Reading and Reference

29 CFR Code of Federal Regulations, Part 1926 Construction Industry, Mangan Communications, Inc. Davenport, Iowa, 2001.

Basic Engineering for Builders, Max Schwartz, Craftsman Book Company, Carlsbad, CA, 1993.

Carpentry and Building Construction, John Feirer and Gilbert Hutchings, Chas A. Bennett Co., Inc. Peoria, Illinois, 1981.

Carpentry, Leonard Koel, American Technical Publishers, Inc., Homewood, IL 60430, 1985.

Engineered Wood Products, edited by Stephen Smulski—available from the PFS Research Foundation, www.pfsf.org, Madison, WI, 1997.

Fire Resistance—Volume 1 & 2—Directory, Underwriters Laboratories Inc., Northbrook, IL, (708) 272-8800, 1995.

Forklifts, The Crane Institute of America Publishing & Products, Inc., Maitland, FL, 2001.

Framing & Rough Carpentry, Scot Simpson, R.S. Means Company, Inc., 63 Smiths Lane, Kingston, MA 02364, (800) 334-3509, www.rsmeans.com.

House Framing, John D. Wagner, Creative Homeowner Press, Upper Saddle River, NJ, 1998.

International Building Code 2000, International Code Council, Inc.—available from the International Code Council, 5203 Leesburg Pike, Suite 600, Falls Church, VA 22041, (703) 931-4533.

International Residential Code for One- and Two-Family Dwellings 2000, International Code Council, Inc.—available from the International Code Council, 5203 Leesburg Pike, Suite 600, Falls Church, VA 22041, (703) 931-4533.

Mobile and Locomotive Cranes, An American National Standard—ASME B30.5-2000—The American Society of Mechanical Engineers, 2000, (800) 843-2563.

Resisting the Forces of Earthquakes, International Conference of Building Officials—available from the International Conference of Building Officials, 5360 Workman Mill Road, Whittier, CA, (800) 423-6587 & Earthquake Engineering Research Institute, 499 14th Street, Suite 320, Oakland, CA 94612, (510) 451-0905.

Roof Framing, H.H. Siegele, Drake Publishing Co., P.O. Box 8524, Bend, OR 97708, 1975.

Roof Framing, Stanley Badzinski, Jr., Prentice-Hall, Inc. Englewood Cliffs, NJ, 1976.

Rough Framing Carpentry, Mark Currie, Craftsman Book Company, Carlsbad, CA.

Stair Layout, Stanley Badzinski, Jr., American Technical Publishers, Inc. Alsip, IL, 1971.

The Art of Roof Cutting, Steve Peters—part of a series of videos.

The One Minute Manager, Spencer Johnson & Kenneth H. Blanchard, Berkley Publishing Group, New York, NY, 1983.

The Very Efficient Framer, Larry Haun, The Taunton Press, Inc. Newtown, CT, 1992.

Wood Construction Connectors, The Simpson Strong Tie Company—Catalog C-2002—(800) 999-5099, www.strongtie.com.

Wood Engineering and Construction Handbook, second edition, Keith F. Faherty & Thomas G. Williamson, McGraw-Hill, Inc. New York, NY, 1995.

Wood Frame Construction Manual, High Wind Edition, 1995 SBC, American Forest & Paper Association American Wood Council, Washington, DC, 1996.

Wood Framing Portable Handbook, Jonathan F. Hutchings, McGraw-Hill, New York, NY, 2000.

Working With Difficult People, Muriel Solomon, Prentice Hall, Paramus, NJ, 1990.

Index

Notes

Notes

Notes

Notes